How To Live
An Awesome Life

*The 11 Step Formula for Fulfilment
and Success*

BEN COOMBER

JOHN
MURRAY
LEARNING

First published in Great Britain by John Murray Learning in 2023
An imprint of John Murray Press
A division of Hodder & Stoughton Ltd,
An Hachette UK company

1

This book is for information or educational purposes only and is
not intended to act as a substitute for medical advice or treatment.
Any person with a condition requiring medical attention should
consult a qualified medical practitioner or suitable therapist.

A CIP catalogue record for this title is available from the British Library

Trade Paperback ISBN 978 1 399 80005 1
eBook ISBN 978 1 399 80010 5

Typeset in Celeste by Hewer Text UK Ltd, Edinburgh
Printed and bound in Great Britain by Clays Ltd, Elcograf S.p.A.

John Murray Press policy is to use papers that are natural, renewable
and recyclable products and made from wood grown in sustainable
forests. The logging and manufacturing processes are expected to
conform to the environmental regulations of the country of origin.

John Murray Press
Carmelite House
50 Victoria Embankment
London EC4Y 0DZ

www.johnmurraypress.co.uk

Contents

What this book is about . . . and what it's not

I don't know about you, but I want to live an awesome life, and be my most awesome self.

Sounds simple, right? Yet somewhat arbitrary, like a dream written on a napkin after a few beers. After all, life always seems awesome after a few drinks, setting the world to rights with a friend, right until we wake up in the morning with a sore head, sleeping through the alarm and chasing our tail just to make it through the day, all while saying to ourselves, 'What on earth was I thinking last night? None of that's possible! Back to reality.'

Now let's level with each other right out the gate: who doesn't want to live their best life? You'd be foolish to say no, right?

Hopefully you're reading this and saying to yourself . . .

'Yes, Ben, ME, I do.'

You see, I am just an ordinary guy that took life by the horns and owned it; and you can do the same – if you follow the formula in this book.

Everything you want in life *you can have*. It starts with dreaming (which most of us do), writing things down and making a plan of action (which some of us do), then taking action (which very few of us do).

The dreaming and writing down part of the process is one that most of us enjoy. I find writing down my dreams and goals and working out how I'm going to get there super exciting. I also love doing this when I'm on holiday, and I have a sense of freedom and space, and I'm relaxed enough to really dream and take the time to explore my thoughts without any external influences or demands on my time.

But for most of us, this is when the fear creeps in, when we question whether we can do it, when friends have a joke at our expense, when we have to do some things outside our comfort zone, when we have to work harder. That's normally when we stop, retreat, and go back to the comfort of the status quo.

Yet we remain unhappy, frustrated and dissatisfied, thinking 'I WANT MORE FROM LIFE', and making those familiar BS excuses for why *it* hasn't happened yet.

BUT there is another way, and I promise you it's possible. I've done it, you can do it.

And when I say you can do *it*, I literally mean everything and anything. Everything life has to offer you can do; it's simply you choosing to do it and taking the time to execute on the plan.

See, I want to live my most awesome life, to have it all. I want . . .

- to have a fit and strong body
- to live with vitality and good health
- to go on adventures and travel the world
- to have an amazing relationship with my wife
- to have awesome kids that grow up to be fulfilled and happy
- to have a career that gives me purpose and meaning
- to spend time doing what I love
- to feel free to live the life I want to live

- to have enough money to not worry about things
- to be able to enjoy life and all that it offers
- to live well into old age . . .

. . . and MORE.

> I want it all, and I want YOU to believe you can have it all, too.

This book is about BIG achievable goals that shape the life you want to live. That's why it's called *How to Life an Awesome Life*. It's a book with a big target: it aims to inspire you to go big with your life, to dream and take action; to have it all, whatever your goals and dreams might be.

The reality is that few of us are *truly* living our best life. Instead, we're hiding behind upbeat selfies and pictures of the life we want our social media to portray, or the narrative we keep telling our friends over a drink through a broken, half-hearted smile.

Be honest with me, and yourself. Are you truly living the most Awesome Life possible? Your answers to the following questions might help you work this out.

- Do you feel happy that life is on track and all is good, or that you are at least working towards that?
- Do you have energy and passion for life?
- Do you feel strong mentally and physically?
- Do you feel positive most days?
- Do you feel confident as a person and comfortable with who you are?
- Do you go to work every day feeling inspired and excited, putting out your best self?
- Do you have enough money to do the things you want?
- Do you have the body and fitness you want?

- Do you have the house, car and things you want, or a method to get them over time?
- Do you feel you are making an impact on others' lives?
- Do you feel alive and have a lust for life?
- Do you get up excited and curious to face the day?

You might have answered yes to some of the above and have fulfilment in some areas of your life, or you may feel you have none of the above. Either way, with this book and its 11-step formula I'm going to inspire you with your own potential, help you create an action plan, and set you on the first steps of your journey and beyond.

Notice I am not using the word 'success', which you may see in many books like this. Success is defined as 'the accomplishment of an aim or purpose'. The reason I'm not a huge fan of the word 'success', despite everyone feeling like they know what it means, is that it often has fixed criteria, and it's not open to intuitive feedback or individual interpretation (you knowing if you have achieved the goal or not).

If we have a goal, it's often shaped by a number, like 'I want to lose four stone', and it's only when you have lost those four stone that you will be happy and feel you have achieved success. I would rather the goal be: 'I want to lose weight to the point where I look and feel my best self, where I fit into the clothes I want to wear, feel good in my skin, and feel fit and strong. I think this is around four stone, but this number is only a rough target. I will know when I am happy with my weight loss because I will FEEL like I've completed this journey.'

This is why I prefer the word 'fulfilment' over 'success'. Many things can make us fulfilled, and if we are always fulfilled in life, we are likely happy. I've never met ANYONE truly happy who is simply trying to be successful at things – they are just jumping from one goal to the next, never being in a state of fulfilment.

Hence my statement about what I want for my kids: 'To have awesome kids that grow up to be fulfilled and happy.' So many say, 'I want my kids to be successful.'

What is success anyway? Who is defining it? You? Them? Society?

I want fulfilment. I want my kids to be fulfilled in all that they do. And if they turn up to life and do things right, as I try to do, they will likely be successful by default. But it rarely works the other way round: chasing success rarely leads to fulfilment, but chasing fulfilment and turning up and doing your best every day quite often leads to success.

Right, back to the task at hand . . .

Now I'm not going to bullsh*t you, there is a lot of work ahead. This is half the reason people fail: they retreat when it gets a little tough. And working on BIG goals isn't always easy.

Getting really fit means you'll have to do some tough workouts.

- Losing weight means you'll have to say no to some food sometimes.
- Earning more money means you'll have to put some extra hours in or make some tough decisions about your career.
- Changing who you are means you have to look at yourself as well as your current beliefs and behaviours (which is really hard – but often needed).
- Developing deep and meaningful relationships takes time, hard work, and an understanding of others and what makes them happy.

All of this takes time, way longer than most of us think or will allow.

If you're reading this book thinking I've got a load of secrets to fast-track you to get all the above in six months' time, unfortunately you'll be disappointed. Shaping your dreams and living your most Awesome Life requires patience; you've got to be willing to play the long game. With that being said, I hope to get you there much faster, and some of the things listed above can be achieved really quickly . . .

More happiness? It starts with a shift in your mindset.

Better health? It starts with eating better and looking after yourself.

Fitter and stronger? It starts with exercise.

You can have so much so quickly if you're prepared to work with this book, shift your perspective, make the time for new things, and discard old things (this book isn't just about adding new things, or creating a new plan; it's also about ditching things that aren't working or serving you). But some of the other things like fulfilment in your career or relationship, building wealth, going on adventures, or growing as a person take far longer, and you need to take a five to ten-year view on some of these things.

What I hope you notice here is that all the stuff that really matters in life doesn't take as much time as you think it does to achieve. When people focus on dreams and change, they often focus on *things*. A house. A car. New clothes. And while all these things are nice and good goals to have – everyone likes having nice things – ultimately living an awesome life simply comes down to . . .

> YOU.

Living an awesome life is a physical and mental state of being, something more ethereal than it is material. It's a state of being, where you are happy, fulfilled, challenged, loved, having fun and doing what you love, all while continuing grow as a person. This makes you feel alive and thus makes you feel AWESOME. So, while you might have goals like buying your dream home, or going travelling, or changing career, or having kids, you can be happy working towards it, you can enjoy the *process.*

After all, everything in life is a process. We are always moving towards things so it's important to choose what we move towards and then enjoy the process, the journey and what it does for us. Life is actually quite long; most people live past 80 years old, so you have to enjoy the journey as it's a long one (though paradoxically it also seems to flash by and not all of us are lucky to hit these ages, so we need to make the most of it!).

This approach to life is often framed as a growth mindset, being willing and open to change, always developing as a person and enjoying the process of becoming greater, but in the same breath being grateful for what you have, including the simple things like your health, and being fulfilled with where you are at and what you are doing in life. It's taking stepping stones towards the future while never taking your eye off the beauty of the present.

Building a business is a good example. Building a business never stops unless you retire or sell; there isn't a clear end point for the company or for yourself. You keep growing into the person that can manage it all and get to the next step. I sit here now, writing this as a business owner, someone constantly moving forward learning the next steps. It's all a journey, and every day I relish the prospect of being challenged by what's coming next. It's also because life isn't a picnic. Life can be really tough at times, so it's important to develop resilience, to be able to take challenges head on, and to know that whatever that challenge may be, you will become a better and stronger person as a result.

> You either let life shape you into a strong, able and AWESOME person, who can live a bigger and better life, or you let life control and defeat you, ending up having a small, limited, unfulfilling life.

I know which one I choose . . .

If you read this book and implement the 11 core Awesome life pillars, you can have all you dream of and become everything you want to be as a person; but the key thing is that you have to choose to do the work and apply the lessons in this book – however uncomfortable or hard that work might be.

Now I must repeat (and I will say this a lot), this whole process starts and ends with you. No one in life is going to give you permission to succeed or be fulfilled, you have to give yourself permission. No holy voice is going to sound out through the sky and say 'Yes, you may now go live your best life, don't worry about him, or her, or that, or what happened in the past, go achieve and be.' That stuff might happen in the movies, or in your dreams, but not here on Earth In reality, we CHOOSE to live our best life. It's time for *you* to choose.

I recognize and appreciate this doesn't feel as simple to do as it is to say in this moment. You may have had parents that weren't always the most supportive of you as a kid. Or teachers that told you that you would never amount to anything. Or friends that always dismissed anything you ever said you'd to as being daft. These are all things we need to work through, but they are not excuses to settle with a life we don't want. Every one of us has had challenges in life, and while some people do have it easier or harder than others, we have to play the hand we're dealt and make it as good as it can be for ourselves and our families. This book isn't about comparing yourself to me or anyone else you know; it's about you, only you, and optimizing what you've got. It's that simple.

It's the job of this book to help you maximize your personal strengths and abilities while nullifying your sabotaging ways. You likely have some fears and self-doubt, lack long-term thinking and planning, or don't know how to say 'no' to others and 'yes' to yourself. This is what this book aims to do. To either get rid of all that, or at least shape and control it so it doesn't hold you back.

Because I promise you, I literally cannot say this loud enough . . .

YOU CAN DO IT.

YOU CAN ACHIEVE IT.

BUT . . .

YOU HAVE TO DO THE WORK, AND AT TIMES, IT WON'T BE EASY,

TRUST ME.

Alongside giving you a plan and insights, this book is also here to fire you up and motivate you to continue executing that plan with a constant and evolving vision of how you want your life to be.

This is why I use the word 'Awesome' all the time. Because that's what you and I want our lives to be.

So, if you're willing to cut the BS, stop blaming things, other people, or circumstances which are out of your control, and take control, shape your future, design it, and take action on it, then you can have it all.

See, while there are a lot of things out of our control in life, we have control over one thing: our mindset, and as a result the way we respond to these things. The story we tell ourselves about our roadblocks are often far more important for determining our outcomes than the roadblocks themselves, and so while it might be easy – even comforting in a paradoxical way – to tell ourselves that we *can't* because there is something in the way, if we want to

9

make our lives better we have two choices: change the story we tell ourselves and join the millions of people who have turned things around from difficult places, or forever wish we took action. This means we need to combine radical acceptance of who we are and where we are in the world, with a dogged commitment to changing things regardless of the challenge that presents.

It's time to accept who you are, for all that you are.

To accept the situation you are in, whatever has happened in the past.

And to make a plan to change it and execute boldly on that plan.

Because this is how you become fulfilled *and* successful and live your most Awesome Life.

This is also why the first half of this book, which sets that stage for the 11-step formula, is quite long. You might have had a flick through and thought 'Why take so long to get to the 11 steps and to the real action, Ben?'

The reason for this is based on my experience as a coach. Change isn't easy. We have fears. We have problems. We have roadblocks. We have excuses. And most of the things we want to change we have attempted before. So just giving you a roadmap won't cut it. I did this with clients in my early years as a coach and it very rarely works. I need to help you break down fears, teach you to effectively problem solve, help you shift your mindset, and clear the way for the change. So yeah, you could skip to the 11 steps or even skip to the chapter or even skip to the chapter summaries, but that will only give you the highlights and not the context and skills to be able to pave the way for BIG, long-lasting change.

So, skip ahead by all means, but if you are in the same position in six months' time, and haven't made the changes you wanted, that might be why.

This book is not going to try to change you; it is simply here to help you optimize. You are you. I am me. My strengths and weaknesses as a person are personal to me, and the same can be said for you. So, it's not a case of you becoming like me, or someone else you deem to be successful, because success and living your most Awesome Life comes in many forms. I am not here to judge or say how that should look; I am here to show you what is possible, how it is possible, and to help you to go away and create that life for yourself over time.

Because it will take some time. Big life goals, big change, it happens over months and years. I know this first-hand. Some of my big personal goals took a bit of time. For example, it took me . . .

- six months to lose five stone of body fat, and another three months to lose the last half stone
- three years to put on three stone of muscle
- three years to build a coaching business online before it earned enough money for me to go full time, and six years of working on that business before I had enough money to buy my first home
- seven years to learn how to get over my fear of hurting the woman I love and committing to the relationship and to her despite my fears
- ten years to build the financial security I wanted before I had kids
- many, many years to learn how to be happy and content with what I have, while still striving to grow as a person in an enjoyable, patient and content way.

The big things in life often do take time. Please know that. But being 100 per cent honest, you should be able to do it a bit more quickly than I did because you are holding this book. All the things above that I struggled with for years and years you could do faster because I am going to detail what I learned throughout these pages. Don't struggle any more than you have to. Apply the lessons in this book and go crush life way faster than I did.

But I have a caveat: don't try to go too quickly because a lot of the benefits are in in the process, in the journey. This isn't a book just about achieving things; it's about growing into the *king of person who achieves things and is fulfilled*. A lot of the things I have achieved taught me valuable lessons along the way. For example:

- The process of building muscle develops a confident gym goer in the process.
- The process of losing body fat and keeping it off develops a confident person in the kitchen, and nurtures a healthy relationship with food.
- The process of building a business develops a good leader and service provider.
- The process of saving for something makes you learn about investing and putting money away for your future.
- The process of achieving one goal gives you the confidence to achieve more . . . and so the cycle continues.

Yes, the end goal is satisfying – achieving that milestone is something to be celebrated – but the process is where so much of the reward comes from. The journey shapes you, makes you more able, and who doesn't want to be someone who is confident, able, knowledgeable, aware, knowing and loving?

I do.

And I know you do, too.

As I write this book at the age of 35 having achieved a lot, I know I am only a third of the way through my journey (I aim to live to over 100) and I'm excited for the journey to come. Yes, I'll achieve more, but more importantly I'll grow more as a person. And as I grow, I can help myself more, help my friends more, support my family more, contribute to society and my communities more, and that is AWESOME.

For me, that is a fulfilling life.

And what underpins your level of life fulfilment?

YOU.

You are the asset that you need to develop. I've read countless books on personal development over the years because of the value they can bring to your life, and now I'm the guy writing one after having had the dream of doing it for so long; but it all started with a weight loss goal and simply wanting to better myself.

Where will your journey start, or end? Only you can decide.

That's the awesome thing about life, it's only going to take you exciting places when you go 'all in' and choose to become the best version of yourself.

I promise that when you choose yourself, when you challenge yourself, when you develop yourself, when you are constantly learning and evolving and willing to change, you will be living an Awesome Life.

Life should evolve, life should change, life should go through stages, life should go up and down and around. And that's what makes life interesting.

How many people do you see as stuck in life, stagnant, just going through the motions, not necessarily sad, but also not happy, just 'meh'? They don't have enough to look forward to, they aren't moving towards a new goal, they aren't growing or being challenged with what's next. Maybe you feel that way right now.

Please don't think that you need to always be working towards something grand in life – you don't. Life isn't a perpetual race to acquire more things, titles and acclaim. When I say we want to be moving forward with life by growing and being challenged, it might be you learning how to grow your business, but it might also be you working to bring your local community together more, to be a better parent, to forge stronger relationships, or how to grow a vegetable patch in your garden so you can show your kids the value of real food. Growing and learning means we are never stagnant, that we are always passionate about life and what it can bring. And if you ever feel that you aren't, change MUST happen.

Now I can give you all the examples in the world, but all this stuff is personal to you and me as individuals. I can tell you what I love, what it means to live an Awesome Life for me, and what I might think will lead you towards an Awesome Life, but ultimately only you can piece this all together and work out what living an Awesome Life means to you. What I want is for you to know what you truly want, and for you to use this book to help you shape your future. Because I don't want you to not go another day not working towards a better future.

You deserve it. We *all* deserve it.

This is the incredible thing about being human in the digital, information age. There is no information we don't have access to anymore; you can learn how to do anything. Medicine has increased our life expectancy. We can travel anywhere and everywhere. We can do any job we care to dream of. We can pretty much contact anyone in the world with enough effort. For many of us, there is an almost obscene amount of abundance and opportunity. And that abundance, those opportunities, are only going to improve as technology levels the playing field even more.

So, I'll ask again, what does living an Awesome Life mean to you?

What do you want? Who do you want to be? What do you want to change?

I'd like you to start to think about that, I want this introduction to start off the process of you dreaming, wishing and wanting. I

don't mind if you even put this book down for a couple of weeks
to think about that, because we are now looking at big life decisions, and such decisions shouldn't be made lightly. It takes time,
so please don't rush it; there's no pressure, not from me anyway,
so please don't put that pressure on yourself. It's often when we
rush things we make the wrong decisions, so take it slow.

> Big things in life take big thinking. Take the time you need.

It's funny that the question of 'what do you want to do in life'
always ends up with someone talking about their career path,
or more specifically that one job. I used to hate that question as
a kid; it was as if you had to say 'I want to be a lawyer/doctor/
accountant [insert whatever high-status, high-paying job you
like]', and that was your life, your future, all done and dusted.

All you were meant to aspire to was your job . . . That was it,
your life. Fuck that.

As people we are not a job, or a career, that is not our whole
identity, that is a small part of it. Life is many things. We are
many things. After all, we are HUMAN.

Life is work.
Life is health.
Life is love.
Life is fun.
Life is adventure.
Life is sleep.
Life is eating.
Life is laughing.
Life is moving.
Life is for growing.
Life is for LIVING.

Life is about SO much more, and this is why there is so much to talk about in this book.

I've been stuck at many points in my life, sat there thinking 'What's next?' But the only way to find out is to carry on and be a little patient. To keep growing and challenging yourself, to keep walking through doors and taking new opportunities that come up, to keep seeking change, challenge and growth. Do that, and you'll find that the path ends up going in a pretty cool direction.

My big life shift was losing 5.5 stone of bodyfat. That transformation of my physical body changed my life, the act of becoming healthier, losing unwanted body fat and getting really fit ... all that was incredible. But it made me curious as to what else I could change; it made me seek MORE. If I could eat less, eat more healthily, adjust my lifestyle to have more healthy habits, and feel this good, then WOW, give me some more. I'm in ...

That one transformation made me want to transform many other areas of my life and turn my body and mind into the ultimate tool. And guess what, it's your turn.

You are the tool.

You are the vehicle.

You are the person that is going to shape your future life with zest and passion.

It's time to unlock your potential.

It's time to develop the tools and insights to succeed, achieve and be fulfilled

It's time to build your Awesome Life.

Ready?

Pumped?

AWESOME. Let's go ...

PART 1

Doing the groundwork

CHAPTER ONE

So what is an Awesome Life?

This book is about you, but at this point I feel I need to introduce myself a little more; otherwise you might not believe me and get what this living an Awesome Life is all about. It could be easy for me to write a book and just *say* these things. To paint the picture but not to have lived the story. But I am writing this book because I feel I have lived an Awesome Life for 15-plus years and I feel empowered to inspire others to do the same.

Once you're convinced that I know what I'm talking about, I'm going to outline why most people hold themselves back, how you can approach your fears, think more critically, and problem-solve, all while telling stories that should give context and real-world meaning to my points. This should set the stage for the next part of this book, which explains the 11 steps in the Awesome Life formula.

So here we go: a little bit more about me.

So why is *my* life so awesome?

I am writing this book with a great feeling of calm, satisfaction and gratitude for my life. If that's not a life being well lived, what is?

You might have picked up this book thinking it was going to be one of those usual motivational/career/money books where the guy or girl writing it, if you checked them out on their social media, is *living the life*.

But I'm not the guy with four five-million-pound homes dotted around the world with garages full of luxury cars, who holidays eight times a year in exotic locations, who buys his partner diamond jewellery on a whim while passing through the airport, who owns every Rolex just because he can, who has a housekeeper do everything around the home, who works just two hours a day trading the markets . . . I am NOT that guy.

Jeeze. That guy sounds painful!

And if that's what you see as successful, as the ultimate goal, as the trappings of having 'arrived' in life, we're in trouble. That's the type of crap you see people flaunt on social media – the watches, the holidays, the houses, the cars, the money stuff. Those are the outlandish purchases that only intimate that a person is 'successful' but doesn't necessarily mean anything beyond that; they just mean that someone has money, and yes, a lot of it.

It's also emblematic of what I feel is is so wrong about the modern age of social media. We can portray the life people want to see whether or not we're actually happy while living it, and a lot of people do that. So, make sure you follow the right people online – because there are a lot of insufferable people out there just playing some warped status game. Trust me, I've spoken to a lot of them, many of them aren't happy, they aren't fulfilled, they are empty inside.

I'm a simple guy with simple, meaningful (to me) dreams.

So, who am I, and what has led me to sitting here feeling a great sense of calm, satisfaction and gratitude for my life?

I am fit, healthy and strong.

I understand myself, my unique abilities, and how to use them to get the most out of life.

I have ADHD, which became an issue when I was studying at university, but got help with it, learned how to manage it, did the work, and now use my ADHD as an asset to my business.

I used to have IBS, eczema and asthma when I was younger (which I worked to solve once I left high school), and spent over 14 months in 2020/2021 battling to recover from long COVID, which also resulted in me having to undergo testosterone therapy, rehabilitate my gut health, and battle back from clinical depression in 2021/2022. I know what health recovery looks like, and how challenging it can be.

I've had a great career to date, being awarded health coach of the year 2019, nutrition coach of the year 2020 and 2021, multiple awards for the supplements I've created (Awesome Supplements should you wish to check them out). I've written for most UK media publications and newspapers, have been on TV and on the news a few times, have had a number-one-rated UK podcast (rated in the top ten globally), which has allowed me to inspire many people and connect with some of the greatest minds on the planet . . .

I've helped thousands of people change their lives via my podcasting, writing, coaching and my online programmes.

I run a group of companies that collectively, in the year of writing, should turn over £2 million, and which, if sold, could see me retire if I wanted to with the money I would net. Otherwise, financially, I never have to worry about money or spending. My wife doesn't have to work and can focus on being a full-time mum to our two daughters. I'm not a millionaire, but I'm comfortable – and day to day I don't want or need for much (funnily enough, a comfortable life like mine takes a lot less money than people think – more on this later).

I've travelled most of Europe, Asia and Central America as well as many other incredible places, both with my work and for pleasure.

I have a happy, healthy family with a beautiful home in a lovely part of the UK, just a few minutes from all our friends and family.

I do work that I am passionate about, and which gets me fired up every day.

I work in a very flexible way, never missing anything to do with my kids, and enjoy every aspect of my life.

I am confident, calm, balanced, happy, fulfilled and constantly excited about the future.

If I did happen to die today, I would die a happy man, knowing that the years I have lived I went 'all on in' and made the most of it.

I see every day as an opportunity to learn, have fun, experience life in all its ups and downs, while continuing to challenge myself.

I am living an Awesome Life.

What I'm saying, in short, is that I'm a pretty normal guy (I think) who has a pretty normal aspiration for living a good (awesome) life. So, what's my criteria for this?

- I want to be happy, content and fulfilled.
- I want to be fit, strong and resilient.
- I want my family to be happy and healthy and laugh lots.
- I want to provide everything my kids need to thrive.

- I want a nice house to enjoy and raise my kids in.
- I want a car that works and I don't have to worry about.
- I want the money to go on adventures and have experiences.
- I want to be able to afford good food, both for health and pleasure.
- I want to be able to help my family when they need it
- I want to not have to worry about money.
- I want to do work I am passionate about and positively affects the world.
- I want to have the freedom of choice and time and not be bound by any external forces
- I want a free mind, devoid of pain, anxiety, clutter or ill feeling towards others.
- *I want it all.*

This for me is living an AWESOME Life. It's a delicate balance of things, experiences and state of mind. I have it, and I want to share with you how you can also have it.

Exercise: What is your Awesome Life?

This is the first exercise of many in this book, where you will define what living an Awesome Life looks like for you. We're also going to revisit this later in the book, as it might change as you read on. As I share more perspectives, insights and teachings, you might find your definition shifts or deepens, or how that life materializes.

So, forgetting what living an Awesome Life is to me, write down below – whether it's a list of bullet points or a paragraph of text – what you think living an Awesome Life is to you:

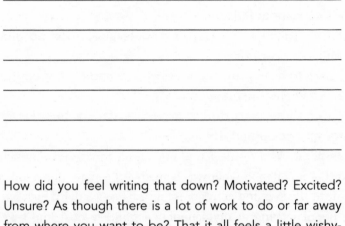

How did you feel writing that down? Motivated? Excited? Unsure? As though there is a lot of work to do or far away from where you want to be? That it all feels a little wishy-washy right now?

I want you to have a mixture of these emotions, because that would be a truthful place to be. There is no point being so motivated and inspired that you're blind to the reality of the path ahead. Because when you know and see what the path is, you will know there is a fair chunk of work to do. But that's OK. As I've said, this stuff isn't going to take a few weeks to put into place. Some bits will – there are plenty of quick wins we can have to get you living a much more Awesome Life quickly – but many other things will take time, and that's expected.

Back to me (we'll focus on *you* really soon)

I don't want to focus on me too much, because this book is about you, but I need you to have confidence you are in good hands. You might have picked up this book on a whim in an airport as your holiday reading and have no idea who I am, or got recommended it by a slightly crazy friend of yours and be reading with trepidation, or got given it as a gift at Christmas and are reading just in case they ask you later what you got out of it. So here goes . . .

I started my own personal development journey at the age of 18. When I finished school, I was very overweight, so much so that I was classified as obese. I also suffered with ADHD, asthma, eczema and IBS, and had done so throughout my teenage years. As a result, I was bullied all through senior school for being 'fat' and what was coined 'a thespian' (a person who is into the arts and acting and quite flamboyant, which wasn't a popular thing at my school – a military boarding school). School, at times, was really tough, and in the back of my mind I always wanted to change, to do something about it, to realize my potential, but I lacked confidence, know-how, and support beyond my mum (who was always awesome and supportive, thanks Mum).

Bullying can do two things: it can make you retreat into yourself (the most common outcome) and cause you to lack self-worth, or it can make you want to fight back, be better, and prove them wrong.

I chose the latter. Screw letting the bullies' words define who I was or who I was going to be.

Once I left school and I got my first job as I started to pursue my dream of becoming an actor I started to have thoughts of change, largely focused on my health and fitness. Early on, I took simple steps. Although I had finished my secondary school, I was still at the military school because my mum worked there, and I was lucky because the school had good facilities we could use (beautiful surroundings, playing fields, gym, swimming pool, etc). So, I started to run a few times a week and visit the school gym. This was me simply starting to say, 'I want to better myself. I don't want to go into the big wide world and continue to get bullied for being overweight, to always be picked last playing sport, to not feel confident in myself'.

During that summer, I got a bit fitter and I lost a tiny bit of weight, but it wasn't a lot at all, maybe 4 or 5 pounds from a whole summer of training. It was frustrating as I was putting in a decent amount of effort, but the thing holding me back was my diet. I wasn't eating well enough, and ultimately I was still eating too much (boarding school does a good job of feeding you up . . .).

After a few months of this we moved. Because I had finished school, my mum felt it was time to move on (she originally got the job because she was divorced and wanted to continue to put my brother and I through private school – what a sacrifice and clever move; thanks, again Mum, I'll be forever grateful). So, with a new partner, they bought a house in our local town, and we all moved from the school to Ipswich, Suffolk, in the east of England.

I continued on this fitness journey while starting to do auditions for drama school. The auditions weren't going well, my weight loss wasn't going well, and in the midst of all that I had a big argument with my brother one day at home – someone I always bullied and argued with because:

1. I was his older brother by four and a half years and you often do that as a big brother.
2. As a deflection of the bullying I used to receive at school, probably to make myself feel better (my brother was a bit chubby, too, at the time, so I deflected the fat jokes I got at school on to him – classic bully behaviour!)

One afternoon I was bullying my brother about his weight while we were making food in the kitchen and something I said was the straw that broke the camel's back. My brother fought back, and rightly so, but this time in a BIG way, saying stuff like 'You're far from perfect, bro. Look how fat you are, look at all this fitness and running you're doing and you're not even losing any weight. You keep getting rejected from drama school, nothing you're doing is working. You're failing, big time, so f*** off!'

After 17 years I can't remember his exact words, but it was along those lines. And guess what, it hurt – badly. But after the frustration and anger wore off, and the facts showed themselves (it was all true), I wanted to react. I wanted to do better, to be better, to find a better way. I knew there was a way. People lose weight and crush their goals all the time, I just had to find out why I wasn't achieving my goals. I had to find out the flaws in my methods. I also considered what this goal would mean for my career. I had been unsuccessful both with my career ambitions my fitness and weight loss ambitions; and perhaps they were connected. Perhaps if I got fit, lost weight, and built up my self-confidence, my chances of acting school success would improve?

Moving on

So I developed this mantra in my head: 'If I get fit and lose weight, I'll be successful in my career.' And that was it. Because I was 18 and in that 'discovering myself' phase of my life this really drove me on. I now had this singular focus to prove everyone wrong, because I'd been told my whole life that acting was a stupid career path to follow, that studying science, maths and English was the way to go – yet I just wasn't good at those things. I was good at the arts, and do you know what? – this made me step up my actions in a big way. It was enough for me to go find the answers I needed. My mindset was half-way there: I was already taking action and doing a lot of work to change my circumstances but my tools were broken. The things I was doing, mainly my eating, weren't right, so if I could find the answers, I could and would be successful with these goals I had for myself.

Side note: If you're not finding success with something in your life, one of two things is ultimately the problem. Either your strategy is wrong, or your tools are inadequate (or both!) For me the effort was there, but my tools were just not up to the job.

This led me to problem-solve and think, 'Where do I find people that know a lot about health, fitness and losing weight?' 'Ah, of course the gym!' So I took a good chunk of my then earnings and I committed to going to the gym and getting the advice I needed to achieve my goals. The effort was there; this was me finding better tools.

When I joined this gym I was very fortunate to get a gym induction by a great coach named Ben Gray (with whom I'm still friends today). He gave me some great lifestyle advice, told me to buy a book that was 'hot' at the time on nutrition called

How to Eat, Move and Be Healthy! by Paul Chek, and wrote me out a fitness plan. The plan consisted of:

- hitting the gym four days per week doing 30 minutes' cardio, and one hour's weight training (I then added 30 minutes' core training too because I wanted a six-pack)
- reading the book and applying the diet advice in it
- getting good sleep
- hydrating well
- being as active as possible day to day
- avoiding drinking too much alcohol.

That was the plan and it was a huge improvement on my previous one, which was not much more than 'Eat more healthily and get more exercise'. This was also alongside starting to play rugby again (as I love sport and it's a great way to meet new friends), which meant training twice per week and playing a game and the weekend. All of this was a little extreme in terms of how much exercise I was doing, but I had the desire and the energy to do it at the time (as well as very few other commitments!), so I went HARD at it. Guess what, it worked: through my improved eating habits, and with weight training rather than just cardio, I lost five stone in six months, with the last half stone taking two to three more months. I was a new man as a result. This saw me grow very quickly as a person: to be a lot more confident in myself, be really fit, get rid of my eczema and reduce my IBS symptoms too, and I started to really believe I was made for great things.

Getting fit and healthy really was a game changer and is ultimately, as you will find in this book, the foundation for everything you want to achieve in your life:

- If you want energy and vitality, you need to be as healthy as possible.
- If you want to lose bodyfat and feel good, you need to eat good food, and less of it to lose weight (no fad diets, just good, normal, balanced meals).
- If you want to be strong (mentally and physically), you need to do things that make you stronger, like lifting heavy things or doing physical and mental challenges.
- If you want to move well, look after your body, take care of it and how it moves.
- If you want to feel good day on day, prioritize good sleep.

The book I read to help with all of this ultimately gave me all the foundations I needed to live a good, productive, healthy life. And because this was such a life-changing book for me, it showed me the power of the written word. Just one book read cover to cover, and its lessons applied to my life *changed* my life – the same could be for you reading this book, too.

Gaining so much value from a book turned me into an avid reader. School had almost made me hate reading because I rarely read anything I actually wanted to read. So much of school was spent reading Shakespeare plays, history about Henry VIII, how to tackle algebra, and the nuances of the periodic table. All the stuff I had to learn just to pass a test or exam (I think the school system needs an overhaul, but that's for another book). The reading I did at school was never felt like it was driven by real interest, or real-world application, so I rarely read any non-fiction books outside of school. But now I had read this book I was hooked. I felt that if this book gave me this much value and had changed my life this much, and it only cost me £15.00, there was an entire world of books out there ready to discover.

I went to the library and found more books on health and fitness (the internet wasn't as much of thing back then like it is now). I devoured what I could for free from the library, then started buying some from the local bookshop. This, along with a few other life events, led me to abandon acting as a career and train to become a personal trainer and nutrition coach. What I had learned and applied to myself was life-changing stuff, and I wanted to coach other people to do the same, to change their lives just as I had changed mine. So, at age 19 I started doing personal training and nutrition courses from the very guy that wrote that very first book, Paul Chek. And because I was working hard doing two jobs, I was able to afford to fly to California and study directly under him at his facility.

A year later, after much study, I became a personal trainer working one to one helping people. But I'll be honest, I didn't get very good results. I felt like I knew what to do and knew how to make a plan, but I had barely scratched the surface. I didn't understand people and the nuances of coaching and behavioural change, so I rarely got people to achieve their goals.

So, I went through the same process again. 'OK, I'm failing here,' I told myself. 'I'm not getting the results I expect, but I am applying effort, so it's not an effort problem but an under-standing problem, a lack of education.'

I made the decision to go to university and study sports coaching and performance. My motivation here was threefold:

1. I knew I wanted to study the human body inside and out so I could be better at my job – a degree that covers aspects of physiology, biology, biomechanics, sports nutrition and coaching would do this.

2. I wanted to go to a place that had lots of opportunities – which universities do. Opportunities I knew I wouldn't get in my hometown continuing to do what I was doing.

3. I wanted to have fun, explore things, people, and the world, and coming from a small town with not a lot going on, I felt moving away to university was a good way to do this. To really fly the nest.

At this point I will cut a long story short and pick up parts of my journey later where they're relevant. The point here is to stress the power that just ONE book had on me and how it stimulated in me the desire to learn, evolve and grow as a person. I've taken this approach to everything I've ever done. If I've wanted to know something, or learn something, I've simply bought a book, or several books on a topic, talked to people who know a lot about the topic, and learned everything I could to get the outcome I wanted.

> **'A book must be an axe for the frozen sea within us.'**
> **Franz Kafka**

A Swiss Army knife approach to life

On that topic, it's important to try not to learn without aim; instead try to learn with purpose. I remember in the early days of personal development, my learning was all about nutrition and fitness, but as soon as I felt I had learned what I needed to learn, first for myself and then to help my clients, I shifted my learning to sports nutrition and behavioural psychology. Then when I started my business, my learning shifted to business, then when I had issues growing my business, it shifted to marketing and sales, and then over time to leadership ... to finance and wealth building ... then, as I prepared to have kids, to parenting and Stoic philosophy (!). Ultimately, we learn things that are relevant to changing or improving our situation, and as we evolve in our lives our learning needs will change, and that's a good thing.

This approach has led me to become a good, and proud, *generalist*. I know a fair bit about nutrition, health, fitness, mindset, behaviour and habit change, career success, business success, relationships, parenting, productivity and technology, but I'm no expert or specialist in any of these areas. I know enough to help 95 per cent of people to improve themselves in these areas, and I've chosen to do this because I want to help a large number of people. It also feeds my ADHD and my brain's huge appetite for stimulation. It's a win–win.

What I want you to get from this book is the skills I have developed as a life generalist. This book won't help you develop any hyper-specific areas of business or your career, for example. I'm no engineer and so I can't help you progress your knowledge in engineering, but what I can help you with is your approach to your career and how you can develop it in a broader way; and this will help you to become a more successful and better engineer. Just like I can help you with your nutrition, fitness, health, relationship building, and many more areas fundamental to being your most awesome self, and building your Awesome Life. It's the broader skillset that's important. The specifics can come later, and are often the easy bits.

Think of this book as a Swiss Army knife for a better life.

CHAPTER TWO

Life imposter syndrome

At this point in the book we need to be super honest with ourselves and say, 'It's not quite that simple is it.' If all it took were some motivational words from someone to live our best, most Awesome Life, we'd all be doing it. Except most of us aren't, so we need to consider why.

We all dream, we all want more, we've all made grand plans before, but where do the plans go, why do they fade, what happens?

The fear of being judged

Perhaps the most difficult thing to deal with is when fear, doubt and imposter syndrome kick in and make us back down, stopping us from taking action on the plans we make. They hold us back because we think that our doubts are evidence of our inadequacy, yet these emotions, these fears, are totally normal, and if you're willing to get close to them and understand them for what they are, you can still do the thing you want to do in spite of them.

Emotions don't work in isolation. People look at successful people and think, 'Oh they don't feel these emotions, these fears; they must just not have them and have the ability to just DO things.'

Incorrect. We are all human, and it's human to feel an array of emotions, both positive and negative, all at the same time. The simple difference that allows someone to be successful, breaking the pattern of negative thinking and creating positive outcomes, is the ability to build up enough courage to break through the moment of paralysis.

Let's take the example of public speaking. Very few people are comfortable speaking in public, for many this is true even if it's in a small group and they just have to say a few words. Even the thought of public speaking gives many people dry mouth and sweaty palms. Common sentiments that I've encountered in people who have asked me for advice include: 'If I stand up there and speak, what will people think of me? . . . What if what I say is silly? . . . OMG, look at what I'm wearing! . . . I'll likely stutter and then they'll think I'm an idiot . . .'. These fears can be debilitating, and so people avoid public speaking.

The experience in our head of how people will judge us is a powerful stimulus for inaction, unless we are in an environment with people we *really* know, trust, and feel comfortable with, meaning we won't be judged for what we say.

Side note: And the honest truth is that (at least in the moment), we will be judged. We all judge people all the time. It's a natural process that we do in order to work out the social hierarchy in any given situation and, importantly, our place in it. We also do this to simply make sense of the world and the people in it. We use the process of judgement to work out who this person is, what they look like, if they might be someone we might want to talk to, if they feel like a peer, or someone we should avoid. It's a natural process the brain goes through even when we just glance at someone.

I tell you this because I want you to draw comfort from this. If we are all doing it, and it's 100 per cent natural, we can all relax. It's not something only other people are doing to us when we enter a room, you and I are doing it, too – it's a process we *all* go through and, importantly, we all forget about our judgement almost as soon as we leave the situation in question. I'd like you to take comfort in knowing that it's always happening, and you can't stop it, all we can do is grow to accept that we can't control other people's judgements, and that those who judge us will forget their judgement sas soon as they move on to judge someone else.

So back to our public speaking example. When we look at the fear of public speaking, we need to break down the fear. We've looked at one element of it, people judging us and that stopping us from doing something like speaking publicly, but another big aspect of this is us feeling like a fraud, that we can't do or say something of value. This is imposter syndrome – an individual, you or me, doubting our skills or talents and our ability to say something of value. What this culminates in is us feeling like a 'fraud'. 'Oh, if I get up there, and say something wrong, or silly, or incorrect, they will realize that I don't know what I'm talking about, that I'm not clever, that I don't know my subject matter, that I shouldn't be in front of others like this.'

So, we stop, we freeze, we don't speak up, we don't take the opportunity, and we shrink, we miss the opportunity, and we don't progress.

Now public speaking is on the extreme end of this 'speaking up' spectrum. There are many moments in our daily lives where people don't speak up as a result of imposter syndrome or a fear of being judged. This happens in one-to-one conversations, in digital conversations, and in small and large groups. So many people could be living much bigger, more rewarding lives if they found the courage to back themselves, trust their ability, see themselves as someone of value in the world and to others, and speak up.

> Please have the courage to speak up, to back yourself, and step up to a bigger, more AWESOME LIFE.

Life imposter syndrome

Having worked as a coach for over 15 years I've heard a lot of fears from people who struggle with changing to the person they want to be and to live the life they want to live. This is why I call it 'life imposter syndrome': people are scared to move on to a new, bigger life, despite evidence all around them that they deserve more and want more, and that others around them want it for them (if people don't want it for you, they wouldn't be your friends, would they?).

Fears can often be multi-layered and need to be tackled in parts. This is because we stack fears and reasons together, sometimes because there are multiple reasons our brain is saying no and there are several genuine fears at play. But sometimes our brain does it to protect us, to create an overwhelming reason to *not* do something. As a result, we stack reasons together to keep ourselves safe.

But we must ask ourselves, 'Are the reasons I am saying I should not do this thing grounded in facts, in reality, and are they going to serve me long term?' Many fears keep us safe – short term, they protect us from the potential embarrassment, or the feeling of stepping outside our comfort zone into the unknown – but the reality is in 99 per cent of cases these fears don't serve us in the long term, and we must find a way to break through.

I repeat: we MUST find a way to break through.

Our most Awesome Life depends on it!

Here are some of the fears I've heard from clients, which might resonate with you, together with my own feedback breaking down those fears into what lies behind them:

'I'm scared of getting into a healthy lifestyle too much. I did a diet before and everyone thought I was obsessed and boring.'

As you say this fear to yourself, can you see what this fear is actually rooted in? It's judgement from others, a shift from your known identify to a new identity as a healthier person, and feeling like an outsider to the environment you are accustomed to.

'I don't want to go for that new job. Last time I failed the interview my team found out, and it's a ten-minute longer commute from my house so it's not worth it anyway.'

As you say this fear to yourself, can you see what it is actually rooted in? It's judgement from others, not being comfortable with failing/getting rejected, doubting your ability to step up to the new responsibilities, and a lack of self-worth and thus feeling like you aren't deserving of a better job.

Side note: Do we ever learn to be better from success? No, we learn to be better from failing. It's time to get comfortable with failure – it's life's only teacher.

'I can't make time to get fit. I always have to work late, I have family responsibilities when I get home and after that I'm just too tired.'

As you say this fear to yourself, can you see what this fear is actually rooted in? It's fear of speaking to your boss to readjust your workload so you can have a better work–life balance, lack of self-worth and thus a lack of desire to value health, fitness and wellbeing and to re-prioritize your time, and potentially a lack of support from their partner to share parental responsibilities more so you can stay fit and healthy.

These are just three examples, but hopefully three examples that start to make you think about some of the fears you might have around change, and what they might be rooted in. It's really important we develop the ability to look at our fears rationally, break them down, and find a path to work around them for the benefits of what's on the other side.

So many of our fears lead to negative thought processes that ultimately turn us away from action. The decision to avoid taking the next step becomes a habit. It's time to break these habits holding you back, because your Awesome Life will still involve these fears – what we need is the courage to do things anyway.

It's time to get rid of life imposter syndrome.

My own fears

Let me use myself as an example in this. I have life imposter syndrome right now writing this book. Not so much now in this moment, but before I wrote this book and periodically as I approached certain topics. In fact, imposter syndrome to some degree stopped me starting this book sooner than I should have. I was thinking . . .

- 'Will this book be good enough? Will people read it?'
- 'What if it's not as good as other books and it just sits on the shelves and gathers dust?'
- 'What if people think I'm a crap coach, that I'm just full of hot air and actually don't know what I'm doing?'
- 'What if I say something wrong, make loads of errors, and people think I'm an idiot?'
- 'Do I have enough experience and pedigree to talk about that topic? Should I have gone to university and got another degree to be "informed" enough to speak on this topic?'
- 'Once the book is released and I'm in the public eye more, what if I can't explain things properly? What if I go on a radio show to talk about the book and just can't get my words out and just fluff it?'
- 'I'm about to write a book and my health isn't 100 per cent right now. If I can't get my health right, how can I teach others to?'

These are all legitimate, fair and rational thought processes, and rather than run away from them, or be scared of them and para-lysed by them and not take action, I can take a logical approach to dealing with each element of my imposter syndrome and fears and find a way to take action. So, what I will now do is take each thought process, find an opposing argument, and prove to myself that I can do it and have the ability to do so.

This process can give you enough confidence to take a step, and that step will snowball.

> We all have fears, but we must find the courage to do things despite them, because the reward is worth it.

Let's go through my fears one by one. What we can do to work through them is use both direct questioning to find out where the truth lies, or provide counter-arguments for the fear with evidence from past experience, or do a mixture of both. This is a process I am acting out on myself so you can learn from this process, so please take note, because I want you to use this technique on yourself, to break through your life imposter syndrome and fears, and step into your Awesome Life. You might have life imposter syndrome about being a good parent, or taking a new job, or trying a new sport, or going to the gym . . . who knows? What I want you to do is extrapolate from this example and the technique I am using and use it on your own current life imposter syndrome narrative.

'WILL THIS BOOK BE GOOD ENOUGH? WILL PEOPLE READ IT?'

First, this is two fears worded as one in my head, so we need to separate these out. This is a very common thing for people to do: phrasing multiple fears in their head so it incites a more overwhelming response in us to simply say no and not take action, thus keeping us safe and in our comfort zone. This isn't good and highlights why this process is so important if we are able to break through fears and take action.

So, breaking it in half . . .

'Will this book be good enough?'

My response to this fear . . . This is ultimately on me. I've been wanting to write this book for years, and I have been chosen by a publisher to write this book. Because of this, the publisher sees from my pedigree, my coaching background, my track record, and current information I put out on social media as just cause for me to be able to write a book like this. I can also take my time to get it right. I can do the right research, edit, ask friends to proof it, and ensure I can get it to be as perfect as possible. I have also read many books that are for sale, that have done well, and I feel my book could surpass those books in terms of content, delivery and impact. Thus, for these reasons I feel that YES, I can make this book good enough to have an impact on other people.

'Will people read it?'

My response to this fear . . . This is partly a me problem, and partly a publisher problem, as we are both charged with promotion. Understanding this, I know I need to work hard at promoting it on my social media, I need to do as many interviews as possible, I need to use the power of my network, I need to do what I can, and what the publisher tells me to do to help with book sales. I actually feel that, if I do the first bit right, write a good book, it will sell itself over time. I don't have a huge social media presence like some people do, so I can't expect it to be a bestseller overnight, but what I can do is write a book that's so good, and put so much emphasis on that, that it helps people in a way that it gets recommended to more and more people over time. Ultimately, all I can do is try my best, and if I even help, say, a thousand people with this book, then I will be happy. So, in response to this fear, YES, I shall do everything in my power to get this book into people's hands, and I hope the strength and power of the book continues to sell it through recommendation.

Let's review this fear so far . . .

Based on my responses to the above fears, and the process I can embark on to write what I believe will be an awesome book, am I happy to see beyond this fear and take action?

YES.

Now what you have seen me do here is not ignore the fear, to not try pretend it's not real; I have simply taken a very logical approach to tackling it. To overcome fears, it's important not just to ignore them completely, but to find reasons to overcome them by focusing on what is on the other side of the fear, by being aware of the upside, rather than putting all the focus and energy into the downside. In this instance, if I stopped here, if I didn't write this book, if I retreated, I wouldn't have got to do something I have always dreamed of and I'd have missed the chance to help thousands more people.

This is enough for me to focus on the upside and take action, action that will lead me to a more fulfilling future. Let's do this again with my next fear . . .

'WHAT IF IT'S NOT AS GOOD AS OTHER BOOKS, AND IT JUST SITS ON THE SHELVES AND GATHERS DUST?'

Again, this fear needs to be broken in two. My head, once again, has coupled fears together to make things feel more overwhelming and keep me safe and in my comfort zone by not taking action. So first let's separate the fear into its two components so we can deal with it more logically and pragmatically . . .

'What if it's not as good as other books?'

With this fear and how it's worded I want to ask myself some questions because it now sounds like I am comparing myself to others. This is a dangerous place to get into because it's never-ending. In life there are always people who will be better than you in some way; comparison is the biggest zero-sum game there is. There will always be someone healthier than you, cleverer than you, fitter than you, taller than you, skinnier than you, more muscular than you, better-spoken than you, richer than you . . . Comparison is a dangerous game. Don't even start to play it: it's endless and ultimately the thief of progress and joy.

So, a few questions for myself, then I will work on a response to my fear . . .

1. 'When I say "other books", is there a particular book I am thinking of?'
2. When I compare my book to other books, what is the core reason I am doing this? Do I want to ensure I can write a book that can stand side by side with others I admire and respect?'
3. 'Who is defining good? What is the metric of comparison I am using here? Book sales?'

As we can see, there's a lot to unpack here, but hopefully now you are seeing the value of writing this down, and then asking yourself the right questions. Me writing this down right now, in this moment, is a form of self-therapy. By physically writing down thoughts rather than leaving them in my head, I am able to see, logically, why I should do what it is that I want to do – which is write this book – and not listen to the fears I have. If I had chosen to not write this down, I would have kept the fears inside my head and they would have won because I wouldn't have allowed logic and pragmatism to win the day over emotion.

This is why writing things down, and talking to people who can support and help you, can give you the insight and help you need. I often recommend writing and reflection first, then talking to someone afterwards. That way, you have ironed out the problem partially already, so that when you do chat to someone you have a better understanding and better level of clarity, which in turn usually leads to a more productive conversation . . .

But writing down how you feel seems odd so it's rarely done, and we have to sit with our fears and emotions running riot in our heads 24 hours per day. That's not a good place to be, so I implore you from this point forward:

1. Take 10 minutes to write down what you are thinking and feeling. Ask logical, pragmatic and probing questions to get to the root cause of a fear, and outline reasons to do what it is you want to do, focusing on the upside of taking action, rather than on the downside.
2. After you have more clarity yourself, talk to someone you trust and respect, someone who can give you objective and fair feedback on your fears, and ask you the right questions to help you get to the root cause and set out an action plan that will enable you to break through.

Doing this will allow you to see your fears and the things that hold you back in a totally different light. It will feel like you are an observer outside your fears, someone looking in on the problem rather than being inside it.

Right, time to get back to those questions underlying the broader fear 'What if it's not as good as other books?' The best thing to do would be to answer each individually. Yes, I know, this is taking us more time, but this is an important problem. Imagine if you were going through this process to decide whether you should try to change jobs or to work out whether to have kids. Wouldn't taking time to explore the problem, maybe taking days or weeks, be worth it? Big life decisions *should* be given big amounts of time. Me sitting here working out whether to write this book or not is a big life decision. If I was able to write a book that was the way I wanted it to be, it would be a game changer for my life. I could inspire thousands of people, I could change their lives. I could change my life, too. This 100 per cent deserves a lot of my time.

I really hope you can see the value of this process. I've spoken to thousands of people over the years as a coach, whether it's been in a one-to-one setting, in a group setting, or just having a chat on social media. And the number-one reason people do not change is not because they don't know how – most people know how to change, at least to some extent – it's because of a fear, or several fears. At some point in the process, whether it's at the beginning, or when they get halfway there, the fear creeps in, they retreat, and never achieve what it is they set out to achieve. And that makes me sad. To know that people have dreams, have desires, have wants, have needs, have things they really want, and they can feel it, that they really want it, but are simply held back by a fear, often because of a situation that has happened in their life that has scarred them and stayed with them. (And that's another reason I want to write this book! If I can help you start to approach that fear,

47

and conquer that fear, then that's enough of a reason for me to sit at this desk, at this computer, for weeks on end writing this book.)

OK. Another tangent. Let's get back on track. We were about to look at each of my three questions and conquer them one by one, logically, pragmatically.

'When I say other books, is there a particular book I am thinking of?' No, not one in particular, but a group of books I personally hold in high regard that have changed my life, and I would love it if I could write a book that even came 10 per cent close to this list.

Knowing this, I want to ask myself a direct question, one I want to feel the answer to and be able to see it in black and white and use it to empower me to take action . . .

'Based on what I know, the books I have read to date, my experience as a coach, the people I have helped, the methods I use, my ability to make things simple for people, do I feel I have the ability to write a book that could come even 10 per cent close to the group of books I have used to inspire me in my life.'

My short answer: 'Yes.'

My longer answer: based on what I know, the experience I've got, the books I have read, the people I have helped, yes, I do genuinely feel that if I take time and do the work, I can write a book that can change a lot of people's lives for the better. I also know I have good people around me who can help guide me, help proofread bits I am unsure of, and help steer this book to be the best it can be. If I am ever unsure I'm reaching the standard I expect of myself, the standard I am comparing my book to, I can simply sit down, flick through these books and use these books to guide me and up the standard of my book, using them as an example to help shape my writing to be better.

Can you see what's happened here?

I've coached myself to take action by writing down this problem, to directly answer the question 'Can I write this book?' And I've done it by being logical and pragmatic, asking the right questions, and outlining why I can and should write this book.

The beautiful thing is I now feel I don't need to break down every one of those fears. Above I wrote down seven fears that were knocking around in my head. We can actually now see the repetition and my brain doing the thing which many of us do, taking a small group of fears and rewording them in multiple ways to keep us safe by making the volume of reasons overwhelming, keeping us in our comfort zone, and stopping us from taking action. Let me show you these seven fears again and let's see the commonality in them . . .

- 'Will this book be good enough? Will people read it?'
- 'What if it's not as good as other books and it just sits on the shelves and gathers dust?'
- 'What if people think I'm a crap coach, that I'm just full of hot air and actually don't know what I'm doing?'
- 'What if I say something wrong, make loads of errors, and people think I'm an idiot?'
- 'Do I have enough experience and pedigree to talk about that topic? Should I have gone to university and got a degree to be "informed" enough to speak on this topic?'
- 'Once the book is released and I'm in the public eye more, what if I can't explain things properly? What if I go on a radio show to talk about the book and just can't get my words out, I just fluff it?'
- 'I'm about to write a book and my health isn't 100 per cent right now. If I can't get my health right, how can I teach others to?'

So, in reviewing the above seven original fears and the way that I had framed them, you can see the repetition and overlap, and you can see that, in the process of writing them down, asking questions, and being pragmatic about the answers, we have dealt with some of my fears, but not others. So let's be logical and pragmatic and see what we have dealt with, and what we have yet to deal with. I feel we have dealt with:

Should I write this book/do I have the experience to write this book? Based on my above answers, yes, I feel I have justified my ability to write a book and have the experience to do so, and am excited about doing so.

When comparing my book to others, do I think I can write a book that can sit alongside others and do itself proud? Yes, I do. I've read enough books to know what a good book is. I've got good people around me to guide me, and I shall take the right amount of time to ensure this is a book to be proud of and will change many people's lives.

Will people read this book? I will simply do my best to ensure that as many people as possible do read my book. I will work hard to market and sell this book, working alongside my publisher in this process, but ultimately my number-one focus in getting people to read this book is to simply write an awesome book.

What if I say something wrong or make errors? That is the good thing about writing a book. You can take your time and use good people around you to pick up the errors. So yes, I am confident I will take the appropriate amount of time and use the right people to make this book as good as it can be.

Re-reading the above, I am satisfied I have answered my fears. I feel confident I can do my best to navigate them, and the upside now outweighs the downside. As a result, this is filling me with confidence in my ability, and I am excited and happy to write this book. And, ultimately, all I can do is try my best, and that's all we can ever ask of ourselves.

> Life isn't about winning a race against others; it's about winning all by ourselves, to make the best of our abilities, talents and opportunities.

OK, so now we need to work out what we have *not* solved, and work to solve that and ensure that we . . . I . . . have confidence in embarking on this process, from start to finish. Some of my fears were rooted in 'Shall I start this book?' and 'Shall I write this book?', and some were rooted in 'What happens *after* I write this book?' and 'What about my health?', so let's now attack those and leave no stone unturned in the process, because, as I've said, this is important, and whatever problem you look to solve with this process in your life will be big and important, because we don't want to live with fear.

Right, back to one of the fears I had yet to deal with . . .

'DO I HAVE ENOUGH EXPERIENCE AND PEDIGREE TO TALK ABOUT THAT TOPIC? SHOULD I HAVE GONE TO UNIVERSITY AND GOT A DEGREE TO BE "INFORMED" ENOUGH TO SPEAK ON THIS TOPIC?'

I feel I have half answered this question, so I am going to split this problem in two and answer the half I feel I have yet to answer as succinctly as possible: 'Should I have gone to university and got a degree to be "informed" enough to speak on this topic?'

This fear isn't rooted in any actual fear I have, but is a societal norm my brain has attached itself to in an attempt to create yet another reason/fear not to do something. University degrees are *one* way to get knowledge in a career path; there are many others. And because they are considered one of the gold standards in traditional education, it's easy to have it in your brain that a degree is something you need to have if you are going to be knowledgeable in an area and on a guaranteed path to career success. But I'd argue that this isn't the case: I've met many awesome people with and without degrees, so it's certainly not the only path to success.

There are many other ways to master a topic area. You could study outside university, on the job or through books and other, non-university courses. But if I'm being honest, based on my experience to date having been in the fitness and health industry for 15 years, some of the most intelligent people I know make the worst coaches (of course, we need to define intelligence here). This has been shown to me to be true over and over again in the world of nutrition. People focus so much on specific science they often miss the broader picture and how it is applied in the real world. Of course, this isn't universally true, but I've seen it play out a lot in my industry. It's my job, I feel, to know enough about a topic (let's use nutrition as an example), and the science behind it, to help someone. Some of the best PhD researchers in nutrition I know make the worst coaches because their knowledge is so science based and so narrow it's no longer applicable to many of the basic problems people have; they simply aren't pairing this nutrition science knowledge with the science of coaching and behaviour change.

So, while a degree in nutrition might be beneficial to understanding and mastering a topic, it is by no means essential to helping other people with their nutrition. Most people in my experience need pretty basic advice when it comes to improving their nutrition, advice such as: eat more vegetables, focus your diet on real food, eat less if you want to lose weight, eat balanced meals to balance your blood sugar, moderate alcohol and processed foods so they don't lead to negative effects, time your foods around exercise so you have the energy to perform, eat enough protein at all key meals, and make sure you are well hydrated. This basic advice would serve 95 per cent of people really well, and could be understood in full, along with all the nuance and complexity to apply it to others, on a decent nutrition course lasting 6–12 months. Would going to university and knowing all the ins and outs of the human body, being able to recite the enzymes in the Krebs cycle, help me coach and empower the people I want to help? Not really. It will aid in helping some people with very specific needs or be useful in the realm of advanced sports nutrition, but that's very few people. My work is largely focused on helping people master the basics, not understand and implement the deep specifics.

My point here isn't to justify my fear, because I don't feel it's based in an actual fear I have; it is my brain stacking reasons together not to take action on something and attaching itself to an outdated societal norm to compound the reasons I shouldn't progress with my goal, to keep me comfortable, nice and cosy in my comfort zone.

Ultimately, degrees *can* give you a good basis and understanding in a specific topic area, often to progress you along a specific career path. But, in my opinion, some of the best skills you or I will ever pick up in life is by learning from books, people, life itself and being on the job. Sure, learning the theory is important, but living it is just as important. The art of coaching and the coach is part science, part art, and I know enough about the science to write this book, but my job is to shape it in a particular way, using the right words and with an understanding of people and the process of change, to actually drive change in you, the person reading this book. If this book was just full of dry science, it wouldn't drive change, but pair it with stories, practical advice, and an understanding of people and behaviour, then that's a winning recipe.

When we are presented with science, we rarely change. People need more than data to act, people need a *why*, something emotive that spurs them on to make the changes they need or want to make. A simple example would be a doctor telling a patient, 'You need to make some lifestyle changes. If you don't, you could be at risk of dying early.' Statistically, not many people actually change after a discussion like this with a doctor. But with some more emotive wording, the outcome could be completely different: 'You need to make some lifestyle changes. Your heart is under pressure and your recent tests aren't looking great. From my experience people with your condition die 10–15 years earlier than they should, but they also have a huge reduction in their quality of life at the same time. So you might want to start to think about these changes because otherwise you might not see your grandchild's tenth birthday.'

I'm not saying doctors can and should deliver their diagnoses like this, but I hope you get my point, which is that knowing facts is one thing, communicating them so they drive someone to change their behaviour is a completely different thing. One of the reasons I made all the changes I wanted in my life so early on is because of my *why*. I felt that, if I didn't, I wouldn't be successful in my career path, and as a young and ambitious man I didn't want that for myself. I wanted a long and successful career so I made changes with my health and weight to ensure that I did.

A final note on degrees and going to university. When I went to university, there were 140 people in my year on my course, Sports Coaching and Performance. We had a reunion a few years later and worked out that seven out of 140 were actually working in a career path related to their degree. So, ultimately, whatever you do in life, you need to want it, work for it, and put whatever you know to good use; because as we can see from my example (which I appreciate is just one example), having a degree isn't an automatic right to your chosen career path, nor does it mean you are good at what you do.

Let's leave that fear there, as we can see it's not an actual rational fear of mine; it was just my brain playing tricks on me. Let's move on to another one that I had . . .

'ONCE THE BOOK IS RELEASED AND I'M IN THE PUBLIC EYE MORE, WHAT IF I CAN'T EXPLAIN THINGS PROPERLY, WHAT IF I GO ON A RADIO SHOW TO TALK ABOUT THE BOOK AND JUST CAN'T GET MY WORDS OUT AND JUST FLUFF IT?'

I'm now already feeling more confident. As you go through this process, you should feel your ability to do this improve because, as you are forced to ask hard questions, think through the problems, and find reasons to do what it is you want to do, you are getting more positive answers and growing in confidence and the whole thing gets easier in a kind of virtuous circle. So, for me right now I feel I can quickly tackle this fear head on. Like anything, the more you prove to yourself you have ability and are worthy, the easier other things in life are.

So, my response to this fear . . . I have been in the public eye since 2008 when I first set up a Facebook account. It was that day that I decided to 'put myself out there'. And on that journey, I have had many screw-ups. I've said some things I regret. I've said some things that weren't true. I've said some things in a way that I regret because it caused offence I didn't intend, but I am still here today 'putting myself out there'. The reason I carry on and haven't been crushed by my past failures is because I honour the fact that I am human and that we all make mistakes. The error many people make is in not identifying the mistake, or being honest and admitting to it, telling the people you need to tell that you're sorry, and as a result learning from that experience.

If you have followed me for some time on social media, you might have seen me apologize before. It's something I do now and again because I have made a mistake. I may have said something out of turn, or that I regretted, and I was super honest and made a revised 'post' that said, 'I'm sorry, here is why . . .' And do you know what? This is the best thing you can do both for yourself and to earn the respect of other people.

People *love* it when you say sorry (assuming you mean it), because it's *the right thing to do.* It earns respect. If I can admit when I've been wrong, when I could have done better, and make the promise to do better in the future, then people respect that; they tip their hat to you and think, 'This is someone I can trust. They are willing to own up to what they might have said or done wrong. I can respect and appreciate that.' And so, all you actually do by admitting a fault, and in the same breath saying you will do better, is honour yourself as a human being in occasionally getting things wrong, and honour what others want to see in people – honesty and integrity.

'My first world is humanity. My second world is human-
ism. And, I live in the third world merely being a human.'
Santosh Kalwar

So let's summarize how I am going to handle this fear. If this does happen (and it is rare that it happens), I will simply stop, tell the interviewer I've made an error, and reframe my response in the way that I want or intended it to be worded, and not try bluff my way through it. I will aim to honour it in the moment, where possible, and hold myself to account. If I miss it in the moment, I will do what I have always done and apologize, putting out a public statement about what I am apologizing for, and how I want or wish it to be corrected.

Am I happy I can conquer this fear, based on past experience and my track record?

YES.

Fear crushed!

Let's squash another fear from my list, which, as we can now see, has some similarities to previously framed fears but is actually very much a distinct problem – the fear of being personally attacked.

'WHAT IF PEOPLE THINK I'M A CRAP COACH, I'M JUST FULL OF HOT AIR AND ACTUALLY DON'T KNOW WHAT I'M DOING?'

Again there are two components here. So let's start with the first . . .

'What if people think I'm a crap coach?'

This is me inflating the strength of the fear and stacking fears together, as identified earlier. Our brains are *really* good at doing this to protect us, to keep us safe in our comfort zones. Talk to a friend about a decision they are trying to make and you often find the reasons they give not to do something a little scary because they just keep on coming and get wilder and more absurd; this is their brain searching for more reasons to avoid doing something and keep them safe. But we must stop this, it doesn't serve us, and we must squash these irrational, non-factual fears and hone in on the two or three problems that are really there, for which we just need solutions, tactics or a shift in our mindset.

So, I ask myself a question: 'Do I feel I am a good coach and can coach others on the topics within this book?'

HELL YES.

Goodbye, irrational fear, you don't need to protect me. I'm awesome at what I do.

(I'm moving quicker through this process now as confidence builds and I see the increasing absurdity of my manufactured fears.)

Time to break down the second half . . .

'I'm just full of hot air and actually don't know what I'm doing'

This is actually a deep-rooted fear of mine, one that brings up a lot of painful memories. I have mostly dealt with those memories, but of course my brain still has them and so now and again they raise their ugly head. This is also a common fear for a lot of people – other people, in short, being mean, calling you names, saying you're stupid, saying your crap at something, saying you're a waste of space, and so on. Many of us got bullied at school, or at least had some hurtful things said to us at times. Maybe people in the workplace have been horrible to you. Maybe even people close to you have been horrible to you over the years. Whatever the situation, bullying can have a really profound effect on a lot of people. It can make you feel unworthy, cause you to lose some of your self-efficacy, and keep you from getting more fulfilment in life. So, it's important we deal with this and develop a greater sense of self-belief and self-worth.

In 2016, I started to get attacked online by someone in the nutrition industry, the industry in which I have spent most of my career coaching, teaching and educating. This individual started attacking me on Facebook, saying a lot of things personally and professionally about me and why I shouldn't be listened to. As you can imagine, this was a hard time for me: it took up a lot of my time and energy and affected my mental wellbeing. This continued through 2017, 2018 and some of 2019 and got so bad that this person was filming me on stage when I was speaking just so he could edit clips in such a way as to discredit my name and then post them online. The problem was compounded because I spent 2017 fighting bankruptcy, which to date is still the most difficult year of my life (actually maybe 2020 was – they were both very dark times in my life, but we can talk about that later).

Because of these two things I got beaten into the ground in 2017 and became very reclusive in many ways. But I couldn't and didn't fade into the abyss. I had a team under my leadership, I had a company to run, I had clients to serve, and I had to keep the roof over my family's heads. I also had so many engrained behaviours and habits that kept me going and doing the work I needed to do to get out of the situation I was in. So, every day I put on a brave face, turned up, and did what was needed to get myself out of this situation and not fail.

Because I was attacked for doing exactly what I'm doing in this book, you can see why there might be a deep-rooted fear there, one that could, if not approached logically and pragmatically, take over and stop me from taking action.

> 'To see what is right and not do it is a lack of courage.'
> **Confucius**

For me, the right thing to do was stand up to the claims. Many of the things I was being attacked on were untrue, so I had to stand up and fight. Unfortunately, I wasn't given the chance – and that is an issue with social media, you can have your comments blocked and deleted and thus many never get to see your defence – all I could do was continue to do good work and simply fight it in any way I could using my own platform and influence.

But – and here is the *big* but – in between some of the false criticisms there was some truth: I had said some incorrect things, I did have some statements out there that needed to be put right, I had put my foot in it in a few ways. So at this point in time, I had a choice: either stand up to those criticisms, admit where there was fault, and do what was needed to course-correct; or to just lie low and lose credibility and trust.

And I took the first option as this, I knew, was the right thing to do.

I admitted where I was wrong.

I admitted where I could have said or done things better.

I apologized openly about the things I had said or done wrong.

And then I did the work to improve as a person. These attacks – or, better, my response to them – made me a better coach, made me a better person, and made me a better business owner. I set out to improve the professional things that were in my control, and could be improved upon, but how about the more personal things? How would I deal with those?

When you are criticized, it's important to do what we've been doing all along in this chapter, to break the criticism down. Is the criticism personal, and if so, can we completely disregard it as just a personal attack, and thus of no value? Or does it have elements of truth in it, based on our character and how we go about some things, or the way we do, say or talk about some things?

It's important to know because we can then deal with it in different ways.

If someone calls you something online or offline, perhaps it's true, perhaps it isn't; either way, you must look at yourself and ask *why* would this person say this thing, and do the work to improve personally or professionally to stop it happening on a broader scale.

If I say something online that is incorrect, and someone points it out, it's my job to correct that, understand the truth behind it, and be more truthful or tactful in the future.

If I say something in a way that offends a lot of people, it is my responsibility to look at why. Was I clouded by bias, was I disrespectful to a certain group of people, was I speaking in a derogatory tone, was I missing some of the context of the situation, was I being naive based on my lack of experience around a topic and speaking outside my lane of expertise?

Whatever it was, if I am someone that wants to constantly improve, to do better, to be better, I need to do the work to understand the above issue, and course-correct. And as long as I apologize where appropriate, and move forward in a better light, I have done all that I can to be better, and that's all we can ask of ourselves.

Lastly, if these comments are simply personal, or once we break down the comments, have dealt with the ones we can and we are left with only the personal, we can then simply discard them. Some people can and will have negative things to say about us, that's life; there are unkind people in the world, that's just a fact. It's just unfortunate our brain latches on to negative comments and drowns out all the nice comments people make as a safety and survival mechanism. And that's why this process of breaking down and thinking critically is so important: it helps us get to the truth.

If there are nasty, unkind people in your life, you ultimately have two choices:

1. Call them out on it, challenge them and ask why they are behaving in that way, enabling you to get to the root cause of the comments and their basis.
2. Treat them as an unkind person who is simply best avoided.

Some people in this world are just nasty, and it's not our job to try make them see differently; it can just become a fruitless task, a waste of energy. These people are simply best avoided.

Once I had done the work to correct what I could professionally, and addressed my past mistakes, all that left me was one choice, to know that I was on the receiving end of a bully's comments, someone who saw me as a target in a business sense, because I was a competitor and pulling me down would pull them up. The reality is this happens all the time in life, when you are farther along a path compared to others, especially in business and in the workplace; people try to bring you down to make themselves look better, and this is exactly what was happening here. So, I had to know this, suck it up, defend myself where I could, and have the courage to continue to do good work and let people decide what they thought was true.

'We can't control everything that happens to us, but we can control how we respond to things we can't control.'
Avis J Williams

Let criticism shape you, not shatter you.

So after another, I think useful, digression, we should look back at that fear I was breaking down: 'What if people think I'm a crap coach, that I'm just full of hot air and actually don't know what I'm doing?'

My response to this . . . I know I'm a good coach. I've coached thousands of people to date and successfully helped them transform their body and mind. If I do get things wrong, I will admit where I am wrong, apologize and learn how to improve, and if someone does choose to attack me online or offline, I will break down the attack, work out what is professional and what is personal, try to get the opportunity to ask for clarification or more context, and do the work to be better. Then, once I am left with the just the personal, I will know that the accusations are just that – personal – and that it's highly likely the person is acting out of sheer jealousy or nastiness, or projecting their insecurities onto me.

Right – done. Now on to the final fear from my list of seven . . . (By now are you starting to feel more confident about challenging and breaking down your own fears? I hope so.)

'I'M ABOUT TO WRITE A BOOK AND MY HEALTH ISN'T 100 PER CENT RIGHT NOW. IF I CAN'T GET MY HEALTH RIGHT, HOW CAN I TEACH OTHERS TO?'

This was actually my biggest and arguably most legitimate fear when I began writing this book, and thus I have saved it to last because it is the one that made me most feel like I was being an imposter. I wrote this book while suffering the after-effects of COVID-19, or long COVID. Now I think I caught COVID-19 in July 2020 along with my wife. My wife lost her taste and smell, and felt a bit tired, and I got what felt like a moderate cold and felt quite fatigued for about a week. We had just had our first child only three months before this, we were living pretty much in 100 per cent self-isolation, protecting ourselves and our first daughter from what was happening in the world, and because our symptoms were also so mild, we just decided to ignore them and put it down to being severely sleep deprived – which all new parents are for a while as they nurse their new baby into the world.

We didn't think anything of it until October, when we were still struggling quite a bit with our sleep as our first daughter wasn't a great sleeper (she really put us through our paces in that first year!) In October 2020 I did a charity event where I walked up and down a hill for nine hours to replicate climbing Everest, and afterwards had a few celebratory beers and a pizza. I woke up the next day not being able to get out of bed.

Now I expected soreness to some extent, but as a pretty fit guy I didn't expect this level of full-body fatigue. It was so bad I almost felt pinned to my bed, as if someone had wrapped weights around my limbs. But I got up, got on with my day, and just moaned a lot about it while taking some painkillers. But then day two came, day three, day four, and so on, and the symptoms just got worse and worse, so much so that I became very alarmed. I couldn't afford to be like this, what with a pandemic raging and running a business, a new baby, and a tired wife doing it all . . . I just couldn't be ill. It was the darkest, hardest, most emotional period of my life. There were times when I would collapse from having no energy, times I would cry over not being able to do normal things, times I would get into such a rut that I simply wondered when and how it would all end. If you know anyone with a chronic illness or have had to battle something yourself, you'll know what it's like – it's harrowing.

When you are ill for such a a long period of time, it's natural to have these thoughts. Anyone would. The longest I had ever been ill before this was a week with a cold or flu, so over a year of what felt like my body shutting down was a very alarming experience.

We now know this condition to be long COVID – essentially chronic fatigue syndrome brought on by a virus (well, that's the working theory in the medical field at the time of writing this book) – a virus setting off a cascade of inflammatory responses that cause many of the body's systems, mainly the immune system, neurological and energy systems, to become dysfunctional.

So, as you can imagine I've had thoughts like:

- 'I can't write a book on health and living your most Awesome Life if I'm ill.'
- 'If I was really that good, why am I ill? Surely my body should just be able to beat this!'
- 'What happens if I am still suffering from long COVID when the book comes out? I'll not be able to perform, keep up, and be seen as a fraud.'

I've thought all of these things and more, but this is where I am at. I am not defined by my current situation in one area of my life. We will all have times in our lives where things go wrong – with our health, with our relationships, with our kids, with our jobs, with family members, with money. No one is immune to these issues, and this book isn't going to get rid of that. I'm not a superhero, and neither are you.

What this book aims to do is make you the most awesome version of yourself so that when s*** does happen, you can deal with it, conquer it as best you can, and have so many other great things to focus on in your life that you take comfort in the fact that this is a blip; it's just a difficult period in your life, and it will get better if you take the right steps, carry them through consistently, and ultimately give yourself the right amount of time to improve.

I know that I am doing everything I can to get better, and that's all I can do. That's all you can do.

It doesn't make me a fraud that I was unfortunate enough, like so many, to catch a rampaging virus in the midst of a global pandemic and develop a state of chronic fatigue that lasted for 14 months. Before that I was healthy, strong, fit, resilient, and did everything I teach in this book, and even if things don't happen in the way I expect them to, I will still not feel a fraud. Why? Because I am doing everything I can, given the time and money I have, to solve and improve the problem. That is what counts. That's one of the core takeaways I want you to get from this book. Whatever your situation, whoever you are, whatever your goals:

- Do your best.
- Have high standards.
- Push past your comfort zone.
- Believe in yourself and in doing the work.
- Where you need to dig in and work hard, dig in and work hard.
- Prioritize your health, eat well and nourish your body.
- Stay fit and strong, and keep your body in good physical condition.
- Think well, feed your mind well, and look after your most powerful asset – your mind.

- Get to bed on time and get good-quality sleep, because this underpins your health.
- Build good-quality, supportive relationships
- Cut all stress where possible, and where not possible look to effectively manage that stress by having effective coping mechanisms.
- Control what you can, stop trying to control what you can't.
- Give your body time to heal, rest and grow when it asks for it.

And at this point in my life, I need to give my body time to rest and heal, and that's OK. That is currently the hand I have been dealt, and I will do the work that is needed to get back to the place I want to get to.

Yes, I know a lot about nutrition, fitness, health, balance, mindset and so forth. But that doesn't make me immune to *everything*. Just because we are good at something doesn't mean we are perfect and can avoid every pitfall; it just stacks the odds in our favour.

Back to those fears (again) and then on to you

Right. Back one last time to those fears that I had, and then it's time to focus on you and your fears and get rid of any symptoms of life imposter syndrome you might have. It's time to quickly review my fears, write a summary in response to those fears to empower me in taking action against them, and show you how you can do the same. My fears again . . .

- 'Will this book be good enough? Will people read it?'
- 'What if it's not as good as other books and it just sits on the shelves and gathers dust?'
- 'What if people think I'm a crap coach, that I'm just full of hot air and actually don't know what I'm doing?'
- 'What if I say something wrong, make loads of errors, and people think I'm an idiot?'
- 'Do I have enough experience and pedigree to talk about that topic? Should I have gone to university and got a degree to be "informed" enough to speak on this topic?'
- 'Once the book is released and I'm in the public eye more, what if I can't explain things properly? What if I go on a radio show to talk about the book and just can't get my words out and just fluff it?'
- 'I'm about to write a book and my health isn't 100 per cent right now. If I can't get my health right, how can I teach others to?'

My statement of intent as a response to my fears . . .

I will write the best book I know how. I will spend the time on it, do the research needed, ask the right people for help, and make it the best I possibly can. If I do this, that's all I can ask of myself, and there is then no point comparing it to others. People won't think I'm a crap coach because I'm not a crap coach, I am a great coach, and this is shown in my results and pedigree, having helped thousands of people to date. If I make an error, factually or of judgement, I will honour that error, admit my fault, make my apology to the right people or publicly, and make a promise to them and myself to not make the same mistake again. I feel I have the authority to talk about the topics I am talking about in this book, as I am living proof of the principles in this book, and have helped many others do the same. I will do everything I can to make this book a success by doing as much work as I can to market and sell the book, but its success ultimately comes down to writing an awesome book, so I will start there. While my health isn't 100 per cent right now after COVID, I will continue to do the work to get better, and that's all I can ask of myself. I now have the confidence, belief and trust in myself to write *How To Live An Awesome Life* by Ben Coomber, and share it with the world. If I'm ever in doubt, I'll read this statement to myself, and feel the belief to carry on.

Now it's your turn. What fear in your life would you like to look at first (because I can imagine there is more than one, most of us have more than one!) Which fear has the biggest impact in holding you back?

There are a lot of very common fears when it comes to self-development, but to progress, to develop oneself, we must conquer them. Here are few common ones:.

THE FEAR OF FAILURE

If you experience this, where might this have come from, a parent, friend, school friends, work colleagues? You might have been mocked in the past, told you weren't good enough, and then stopped trying because you felt it was a lose–lose situation. Whatever caused it, we need to know, because we need to know whether it's False Evidence Appearing Real or not. This is why getting to the truth is key, because fear could, in many instances, be described as False Evidence Appearing Real. We think or believe something based on a life experience or by things we have been told, and it's created a fear in us. But if we want to get to the root cause of the fear, we often find it's based on false evidence, and knowing this and re-learning the route cause, we can quickly quash fears, hopefully meaning we can get over a fear of failure, or similar fears, quickly.

We must also understand and appreciate that failure is a normal part of life: if you don't fail, you don't know how to be better. I fail every day; the difference is I lean into it, accept it, learn from it, and aim not to make that same mistake again.

> Failure is a teacher, success is not.

FEAR OF WHAT OTHERS WILL THINK OF YOU

I feel we've covered this fear well in this chapter. Please know that judgement is a totally normal human thing: we use it to decipher people, the world, and where we sit in the social hierarchy. Someone who verbalizes their thoughts about you, or something you do in an cruel way, isn't a kind person, so screw them, ignore their insecurities and jealousy, and do it anyway, because if you don't do it, you're the one that has to live with the regret, and a life of regret leads only to sadness.

> Screw the naysayers, do it anyway.

YOU FEEL THAT YOU DON'T DESERVE IT

In my experience as a coach, the people who struggle to change very commonly have a self-worth issue. They don't feel they are worthy and deserving of what it is they want, whether that's a better job, losing weight, or getting fit and strong. They have had someone, or many people, in their life tell them how useless they are as a person and it's caused them, maybe you, to have a very poor self-image. This makes me sad because people should just not behave this way. If we want the world to be a better place, we should be kind, supportive and nourishing of people's wants and goals.

> Know this: YOU ARE WORTHY.

Please repeat that to yourself: 'I am worthy of the happiness and change I seek.'

You are an amazing person. You do deserve whatever it is you want to achieve. No person has the right to steal another person's wants and dreams. I am here to build you up. I am here to make you see that you are worthy and that you deserve whatever it is you want. So, if this is a fear you have, it's really important to get under the skin of it, because if it's held you back before, it will hold you back again, *unless* you deal with it.

So, let's now get you to look at a fear, or fears you have, to write them down and view them objectively and pragmatically so you can get to the bottom of them and conquer them in the same way I have just done.

Write down a fear you feel you have.

_____

Now write down, as I did, all the ways you frame this fear in your head:

_____

_____

Now break each one of these fears down (if you need more paper, grab a notebook and spend as much time as you need to do this exercise). Take one of your above fears, or statements, and write it here:

_____

_____

Now break the fear down and separate it into its components, as it might be multi-layered, just like some of mine were.

_____

_____

What is your response, or rebuttal, or what do you know to be true, as to why this fear is **False Evidence Appearing Real?**

_____

_____

If you have many fears, it's time to tackle them one by one. Take another one of your above fears, or statements, and write it below:

_____

_____

Again break the fear down and separate it into its components, as it might be multi-layered, like some of mine were:

_____

_____

What is your response, or rebuttal, or what to you know to be true, as to why this fear is **False Evidence Appearing Real?**

_____

_____

Take another of your above fears, or statements, and write it below:

_____

_____

Again, break the fear down and separate it into its components, as it might be multi-layered, like some of mine were:

_____

_____

What is your response, or rebuttal, or what to you know to be true, as to why this fear is **False Evidence Appearing Real?**

_____

_____

If there are more fears, follow this simple three-step process in a notebook and continue the exercise, working through each fear you have.

Finally, it's time to write a response as a full statement to your fears. Write a statement that empowers you to see your fears for what they are, and go conquer the thing you want to conquer.

_____

_____

Now read the above several times. Really FEEL it and feel empowered by it.

The new, more Awesome you

I hope this chapter has helped you feel more confident about breaking through the fears you have. This won't happen overnight. Conquering your fears will be something you need to practise daily, but this is the start. If we don't break through our fears, there continues to be resistance in our lives. That resistance results in inaction, and we can't have that. You and I shouldn't stand for that: this book is about action, action towards our wants, dreams and goals. So, stare that fear in the face, know that it's False Evidence Appearing Real, and move boldly and courageously towards your goals.

After this process we need to take stock of something else: the process of change you might now embark on and what other people will think. As you evolve as a person, comments from others can go two ways. People may either be supportive, help you, and become cheerleaders for you; or they may criticize you and try to derail you.

At this point I'm going to be direct and quit with the stories. Good friends, people who love you, people who want the best for you, they won't put you down; they will support and encourage you. Bad friends, jealous friends, threatened friends, they will be the ones to criticize you and seek to bring you down.

'Strong people don't put others down, they lift them up.'
Michael P. Watson

Most people don't like change; people seek certainty, and shock horror, this is why so many people are unhappy and unfulfilled. And if people are changing around those who feel unfulfilled, it can often make them feel uncomfortable. They feel bad that others are changing for the better while they aren't, so instead of being supportive they act in ways that sabotage your efforts and keep you where they are, safe, as an equal. Those people . . .

SCREW THEM!

That's why it's fundamental in the process of change for you to lean on the right people when you embark on this journey. You need to know both who and what you want to be so you can stand strong in the face of *any* negativity from others, but also have good people around you to support your journey. Shifting identity can feel strange; we're not always ready for how it's actually going to change our lives, and this can then feel uncomfortable – it can cause us to stop in our tracks, even go back to the person we were.

I personally love it when I see someone I haven't seen for years and they have got really fit, or similar, and they look super happy and healthy, or maybe they've got a new job and are enjoying work again, or have decided to travel loads and experience the world, or are simply glowing brighter because of something positive that has happened recently in their life. I love it because I see confidence and happiness in that person. I see someone chasing their dreams and wants, and it's infectious. I find it inspiring. At no point do I think to bring them down and say something negative, all I want to do is give them a high-five and hear all about it. I get inspired and feed off it.

Positive people are drawn to positive people.

Negative people are drawn to negative people.

Get in with the crowd you want to be in, shape your goals in the way you want, and confidently work towards the new you, proud of the changes you are making, proud of the new identity you are creating, and proud of yourself for doing it.

It's time to let go of the old you and move confidently and boldly towards the new, the more awesome you that is completely focused on living their best, most Awesome Life.

CHAPTER THREE

The truth frees us all

A lot of people find the truth an uncomfortable thing, so we shy away from it, especially when it feels ugly. But I'm hoping that after reading this book you will lean into it and embrace it, however uncomfortable it feels. We must seek it because the truth frees us. If we cannot look at the truth, however painful it is, we cannot progress; we limit ourselves and put time and energy into false beliefs or plans that don't work. For some of us, the truth is also very well hidden; we've hidden it so we can function day to day without facing the pain that truth may bring. But this will never lead to freedom – freedom of choice, freedom of expression, freedom to be who you are and what you want to be.

At this point in the book, I'm going to need to insert a trigger/content warning. This section of the book could get uncomfortable. But only because we are going to look at the truth. You picked up this book and are still reading because you *want* change, you crave better, you want to live your most Awesome Life. And to do this we must peel back the onion and look at the layers we are dealing with.

This can't happen if you ignore fear, or otherwise don't want to face the truth.

The truth freed me, and it can free you.

And yes, it hurt, and, at times, really bloody hurt. Not physically of course – this isn't the kind of pain we experience from a bruise; it's worse, it's the emotional turmoil that comes with facing past errors or elements of our character that are not serving us, but these things have to be known and confronted for us to be fully empowered for the process of change.

So, before we get into some more stories, I want you to make me a promise. If you are going to continue to read this book and go on this journey, you have to be vulnerable, really vulnerable, so vulnerable that, whatever is there, whatever truth you have to confront, you are going to have the strength and courage to do it and be totally honest with yourself. Because if you can't, you cannot truly change. It's as simple as that.

> To be successful in your life you have to take full control
> and ownership of all your problems. There is no room for
> blame, it's all on us.

OK, now we have made this pact and you are still reading, and you are ready and willing and open to change and happy to be vulnerable, let's continue.

The process of change

The process of change, on a deep level, is hard because our past can feel so hard wired into us. The environments we grow up in and how our parents, peers and broader cultural experiences programme us can be powerful. So, I'm not going to lie to you and say it's easy. There may be times where we push back and think, 'No, that's not my fault, it's nothing to do with me', and in a lot of ways, in a lot of cases, this is right. Some of our experiences may have occurred due to no fault of our own, but we still need to face them; perhaps because we need to accept that it wasn't our fault and let go of the guilt, perhaps because we need to stop letting these experiences shape us, recognizing the strength we have to stop these things being what defines us, our thoughts, and our actions.

In the process of change we need to seek out the truth, look at ourselves and our role in the problem or our reaction to it, take absolute ownership of that problem, and do the work to fix it, however long it takes, and however painful that change is.

And this is why we must seek out the truth – *because it frees us.* It frees us to be the person we want to be, without our old ways, old programming, old behaviours holding us back.

I'll repeat this because it's *really* important: some of this won't be easy, and you know this because there will be things you've wanted and tried to change before, perhaps many times over, and it's not worked. So, if something hasn't worked many times, we can work under the assumption that we're going to need to work harder in this area to change ourselves and how we seek progress in this area of our lives.

So, as you progress, be prepared to eat some big s*** sandwiches.

I have, you will. It will be painful, but lean into it, embrace it, and enjoy the journey of you growing to be a better, more fulfilled, more awesome person. It will be worth it.

I know that if I hadn't been through the painful process of looking at myself, my role in the issues I've had in my life, and how my character was causing some of the problems, and did the work to shift my mindset, express other sides of my character more, and put processes in place to bring myself into alignment, I would not be as happy as I am right now.

It's not easy.

You'll need help.

You'll need to be vulnerable.

You'll need to be open to whatever change is needed.

But it *really* is worth it in the long term. Trust me.

'The problem' is rarely the problem

In our search for the truth, I want to cover two more important areas:

1. the problems we face in our lives and how we frame them
2. understanding the role of science in the process of change, by being a more critical thinker.

Over the years as a coach, I've talked to a lot of people and I've learned that when most of us describe what our problem is, it's rarely *the* problem. What I mean by this is that the problem someone is looking to solve is often being looked at in the wrong way, and this is because of a couple of things. First, they're not operating with a wide enough lens: they are just looking at the moment in which they experience the problem and not zooming out to see the pattern of behaviour that led there. Second, they are not aware enough of their behaviours and do not know how to look at themselves or their role honestly. And third, they are stuck in habit loops that are fixing them within the problem, and they are often not ready or really wanting to change these routines to get the outcome they want.

In short, people want the quick fix, the quick answer, the shortcut, and rarely want to look at themselves, their role in the problem, and to do the work to change.

To describe this problem and what I mean, there is an example that always sticks out in my head from an event I once did in my neighbourhood. I got invited by a local gym to do a talk to its members on nutrition and mindset and the process of change required to achieve goals. Around 50 if us were crammed into a small café nearby. It was a great event, it went well, and as a result the questions were really good, each getting to the heart of the issues people felt they had. Then towards the end I got a great question from a local farmer named Chris.

Here is how the conversation went (paraphrased of course):

CHRIS: *Hey, Ben, how can I get over my sugar addiction?*
ME: *What do you mean? What makes you think you're addicted to sugar?*
CHRIS: *Because whenever I snack, all I want to eat are sweet foods; I eat a lot of biscuits and chocolate throughout the day.'*
ME: *Why do you feel you choose those foods?'*
CHRIS: *Well, when I come in from my farm work for a quick break, I grab biscuits or chocolate because that's the quickest thing to do before I carry on.*
ME: *Do you think if there were other foods that were ready, in your fridge or cupboards, that were just as quick to eat, but healthier, that you would eat them?'*
CHRIS: *Sure, I suppose so. I don't mind eating healthy food so that's not a problem.*
ME: *So who does the food shopping, and who buys in all the biscuits and chocolate you eat?*
CHRIS: *My wife does.*

(Luckily his wife was at the event, too, because he had just thrown her under the proverbial bus!)

ME: *What's your wife's name?*

CHRIS: *Judy.*

ME: *Hi, Judy. With your food shopping every week, and buying the food that you buy including the biscuits and the chocolate, why do you buy the food you do?*

JUDY: *Because Chris asks me to. He doesn't really eat breakfast as he heads out early to work, and asks for these biscuits and chocolate for snacks. He just grazes on the stuff all day, though we always sit down for a proper meal in the evening that I cook from scratch.*

ME: *Awesome. So, Chris, do you think you could plan to have different foods in the house, so that when you come in hungry, you eat different food, healthier food, that isn't biscuits and chocolate?*

CHRIS: *Yeah, I suppose so.*

ME: *Could we agree that it's actually your lack of planning that's causing this issue, that you are not planning to have good healthy food in your house, and thus when you come in hungry from work you are eating the biscuits and chocolate purely because that's all that's there, because it's all you've planned to have there?*

CHRIS: *Yeah, that's fair.*

ME: *Could we also agree that you are not valuing your health enough to make that change, to sit down and plan for the food that you want to eat to be healthier?*

CHRIS: *Yeah, that's a fair comment. I should plan better, and I do want to eat more healthily.*

ME: *Why is that?*

CHRIS: *I'm always tired, never satisfied by what I eat, and always feel like I'm chasing my tail and stressed, and I could do* with losing some weight – the key reason I'm here tonight actually.

ME: *So we could agree based on what you have heard today at this talk, the issues you are experiencing, and what we have identified as the problem, that if you sat down with your wife every week, planned your family's food shop better, and made an effort to buy and prepare proper meals every week, that you would eat better? That would likely help you feel better and more energized, you'll be healthier, and probably lose some weight as a result?*

CHRIS: *Aye, you're right.*

JUDY: *To be honest, Ben, I only do what Chris asks of me. I don't work too much, I help on the farm here and there, and paint for some local exhibition halls, so I have the time to prepare better meals for us both. This is what Chris asks for so I get it for him, and often eat breakfast and lunch by myself, and that's often not very good either as I am only making it for one and it often feels pointless going through all the effort for one, so often don't eat well myself either, which I know is bad.*

ME: *Awesome, could we all agree that what's needed here is better teamwork? That you could both work together to eat well, to organize your weekly food shop so that you both eat well, that stopping for regular breaks and meals together and enjoying eating good food together, around the table, in a relaxed and calm environment, is a good plan for both of you?*

CHRIS and JUDY: *Yes, 100 per cent.*

ME: *Awesome. Thanks for asking that question, Chris. It shows really well how the problem we think we have is rarely the problem we face, and that going through this questioning process by zooming out and looking objectively at the problem is really important. And importantly, how coming together to solve the problem, as a team, is powerful.'*

CHRIS and JUDY: *Agreed. Thank you, Ben.*

I hope that you, too, can see how much we have solved in this one conversation, and how we've gone a lot further than handling what was originally a very isolated, perceived, problem Chris thought he had. It turns out that Chris and Judy had got caught up in some bad habits and neither had said, 'Stop, let's look at this, we're not happy here, let's sit down and talk and solve this problem together.' By probing and asking questions I was able to get Chris and Judy to see the real root cause of the problem. In that conversation we were also able to bring Chris and Judy together more to talk and work as a team on creating healthier habits, to help Chris feel less stressed by making him slow down for a break while he ate a proper meal with his wife, and allow Judy to support Chris more by him being involved in the process from the start.

This is why it is so important to ask lots of questions when you face a problem. We need to act like a child would in asking, 'Why, why, why?' so we can go beyond the surface level. We've all experienced the frustrating thousand questions you get from a child, but it's a great way to problem solve . . .

'Why does that thing work the way it does?'

'But why?'

'But how?'

'But doesn't that mean that X won't work?'

'But how do you know that to be true?'

'Are you sure?'

'But I read that X is actually true?'

'When was the last time you tried, do you think it could have changed?'

These questions can be frustrating, and that's why many of us don't ask them. Questions like this probe deeply into what we believe and means that we could be wrong. And unfortunately, society has taught us to try be right as much as possible, that being right is a good thing, and that being wrong is a sign of weakness or stupidity. But it's not. And even if it was the case that being right is a sign of strength, you would still have to actually be right, rather than just convince yourself that you are. If you are wrong, then you are not right, so if you want to be right then you have to seek the truth, and the truth lies at the foot of the problem, not the head.

So, the next time you are faced with a problem, get right to its core, because if you don't, you'll be implementing the wrong solution, and not making headway on the problem.

Let's have a practice using this simple questioning framework. Really take your time with this one:

Write down a problem you feel you currently face.

_____

_____

Why do you feel this is a problem?

_____

_____

Why do you want to solve this problem?

_____

_____

How do you know this is the problem you face? Could it be a small part of something else? What could that be? If it is, put this bigger problem in line one and start again

_____

_____

Is the problem solely yours, or does it involve someone else?

_____

_____

Are there any simple steps you could take immediately to improve (if maybe not fully solve) the problem, for example better planning, time management, or organization?

_____

_____

To solve the problem, are you willing to act on the solution, to put the time and energy into it to get the outcome you want? Do you honestly value it enough to do the work?

_____

_____

How long do you think it would take to solve this problem, realistically?

_____

_____

Do you need the help of someone else to solve this problem?

_____

_____

Is this person usually supportive of helping you?

_____

_____

If not, should you choose someone else, someone more supportive, so that you have a higher chance of solving this problem?

_____

_____

What are the benefits to solving this problem?

_____

_____

Does solving this problem excite you? If so, why?

_____

_____

Have you tried to solve this problem before, and if so, what happened if you didn't solve it, what got in the way?

_____

_____

As you embark on solving this problem, what's the probability of the problem not being solved because of the issue you encountered last time happening again?

_____

_____

If the probability is high that the issue will crop up again, what change or solution can you put in place to increase your chances of success?

_____

_____

If you still have doubts, list and interrogate them. Are they justified? Is there anything you can do to solve or mitigate them? Are there any different strategies you can use to minimize the potential risks?

_____

_____

Is there anything else you need to solve or anticipate so you can 100 per cent guarantee you are going to solve this problem?

_____

_____

Do you now have absolute confidence you can solve this problem, and are closer to your goals and what it is you want to achieve? If not, start the questions again. Dig deeper.

_____

_____

Awesome! It's time to take action.

Do the stress-test

With the above, I asked a lot more questions than I did with Chris and Judy in solving their 'sweet tooth' conundrum, but this is because we need to go through the ultimate stress testing process when looking to solve our own problems. Not every question will be relevant to every problem, but if you ask the question, even if it's met with a 'not applicable', or a simple no, at least you have stress-tested it in that way and done the work, which will increase your confidence, and your actual ability to succeed.

There's nothing worse than embarking on the journey to living a more Awesome Life and putting in all the effort, only for it not to pay off. This often happens because the path, the plan, has not been stress-tested enough to iron out the kinks before starting. I don't want you to be applying a load of effort and working hard, only to get three months down the road and have nothing to show for it. That's demoralizing, and in all likelihood I know you've done it before on other 'plans' you've followed. I certainly have.

So whatever plan you create for yourself as a result of this book, stress-test it and really get to the heart of the problem, or be prepared for failure, because your boat will be rowing in the wrong direction.

CHAPTER FOUR

Critical thinking

I hate to throw another motivational quote at you so soon after the last one, but this one sums up why we need to cover this final aspect of getting to the truth, whether that's our own truth, the truth of the problem, or the scientific truth of whatever it is we are trying to implement.

> 'If we are not prepared to think for ourselves, and to make the effort to learn how to do this well, we will always be in danger of becoming slaves to the ideas and values of others due to our own ignorance.'
>
> **William Hughes**

To make sure we are 100 per cent aligned on both where we have come from and the ground we've covered so far in this book, let's recap really quickly.

First, we looked at ourselves and understood that we are the vehicles of change, that we have to be vulnerable in the process, and to take ownership of whatever it is we want to work on. We know that we deserve the changes we want, but we'll only live our most Awesome Life if we take the necessary steps.

We looked at fears that get in the way – what I called life imposter syndrome – and how to challenge our fears and move boldly and courageously through them to the upside of a better, more fulfilling life.

Then we looked at the problem (and there will likely be many, but it's always good to start with one and go through them in an orderly manner). We did this not by looking at its face value, but at the root cause by using a questioning process to uncover the truth.

So now, lastly, we need to look at the truthfulness of the facts we use to understand our problems, both the causes and the solutions.

Scientific evidence . . . and why it matters

In all realms of life there are people who have beliefs and assumptions about what is and is not true, the difficulty is often working out what is actually evidence based. I've worked in the field of nutrition for 15 years after training to be a nutrition coach at age 20, and I firmly believe that there is no industry that has more half-truths and outright non-truths than the world of nutrition. It's something I bang my head against the wall about daily.

Think about what you believe to be true in this space. The way you eat right now, the foods you believe to be healthy or not, the things you avoid or would tell others to if they asked . . . where did these ideas come from? How do we know they're correct?

Let's use an extreme example to illustrate the point and imagine you are following a diet made up 100 per cent of liquid meal replacements – why?

Perhaps you saw some adverts about it, maybe heard a friend talking about it, or saw an influencer/authority figure you respect backing the claims you've read. Maybe you saw all of this and gave it a go, perhaps this caused you to lose weight. This kind of story is really common.

Perhaps a nutrition coach you sat down and said it would be a great way for you to control your hunger and lose weight, it worked, so now you believe it to be the right diet for others or the best strategy for you?

Did you decide to give it a go after your doctor told you you were pre-diabetic, you went to do some research, found evidence these products could be beneficial, tried it, and got your blood glucose under control?

What I am drawing attention to in the above is the ease with which we can all be bought in by things that aren't as well supported by research as they would ideally be. This matters because as human beings we have evolved a lot of biases, blind spots, and logical fallacies that are useful for surviving in palaeolithic situations but less so in highly advanced, technologically driven societies. In short, it's OK to trust your gut when it comes to avoiding dark alleys, it's less so when trying to answer the question, 'Will this nutritional strategy maximize my physical wellbeing?' That's a question for scientists with laboratories, tools and complex models.

Reading a magazine, speaking to a friend about something, or seeing something on social media, has a low level of credibility compared to the totality of the peer-reviewed research on the same topic. Now that's not to say you should get all your information from scientific research papers because they are hard to read and usually behind paywalls; it's good to be able to look here, but in reality it's impossible to investigate every topic that matters to us on this kind of level as an individual, but what you can do is stress-test the credibility and the validity of the source of information.

Was the person writing the magazine article you read highly qualified, experienced and trustworthy?

Did they reference research papers?

Did the individual use absolute (black-and-white) language, saying this is proven and you should therefore act upon it, or did they acknowledge limitations in the research? It's a mistake to always look for 'balanced views' because this leads us to a *middle ground fallacy*, where we assume there is truth on both sides. If there is 99.9 per cent agreement with one view it is dishonest to present both alternatives with equal credibility; but nonetheless an honest actor will most often use words like 'might', 'could', 'seems to', and 'evidence suggests' rather than 'is', 'will' or 'causes'. If people do use definite language like this, they need a lot of evidence to back them up, and if that's lacking, you're not obligated to trust them.

Does the source or publication have a history of credibly putting out accurate and well-researched information?

Does your source of information have a funding bias, or is it trying to get you to buy something?

Does the individual you listened to have a track record of seeking out the truth and believe in scientific objectivity, or are they just a contrarian?

All of these things can be a good starting point for us when assessing the validity of a source of information. If we don't question the source, if we do not approach information with a critical mindset, if we do not do the required research to stress-test ideas, then we are not behaving in a scientific, truth seeking way. A good tactic is to adopt the 'null hypothesis' and then respect the burden of proof. This is where you assume at the start that there is no causal link between the two things being discussed, in our example above you would assume there is no correlation between the meal replacements and improved health; those trying to convince you to buy them need to meet the burden of proof, meaning that they need to prove you wrong, to show that there is in fact a link. If they don't do that to a degree that gives you a lot of confidence (using the tools above), then it's a good policy to not believe them because the burden of proof doesn't support what they are saying.

This is why science is important: because it aims to find out what happens when things are tested objectively. That is a scientific researcher's job – to stress-test ideas under controlled conditions and present their evidence to their peers. This body of evidence is then used to find effective solutions to problems. Because we're looking to change and solve problems, we should want to get close to science, or at least close to people who have the expertise needed to translate the body of evidence into recommendations.

Some guy on YouTube talking about what they did and why it worked isn't trustworthy unless they are referring to substantial amounts of evidence (one study is not enough!). Personal experience is great, anecdotes are powerful and important – especially when there is a lack of scientific research in an area – but they are just that, anecdotes and experience, and still need to be stress-tested.

Diet is a good example. Say I go on the keto diet and lose weight, and I stand there and say, 'The keto diet is the best diet for fat loss.' And you say to me, 'Why?' and I say, 'Because eating fat burns fat. Just look at my results.'

Here if we look carefully at what I've said, you'll see that I haven't actually justified myself. You asked why the keto diet is the best diet for fat loss, and I answered with a mechanism without explaining how it works or why it's relevant (note that 'burning fat', or using it for energy, and 'losing bodyfat' aren't the same thing – eating more fat and so burning more fat don't make a difference unless you're burning more fat than you're eating, and I haven't given evidence for that in the example above). I've then said 'just look at my results', but because this wasn't a scientific experiment, we have no idea if the change to a keto diet alone caused the change – maybe my calories, protein intake, or activity levels changed, too?

So, while I might not be outright wrong, the keto diet does lead to more fat burning and I did get results while using it, that doesn't mean that it's the best diet for fat loss, not by a long stretch.

So what happens when we look at comparisons between ketogenic diets and non-ketogenic diets in conditions where calories, protein and exercise are controlled? A 2019 review of the scientific literature put it best[1]: 'low- and very-low-[carbohydrate] diets are not superior for weight loss compared with diets with a higher quantity of [carbohydrate] and are difficult to maintain in clinical trials of adults with overweight and obesity, with or without prediabetes or diabetes'. This of course does not mean these kinds of diets don't work, only that there is no good evidence (despite a lot of looking!) that they are more effective for fat or weight loss than other diets, and they may be harder to stick to long term.

This is what truth-hunting looks like. Look at what has been said, look at the way it's been justified, and then (where possible), look to the broad body of research or at least an unbiased source who can tell you what's currently understood.

Take a look at the following figure, known as the hierarchy of evidence.

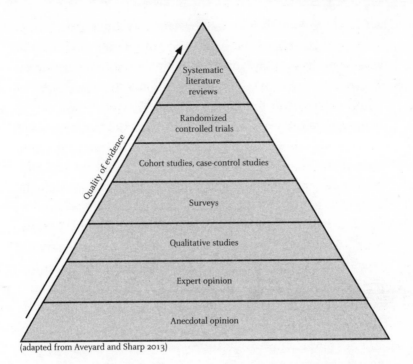

(adapted from Aveyard and Sharp 2013)

As you can see, there are many different sources of evidence, all of which have a different role in informing our actions. There's a lot of interesting nuance to it, but the key thing to take from this is that we as ordinary people should base most of our understanding of the world around systematic reviews (and realistically, summaries of these reviews by organizations like the NHS in the UK who make recommendations around exercise, nutrition and other health-related things).

Unfortunately a lot of people's sources – blogs, videos, social media, friends or people we know and their anecdotes – are very low on the scientific scale. Of course, the people we could be following and taking advice from on social media could be very familiar with the evidence, and they act in a safe, credible and balanced way, and that's OK, but finding those people and fact-checking what they say can be hard, especially when everyone *sounds* so sure of the truth. The unfortunate truth is that lying for profit, being wrong due to your biases and being correct all sound the same and so separating these out can be tough.

This is why critical thinking is so important. Without it we waste time, energy and money, we get taken for a fool, we don't get closer to our goals, and there is a higher chance we lose hope, especially if we have already tried to solve a problem many times, haven't got good information, and repeatedly failed – something that's all too common in the world of fat loss and health. Over 15 years of coaching I've seen many people who have yo-yoed with their diet, repeatedly trying things that haven't worked, or losing weight only to go put most of it back on again. Sometimes this is because their mindset is wrong, but often it's simply because they're acting with full effort on bad information.

If we want results in any area of our lives, the faster we find the truth, the faster we find the best path to get there. We might take a bit longer in the planning phase when we research a few more things, fact-check and be 100 per cent sure we are doing the right thing, but it will save many hours and much heartache farther along the road. Acting on the strongest evidence possible is always the most reliable strategy, the question is how do you find it?

Continuing on with the diet example, if you got really close to the research on the keto diet you would find out that yes, it can be a good diet for fat loss, but it works like any named diet: it causes you to eat fewer calories. In this case this may be because:

1. Increased levels of blood ketones may reduce hunger, though the reason for this isn't fully understood[2], and of course your experience may differ.

2. It's is high in animal protein and fat, and a lot of people like that. Both of these can also help with your appetite, but of course you don't need to adopt a ketogenic diet to eat more protein and fat.

3. It puts people into a strong dieting mindset by having a very clear set of rules, and this can be good for people working towards a clear outcome. It can also be terrible for your relationship with food, though, so it's definitely not for everyone.

4. It can be a good diet for epilepsy, so is medically recommended sometimes in these cases[2].

5. It's a diet that cuts out all sugar, most alcohol and most junk food and thus limits most of the foods people tend to overeat on. Cutting out these foods for a prolonged period of time can help to stop people craving these foods and almost 'reset' their approach to nutrition (it can, however, also do the opposite and cause people to constantly crave these foods and want to binge)

In short, while it can be an effective diet, many diets are effective, and it ultimately works like any other: it makes you eat fewer calories than your body burns and so if it matches your dietary preferences it can work. Just to close this section, no robust long-term evidence has been collected to demonstrate that a ketogenic diet has no downsides for the average population and so it's not a strategy I would personally recommend.

As you can see here, it's useful to take into account anecdote and personal evidence or experience, but because these often miss large parts of the picture they're not reliable. If we want reliable information our best bet is to look to peer-reviewed evidence – the entire body of it, rather than just one study here or there.

Blinded by bias

To finish off this chapter on problem solving and critical think-ing, we need to discuss biases. The definition of a bias taken from a dictionary is 'a particular tendency, trend, inclination, feeling or opinion, especially one that is preconceived or unrea-soned'. What this means in real terms, in the context here, is that we tend to view the world around us through a lens formed by things that we have experienced in life, people we know, the environment we are in, or our proximity to a person or prob-lem, among many other things.

A bias can be thought of as green-coloured glasses attached to your face for your entire life – you don't know they're there and so far as you know that's just how the world looks, but it's only how it looks *to you*. The key thing to keep in mind is that you can't take the glasses off, but by learning that they're there you can get better at understanding that the thing in front of you isn't green, it's white, no matter how it may appear.

'Bias' is often used as a negative term, but I don't think it's good to think of it like that because we all have biases, and they will always be there. It's just that it's our job to know about them and try to work out when our biases are leading us to think in a way that doesn't serve us, or doesn't help us find truth. If we don't do this, our biases can cause us to make poor decisions, not only on a day-to-day level but also on the big, life-changing things, too, and as a result we can end up moving farther away from our goals. Knowing our biases and making better decisions will help with our family life, personal life, professional life and more. As I'm sure you can appreciate, a decision will always be better made knowing all the facts, and accounting for your green glasses (at least as often as you can, anyway).

A quick simple example of a bias might be an argument you are having with friends and family. You might automatically side with your family, even if they are in the wrong, just because they *are* family, and thus your close relationship with them might blind you to the truth.

There are many biases, but the ones below are the ones I've found most common in people I coach, and so these are the ones to pay really close attention to, noticing when you're being driven by them.

CONFIRMATION BIAS

This is where we seek information only to confirm what we already believe to be true, often known as 'cherry picking the research'. Looking at a real-world example, this might be someone who believes that the artificial sweetener aspartame is toxic; rather than neutrally searching for evidence about the health effects of aspartame, they may look for evidence that aspartame causes harm. This is a very subtle difference, but it's a big enough one to lead to different findings, and different interpretations of the same findings. In short, it leads to bad information.

If you want to find the truth on anything in life, you need to consider (as far as possible) *all* the research, *all* the perspectives, *all* the experiences you can find, and then draw a conclusion. Don't just find information that supports your pre-existing beliefs, and pay close attention to when you do it without realizing.

PROXIMITY BIAS

This bias comes down to how being (too) close to someone or something can skew our opinion of the truth. As an example, we might be the captain of a team and know one team member really well, but not another, leading us to think or feel that they are a better player, even if, objectively, this is not the case. Another way that this affects us is that we trust familiar ideas more than unfamiliar ones, even when our familiar ideas are far less supported by evidence. Pay attention. Do you trust the ideas of people you know and ideas you're familiar with a little too uncritically?

AUTHORITY BIAS

This is us choosing to believe or side with someone based on their perceived level of authority. We might be having a conversation with someone at work and choose to side with a manager over a team member just because they are the manager or have a title that suggests their experience or trustworthiness. Do you trust the nutrition advice of someone just because they are a doctor (no matter the area . . .)? Authority bias plays out in all areas of our lives, from daily decision making to political decision making. Just because someone has a title, or wealth, or speaks with confidence, it doesn't make them right. Seek the truth.

THE DUNNING–KRUGER EFFECT

You've probably heard the phrase: 'A little bit of knowledge is a dangerous thing'. Just because we know a little bit about something doesn't mean we really understand it. We humans are good at oversimplifying concepts after we've got a little knowledge under our belts; we've got the nuts and bolts, we have enough understanding to now get us by, and that's it, job done.

This can be dangerous, leading us to settling on that little bit we know as the complete picture, limiting our curiosity about something and stopping us exploring it further.

Don't feel bad about not knowing more about things, or feel that you can't do things with that bit of knowledge you do have. Sometimes a smidgeon of knowledge on a topic is all we need to get started, but just know that to get over the finish line you'll need to get close to a topic, invest time and energy, and know the complexities. A good question is, 'Can I get a degree in this?', and if so, it's usually (though of course not *always*) safe to assume there are some aspects of the topic you don't know about yet.

In short, be honest about what you know and about what you *don't* know. Don't be blinded by a little bit of information and think you can speak with authority on the matter to others, even if you feel like you have enough information to make decisions for yourself.

OPTIMISM OR PESSIMISM BIAS

This bias, for the purpose of this book, can be summed up in these words: 'Don't make big future decisions in a bad mood.' If you're having a bad day, just get through it, and leave the big life decisions until you're having a better day when your mind-set is in a good place and you feel in a good frame of mind to approach problems. The same goes when you're having one of those 'on top of the world' days – good decisions are rarely made after four cups of coffee or eight beers!

Your state of mind when making decisions can very easily skew how you feel the outcome will go and thus you increase your chances of retreating completely, or making risky decisions that may not benefit your long-term future. A clear mind and good mood will see you have optimism about the right decision and its potential for a good outcome while still giving the problem the time it deserves and considering all the angles.

SELF-SERVING BIAS

This is where we assume that when good things happen to us they're because of our hard work and talent, but when bad things happen to us it's because of factors outside our control. This then means that we don't take personal responsibility for the outcome and so seek to do better in the future (something that will benefit us, even if the outcome really WAS at least in part out of our control). As the US podcaster, author and ex-Navy SEAL officer Jocko Willink advises in *Extreme Ownership*, one of my favourite books, take ownership for where you are in your life and what is happening to you; playing the blame game gets you nowhere.

ATTRIBUTION ERROR BIAS

This is similar to self-serving bias, but it's subtly different. Attribution bias happens when we see the best in ourselves but the worst in others, when the same or similar thing or situation happens. For example, if we are late to a meeting, we will look to the full context – a family problem or a traffic jam – and see that the situation may not have been totally in our hands, whereas if a colleague is late, we put it down to them being lazy or not caring or not being organized, that is, to a personal failing that they could reasonably have controlled.

The lesson from these two? Outside forces play into both good and bad outcomes for both us and for other people. We should worry about changing what we can control rather than feeling guilty or blaming others for what we can't control, all the while being compassionate for those who are in the same boat as we are.

YELLOW CAR SYNDROME

This is where something happens, and because we start paying attention we might now notice further recurrences more. It's not that this event is happening more often; it's simply that the brain has now become attuned to that experience or thing. Perhaps you are looking to buy a new car and decide on a yellow one. Typically you will then start to see yellow cars everywhere on the road when you're out driving. Perhaps you've started to think that a certain food is bad for you, or you've started to think it's a bad idea to start a business. Once these ideas have occurred, you're going to see the 'bad' food mentioned more, and hear about more businesses failing even though the frequency hasn't increased at all. The lesson? Try not to let an experience of something fool your decision making, just because your brain is now paying more attention to it. Look for data and make your decisions based on that.

AVAILABILITY BIAS

This bias can be dangerous as it often leans on our memory, which is far more flawed than we think it is. Availability bias leads us to think that things we can recall really easily happen more often than they do. People are hyper-aware of lethal shark encounters because they are so sensationalized; they're less aware of the (400 per cent greater) number of lethal incidents involving cows. This is a problem because we may have forgotten a lot of information, or simply not come across it, so we might start to make decisions based on very limited data. To avoid this, especially if you are considering a big or important life decision, revisit a topic to check you have all the facts available, or flesh it out with someone who knows the topic well.

ADDITIVE BIAS

This is a very common bias in the world of self-development. We believe that adding more and more things, or techniques, or layers of complexity will get us closer to our goal, when what is often needed is subtraction – simplifying or doing less so we can focus on the things that really make a difference.

More doesn't equate to a better outcome. Remember the KISS principle: Keep It Simple, Stupid.

CONTINUED INFLUENCE EFFECT

This occurs when we continue to use misinformation to guide our decisions, even when we know that what we're using is misinformation. Think about the person who doesn't believe in superstition but still touches wood to avoid jinxing things.

A personal example may make this clearer. In my younger years I went on a paleo diet and lost a lot of bodyfat, leading me to believe that the paleo diet and the ideas that underpin it (essentially that a lot of 'modern food' is bad and needs to be removed) was the way to go. I later learned more and changed this belief. Nonetheless, I continued to avoid, at least for a time, a lot of the foods that I had previously cut out. I knew that they were fine to eat, but in the moment I still felt that I shouldn't eat them because I was still using the paleo diet teachings to guide me. It took me far too long to come around to the truth, but that is down to the lasting power of the positive emotion attached to our successful experiences.

Let's put into practice what you have learned about biases and how they can skew your actions and behaviour by interrogating something you believe in and get to the truth. Answer these questions below:

> Write down something you believe to be true, or are maybe questioning whether is true (maybe something current in your life):
>
> _____
>
> _____

How strongly do you believe this on a scale of 1–6, with 6 being 'very strongly'?

_____

_____

What would convince you that this is not true? If you can't think of anything, do you think that this blinds you to the truth?

_____

_____

What evidence do you have for your belief and its truth – do you believe that this evidence is trustworthy or holds some useful truth? Why? Maybe you could point to where it sits on the hierarchy of evidence.

_____

_____

What evidence exists that runs counter to your belief – do you believe that this evidence is trustworthy or holds some useful truth? Why?

_____

_____

Does that counter evidence sit higher on the hierarchy of evidence?

_____

_____

How strongly do you now believe this on a scale of 1–6?

_____

Going through this simple questioning process allows us to quickly interrogate what we believe and get closer to the truth. And as you hopefully now know, this is fundamental in the process of change, because the truth sets us free.

Summarizing biases

As I mentioned above, there are many more kinds of bias, but I picked out these ones because I have seen them be an issue for many, and feel they have the biggest potential negative influence over our ability to change and seek the truth. Understanding these is the first step towards removing their influence over us.

This ties in with our level of self-awareness. We have to be aware of our strengths and weaknesses as people, the environment we live and act in, and the things that can stop us from making what would, long-term, be better decisions. This is why I want you to know what biases can act on you, what character traits you possess and express, and how this combined influences your decision making.

One of the best ways to explore your biases or forces that act upon your decision making is to simply spend more time by yourself, mulling over things, and to then spend time with people who think differently from you. Time alone enables you to think through problems, explore all the angles, do some research, while talking to other people in the know or who have different world views from you opens up your truth horizons further still. Through this process you get as close as possible to the truth through your own critical thinking – which is a good skill to constantly hone – and in talking to others your ideas, problems and conclusions then get challenged.

That said, one of the worst things we can do is to stress-test our problems or ideas with people who think the same as us, or who might be suffering from authority bias. For example, I might have an idea and present it to my team, who only think it's a good idea because they work for me! However, if I was to take that same idea to my wife or business friends, they might look at the problem a lot differently and challenge me a lot more directly because they are very different from me and don't have as much invested in the outcome.

As it happens, I have built a very diverse team that challenges my ideas all the time, but I have done this intentionally by hiring good people and instilling an open and honest culture in my business. I know that in business you get the best outcomes when you have diverse thinking on problems.

But remember, to do this effectively you have to be vulnerable around others and focus on the outcome you want, which is the best possible idea or solution to the problem, rather than simply wanting to be told you're right so your ego gets to feel good.

The best outcome should always be the priority, not confirmation that your idea was a good idea in the first place. It's why having great people around you that challenge you to think differently is so important. These could be work colleges, friends or your partner – whoever they are, converse with them regularly.

'The truth shall set you free is only half the story. You must be willing to accept the truth in order to be truly free.'

Todd Gaster

PART 2

11 steps to your Awesome Life

Are you ready for the 11-step Awesome Life formula?

You've come along way already. High five. That's awesome. I'm glad you're still with me.

And guess what? We haven't even started on the formula, what it is, and how to implement it. It's time to embark on that journey to get into the weeds and do the graft.

I really hope you appreciate the approach I have taken in this book so far. You see, stories are powerful, but so are the things that hold us back. Having been involved in coaching other people for 15-plus years, I know it's never as simple as 'doing the thing'. Nutrition is such a good example of this. We know we should all eat healthily and keep fit, but we don't always do it. But why?

Because things hold us back. Fear creeps in. A lack of knowledge can be a blocker. Faulty belief structures warp our sense of what's true. Stress in our life restricts us. Unsupportive peers make us question the path. We might have been emotionally abused in our younger years and have low self-worth. We've slipped into bad routines and are now struggling to break what feels like a dozen bad habits at once. We're disorganized and can't think where is best to start. We might feel as if we lack money, or we genuinely may do. We tell ourselves that we don't have time . . . The list goes on.

This is why this book couldn't just launch straight into giving you the formula, because that would only work with a small percentage of people. I've drawn up and given plans to thousands of people over the years, but without the coaching that goes along with a plan few people are able to fully execute on it long term. For a plan to work, most of us need to understand how things are going to work, why and where things might get tough, and when and what things need to change . . . oh, and we need accountability and inspiration along the way. We're human beings, not robots, after all.

So please don't be that person who says, 'Just give me the plan, that's all I need.' Because I know in 99 per cent of cases that isn't true. We all benefit from understanding why something works. We all benefit from the stories that support why something works. And we all need the context around how problems are solved and conquered long term. This is why I have taken the approach I have in this book so far. I also wanted to build up your confidence in me as your coach. If you're going to trust in me and this book to truly give you the tools to live your most Awesome Life, then you have to really feel I've been there and done it, and coached many other people to achieve this goal as well. That's why I've told stories. That's why I've tried to 'keep it real', and that's why I've tried to use as many real-life examples as possible, using my own experiences of challenges as a primary context.

I've struggled with stuff, you're struggling with stuff, and I hope my approach is giving you the confidence and belief to make a plan, challenge what you know, and break through.

The rest of this book aims to be more practical, action led, and outcome driven. But I shall continue to tell stories where relevant so you can continue to understand the context behind it all and get a steer on how some of these things can play out in real life.

At this stage in the book, before we move on, I'd like you to go back to Chapter 1 where you wrote down what living an Awesome Life means to you. I'd like you to consider whether what you wrote still feels true.

If it's changed, that's 100 per cent fine. I *expect* it to change for some of you as you read through this book. I want this book to challenge what your truth and future path is. So please don't feel it should have been set in stone; change is good. If it has changed and there's space to cross some things out and scribble down a bit more, do that. If not, grab yourself a nice new notebook and label the cover in big fat letters:

MY BOOK OF BIG AWESOME LIFE GOALS

I love having a good notebook in which to plan and write my thoughts. Writing a goal allows you to think about it more critically, test it, set action plans and hold yourself accountable. If you can attach visual cues or pictures to your plans and goals, then all the better: visualization makes a goal feel more meaningful, and that can help you if you ever start to lose motivation or resolve. I do this at home (in my home office) where I have my goals on a big whiteboard, all my books on display, adjustable standing desk, comfy chair, storage to keep it a clutter free zone, and everything I want to help me work effectively but also to plan my life. I highly recommend having a little space to dream, think and plan.

Right, I hope you're motivated, I hope you're inspired, and I hope you're ready to take the big actions you need to take to reach your goals, because it's time to get stuck into the Awesome Life formula:

Approach

Water

Environment

Sleep

Organize

Movement

Eat

Lifestyle

Inspiration

Finances

Education

To begin with, I have to ask one thing of you: to take things nice and slow. If you read through these 11 steps too quickly, you probably won't fully implement them and make the required changes. I want you to go at a pace that actually allows you to work on implementing what you learn. Slowly does it: real change can only occur at the pace your life can handle.

If your life feels quite busy and stressed right now, it might be even more important to take things slowly, addressing each chapter in turn in a methodical way. Spend time implementing the changes before moving on to the next chapter, to allow your mindset to shift. Give yourself the space and time. This isn't a race; it's about real, lasting change.

Of course, there's no real way to do the work from this book other than the way that feels right for you, in accordance with what you can handle right now. But I do want you to challenge yourself as you go through each chapter because parts will be uncomfortable and you might be inclined to skip that step, to turn the page. But parts of this book *should* feel uncomfortable as these are very likely to be the things that need to change the most.

> Change is uncomfortable. Please do the work this book asks of you and I promise AWESOME things will happen.

On the other hand, we're not after perfect mastery of each step here. Some chapters in this book you can read, start to implement changes, and then move on. The chapter covering Step 1 is a good example. Changing your perspective on how you view life isn't something you can click your fingers and change overnight. You might need a good few months to shift your mindset. As long as you have done the work at each step, setting your intentions and practising daily, you can move on.

It's about balance. You can go too slowly. As I discussed earlier, you need to take time to think about the changes you want to make, to get to the truth, and to think of all the angles. But this isn't permission to procrastinate. Only you will know, but it's important not to make excuses to yourself that you are still thinking, still working things out, still having conversations and still getting things right in your head. While this process is key, once you have all the facts and feel confident about making a decision, make it, back yourself, and take action. No decision will ever be made with 100 per cent certainty – that's not how life works – but if you've factored everything in and you are 70–80 per cent certain about your conclusions, then puff out your chest, stand tall, feel your courage rise, be bold, and take action – because that's all that's left to do.

Don't be all talk and no action BUT do perform the right amount of talk to inform the action.

Right, let's look at Step 1: your approach to life.

Your approach to life

Approach

Water

Environment

Sleep

Organize

Movement

Eat

Lifestyle

Inspiration

Finances

Education

You've no doubt heard the drink in a glass analogy before: are you a glass half full, or a glass half empty kind of person? It's hard to say really, because it depends on the context and can definitely change over time.

With that said we can definitely look at ourselves on average and assess whether the way we tend to respond to situations serves us or not. I hinted at this earlier, but while it can be useful to know that some things aren't your fault, that there's nothing you *could have done* to avoid a bad outcomes, that's not necessarily the place you should stop. This kind of thinking can quickly allow you to spiral into a mentality of victimhood – life happens *to you* rather than it being the case that you're an active participant. You can't change some things, but you can definitely change how you respond to them, and so rather than a glass half full or glass half empty person, it's time to realize that you're the one holding the glass!

As you might suspect from this opener, Step 1 is all about mindset: without the right mindset, the rest of this book might as well not exist.

Building a base level of positivity

I think as a kid I was generally pretty positive, largely because my mum was always so upbeat. For this I'm thankful; some people's parents aren't positive, and that can be one of the most profound influences we have in our life. I do know that I had times as a boy when I struggled to be positive because I was bullied so much and put down by my teachers so often, but once I left school and took life by the horns, I feel as though I have largely been a positive person since. That's not to say there haven't been times where my positivity has taken a severe knock, though. You can't, won't, and probably shouldn't be positive all the time – we all go through some rough phases in our life and dealing with them rather than forcing positivity is healthy – but if we build a base level of positivity in our lives, we never get too far down the glass half empty road.

So here is lesson number 1 in Step 1: we need to build a life that is full of positive things, in order for us to be, or carry on being, a positive person. At the points in my life when I faced the biggest difficulties I maintained a decent level of positivity because there was so much in my life that was already positive. I'm in a happy marriage, have a job I love, have a roof over my head, I'm a self-confident person and trust in my ability to solve problems, and I've a supportive family around me, all contributing to my positive outlook on life even when things get difficult. That's not, of course, to say you need a long list of things to remain positive, but practising gratitude for the things we do have and paying close attention to what truly matters can help us gain perspective, and add things to our list. Do the following quick exercise to help you feel more grateful and positive for all that's in your life right now.

Write down all the things that you are grateful for, and that are positive things in your life right now:

_____

_____

_____

_____

_____

_____

_____

_____

_____

_____

Turning things around

Now consider the flipside of the list you have written down. Think about some of the things in your life that might be weighing down your positivity:

- You've got a job you hate.
- You dislike your work colleagues.
- You feel your parents are always on at you.
- You are struggling for money.
- You're really low in energy and motivation because you're eating poorly, not exercising much and going to bed late
- You've a bad injury and can't play the sport you love.
- You feel stuck in life, like there isn't a path to a happy future.

There could be all manner of things going on in your life that feel negative, but how can you turn them around? This is where we need to be solution focused rather than problem focused. This is tough because when you are in a rut you often focus on the problem. But, as, Tony Robbins, says:

'Where focus goes, energy flows.'

If you keep focusing on the problem, that's where your energy will go, and your energy will remain negative.

So, let's take a really blunt, direct, solution-focused approach to each of the above problems. It's high time to go for the jugular!

YOU'VE GOT A JOB YOU HATE

Why do you hate your job? Can you change it? Can you move departments? Can you ask for a change in responsibilities? Can you embark on some professional development to improve how well you perform in your role? Can you speak to your boss, be honest with them and share this insight and work together to create a plan so that you can enjoy your job again? Could you work from home some of the time as half of the problem may be how long you spend commuting every day? Is there a way you can frame your job as a stepping-stone, or necessary evil that will allow you to do what you need to do, rather than only a burden?

I don't know the root cause here, but remember, a solution focused mindset may mean changing your life situation today, or it might mean laying the foundation for changes in the future with a change of perspective.

YOU DISLIKE YOUR WORK COLLEAGUES

Why? What can you do about it; maybe communication could be improved? Maybe you could spend time nurturing those relationships so you understand your colleagues better? Maybe you could distance yourself from the one or two problematic characters? Could you move departments? Could you have an honest chat with those problematic people and find a way to work more effectively together? Could the things that are annoying you actually be a reflection of how you work and how they make you react? Is it them, or is it you? Can you change your reaction to their behaviour? Do you have to get annoyed? Could you speak to your manager or boss about it?

I don't know the root cause of your work colleague problem, but without addressing it these relationships will continue to make your life worse.

YOU FEEL YOUR PARENTS ARE ALWAYS ON AT YOU

Why do you feel like that? Is it them, or is it you and your behaviour? Perhaps you should stop sharing updates or stories about the things that they moan about you for? Perhaps you distance yourself from them for a bit and just let the situation cool off? Perhaps you could up your game and prove them wrong? Perhaps you just sit down and talk to them and really get to the heart of the issue? What do you think is the root cause of the friction and can that be resolved? Or can you change your perspective on why they approach the issue the way they do?

I don't know the root cause of the problems you have with your parents, or if they can be solved, but if you want them to be then we need to take a solution-focused approach.

YOU ARE STRUGGLING FOR MONEY

Why? Are you spending too much? Are you trying to 'keep up with the Joneses' and buy stuff you don't need? Have you over-committed to things financially? Do you know how to budget? If your financial literacy is great but you have a low-paying job, could you ask your boss for a pay rise? Could you ask how you can put yourself on the path to promotion? Could you get a second job? Could you move jobs? Can you start a side hustle?

Is there a way you could upskill and work towards better employment at some point in the future?

I don't know the root cause of your money problem, but the only way to improve your situation is to take a solutions-focused approach to thinking about it.

YOU'RE REALLY LOW IN ENERGY AND MOTIVATION BECAUSE YOU'RE EATING POORLY, NOT EXERCISING MUCH AND GOING TO BED LATE

What's stopping you from taking action to improve your health and fitness? Is it money that's holding you back from working on your health? Is lack of time holding you back? Do you value your health enough to change it? Is your partner an issue because they have some bad habits or you've developed some together? Why are you staying up late and not sleeping well? Is going to bed late serving you? What simple steps could you take to get fitter? Could you just start to walk more?

I don't know the root cause of your health and lifestyle problems, but I want you to take a solution-focused mindset to solving them, because sleep, your health and your level of fitness will dramatically improve your experience of life and how much you can achieve in other areas of your life.

YOU'VE A BAD INJURY AND CAN'T PLAY THE SPORT YOU LOVE

What other interest or hobby can you pour your time into? What opportunity has this extra free time created? Could this be an opportunity to work on some weaknesses you have in your sport or in the gym? Perhaps it's time to retire from that sport or try a different one? Perhaps your body is telling you something? Perhaps there's an opportunity here and you're just not seeing it? Could you rehabilitate the injury if you put your mind to it?

I don't know the root cause of your injury problem, but I want you to take a solution-focused mindset to solving it.

PROBLEMS AND SOLUTIONS

Problems and solutions should always be part and parcel of the same discussion; otherwise you're just moaning. And trust me, I've been in a rut, I know what it feels like. I know how thoughts can race through your head and the hole feels too deep to get out of. But you have to see solutions, you have to see opportunity, you have to notice what your life is telling you and plot a different course of action.

When I was fighting going bankrupt in 2017, life was telling me something:

- I was focused on the wrong things.
- I had the wrong people managing the company's money.
- I had entrusted the wrong people with the decision making.
- I had taken my eye off the ball and wasn't checking in often enough or with enough of a critical eye.
- I hired out of fear rather than out of opportunity, so hadn't been diligent enough when hiring a key person.
- I made the original business decision while drunk – a *terrible* way to make a decision.

Only I could make the decision to accept my responsibility in this failure, to accept what had happened, and do the work to implement solutions and learn from my mistakes.

> Own your problems.

In 2020, when I was battling my way back to full health from long COVID and was in the biggest health rut I have ever been in, I had to accept that:

- The virus had made me ill and it was the straw that broke the camel's back.
- My gut health was compromised and needed work – a key reason my immune system was weak.
- I was living life at 100mph and I needed to slow down – my response to the virus was telling me to slow down.
- I needed to become more patient. As someone with ADHD who was now a parent, and with a business that needed me to be a clear-thinking CEO, I now more than ever needed to work on my patience and pace of life.
- My illness was telling me to get a better perspective on life, on where my time and energy should truly be.

Only I could accept the harsh realities of what this health problem was telling me, work on the solutions, and do the work to become a better person, parent and business owner.

Life is going to throw us all a huge number of curveballs and bad situations we're going to have to deal with. I've had many, you've had many, and we will both continue to have them. The difference, ultimately, between success and failure and whether we become stronger or weaker because of our experiences is how we react to them. Do we let these experiences win, or do we rise to the challenge and take them head on, in as positive a way as possible?

Both 2017 and 2020 made me a better parent, person and leader for my business. I'm forever grateful for these painful

experiences now because of the lessons they taught me. I know
they will help me take on other challenges in life.

We all go through the frustration, pain and anger phases of
problems, but the mark of success is how quickly we shake
these phases off and focus on the solutions, not the problems.
This way, over time, if we let them, our problems can shape us
into better, more resilient people.

(Re)gaining momentum and perspective

When we are in a rut with a problem, there can be a real lack
of momentum: we feel stuck, and that often makes us do nothing. We can feel paralysed even when a solution is obvious.
This is where one simple step could get us out of that rut and
change our course. For me, this can be just going for a walk in
nature, taking the time to move, get fresh air, get momentum
(or the feeling of it from walking), and taking time to think and
find solutions – maybe first by yourself, to get some personal
thinking time, then the following time with a trusted friend
who can give you advice and maybe add a fresh perspective.

A walk by myself and/or with a good friend is one of the
simplest ways to get perspective and momentum back into my
life. For you, that first simple step out of your rut or negative
feelings could be something different – from open-water swimming to a trip to an art gallery. Anything that gets you, your
thoughts, and your mindset moving again so you can focus on
something different and/or fun.

Now let me be clear. If you do this by meeting up with a
friend, it isn't a chance to moan. That's not allowed. To be positive and to find solutions you need to take a problem-solving
attitude, not a moaning-about-the-problem attitude. That's the

glass half empty, 'I'm a victim' approach to problem solving, and it's one of the most common character traits I've seen in clients over the years that keeps them stuck. It feels good to complain, but it doesn't help you achieve your Awesome Life.

> Everything is in our control.

We have the power either to change things or change our mind-set towards the problem. So yes, you might not be able to materially change the issue, but you can change how you view it.

These are some of the phrases I commonly hear from people who play the victim:

- 'I don't have enough time.'
- 'I'm not talented enough.'
- 'I'm not clever enough.'
- 'I don't have enough energy.'
- I don't have enough money.'

Perhaps you have something you often say that holds you back from taking action in your life? This is where I have to tell you something straight up: your life will change significantly when you realize that life is happening *for* you, not *to* you.

The American psychologist Carol Dweck, author of *Mindset*, has a brilliant solution to the victim mentality: to any of the above phrases, you simply add the word 'yet'.

- 'I don't have enough time, yet.'
- 'I'm not talented enough, yet.'
- 'I'm not clever enough, yet.'
- 'I don't have enough energy, yet.'
- I don't have enough money, yet.'

This one little word shifts you from a problem-focused mindset to a solution-focused mindset. The problem, rather than intractable, becomes something that we can now work on so we can have what we want in the future. Sure, you might not have the time or the money to do something right now, but you can work towards having the time and the money to do something, *if you choose to.*

Telling stories

The stories we tell ourselves make or break our happiness, our future, and our potential.

If you wake up and tell yourself the story 'I'm tired. I'm bored. I'm ugly. I'm not talented. I'll never get paid very much . . .', then that's the story of your life. That's how your life will play out.

What would happen if you woke up every morning and told yourself a different story? 'I'm strong. I am talented. I'm going to work towards the future I want. I have skills that can benefit people and this world. I'm not going to limit myself. I'm going to approach life positively from a place of gratitude and love. I'm going to push myself. I'm going to enjoy this journey that is life and I'm going to have as much fun as possible in the process.' What could your life look like if you let this different story play out?

Let me repeat:

> The story you tell yourself is the story that will unfold in your life.

The question is, are you willing to start to write a different, new story?

At this point I think a quick exercise is in order. Now this will feel uncomfortable, but it's really important that you do this because I want you to see how you currently view yourself. Write below some of the thoughts that regularly go through your head: the *stories* that you tell yourself. Whatever these stories are, however ugly some of these thoughts might be, however uncomfortable they make you feel, do this! No one is going to read this, this is your book, so don't worry about the judgement of others. The process of writing this stuff down rather than keeping it in your head is transformative, so please, please don't skip this.

Write below, whether it's a paragraph or a list of bullet points, the thoughts and stories that regularly go through your head and that you feel you have to battle with/against:

_____

_____

_____

_____

_____

_____

How did it feel writing those things down?

Perhaps it's all positive, in which case high five, but I suspect that some of these thoughts and stories made you feel a little sad. You may be even shocked that you are so negative about yourself. Either way, don't shy away from whatever you've written (this book is about facing up to the truth, after all). Accept it for what it is, and now, importantly, choose to change it.

So, Step 1 is about being honest and identifying what these thoughts and stories are, and Step 2 is simply deciding what we want to change these thoughts and stories to. What story do you want to write for yourself? What do you deep down feel and believe is inherent within you? If you were to live your truth, or change your truth to make things better, what would that look like? If nothing was holding you back, what would life look like for you?

It's time to write below how you want your thoughts to be going forward, what you want your new story to be:

_____

_____

_____

_____

_____

_____

Having written that, how do you feel?

Again, I would expect you to be feeling a mix of emotions here. On one hand, you are probably feeling motivated – like your words could be true, that you want them to be true – but you are also probably feeling a certain level of trepidation and disbelief. And that's good, that's fine, that's human to have this mix of emotions. Our job now is to focus on the strength and desire underpinning the new story, to have the story playing in our heads, front of mind, while we deal with the demons that might be holding us back.

One important reminder: this book isn't about blind motivation, just getting pumped up for action and not dealing with the things that have previously held us back. That's simply foolish, because once the motivation wears off, the same old demons will rear their ugly heads again. So, it's important we both focus on the future and what we want to change, and work on dealing with whatever demons are there, in whatever form they take.

They could be fears we have that we need to come to terms with, whether real or imaginary. They could be people in our lives who hold us back. It could be the situation we are in at the moment with which we need to be a little patient and allow things to play out. It might be where we live or the job we have. So many things will be there that we want to change, and while we can't click our fingers and change it all, we can set the intention to change it and start making the moves, all while having our new story front of mind the whole time.

Before moving on (slowly does it, remember!), let's do a quick recap.

First, we've set out to understand where we are on the positivity scale and how we can become a truly glass-half-full kind of person. Second, we looked to flip our mindset from a problem-focused to a solution-focused approach. We then took a look at how we need to accept that everything is in our control, or at least that we have control over our reaction to problems. And we've just now looked at the stories that play out in our head and how they might hold us back, along with how we can start to rewrite the story to be the one we ultimately want to live.

Now, to continue this journey of ours, it's time to look at what you value in life.

Your values

Values are another important piece of the puzzle because they, too, can help to steer us back to our truth. If we fully understand and appreciate what we value in life, we can start to make decisions that are in alignment with who we are as people. If we are making decision about a new job, or whether to break up with someone, or even something as simple as what book to read next, we can run it through our values filter and see where we need to be. This can also help us develop a 'do not do' list.

Self-help books commonly ask you to *add* things to your life, such as 'Do this new healthy habit' or 'Start doing X for mega results'. And while I *am* asking you to add new things to your routine and life with the goal of improving it, we also need to take things away to have the same effect.

If something isn't serving you in your life anymore, you have to have the strength to see this and make the call to stop doing it. The reality is there is only so much time in the day, week or month, and time is our most valuable resource – we don't get it back. We need to be filling our time with things we value, because if we stretch ourselves too thin we become over-whelmed, frustrated or angry, and can't give our love and atten-tion to the things that really matter.

So let's first create a list of values. I want to recentre you, make you feel more whole and aligned, and clear out any stuff or commitments that are no longer serving you, so you can approach life in a truer way and with more time to give to the things you care about.

To help with your values list, the following is a list of values, or things that you might want to value. Circle the ones that speak to you. Try to choose no less than three but no more than five or six. There is space to add any that aren't included here

Honesty	Love
Integrity	Diversity
Health	Loyalty
Fitness	Learning
Open communication	Contribution
Family freedom	Strength
Respect	Speed
Connection to others	Power
Intelligence	Endurance
Generosity	Wealth
Security	Money
Creativity	Friendship
Career Success	Contentment
Fun	Leadership
Travel	Courage
Openness	Gratitude
Respect	Self-respect
Work–life balance	Happiness
Teamwork	Peace

Can you think of any more . . .?

_____

_____

_____

_____

Now look back over the values you have highlighted as those you want to live your life by. Then look back over the story that is playing out in your life currently, and the story that you want to play out in your life. Can you see where you are not aligned with your values? Can you see what is not serving you? Can you see what needs to change, what you have to stop doing?

It's time to have the confidence to change that, so you can live in alignment with your values, and the story you want your life to be.

Your 'do not do' list

Now it's time to write your 'do not do' list. Below, write all the things you want to stop doing, or thinking, or attracting into your life. Make it a complete list, not just a list of physical activities, but a mental list, too. If you struggle with this list, it's completely normal. It takes a lot of strength to start to say no to things in your life that are not serving you, that you have maybe done for many years and are now a habit. If this is the case, keep this exercise in your mind, put down this book for a few days with a book mark in, and every time you think of something or come across something in your day that should be on the list, come back to this page, and write it in the list below. Remember, these are things you want to stop doing or thinking, not things you don't like – using the colleague example from above, you might write about how you always escalate when they give snide remarks, rather than about how you want to stop working with mean people. Be solutions focused!

And, MOST IMPORTANTLY, take that first brave step towards NOT doing it.

Do not do list

_____

_____

_____

_____

_____

_____

_____

The area most people struggle with in this process is letting *other people* know you can no longer do something. Maybe it's as simple as not turning up to help at coaching practice at your children's school because it's one extra thing that's draining your time or energy. Or perhaps it's a chat you need to have with your partner because you've reflected and been honest with yourself about things not working anymore. Or you need to speak to your boss about your job because it's something you no longer enjoy.

The reason I find people struggle with this is because they try to find the best way to deliver the news without hurting or offending the other person. They try to dress up the news in a way that will leave them on as good terms as possible.

But, in my opinion, this is wrong. Let me show you why.

The importance of honesty

I bet in the list of values above you highlighted either integrity or honesty. It's why I put it at the top of the list, because most people do say they value it, want more of it in their lives, but aren't actually living it. If you truly believed in those values, you would deliver your news with honesty and integrity. Also, people aren't stupid. If you lie and try to dress something up as something it's not, people will see and feel that, and then in their eyes you won't be honest, you won't have had integrity in that process, and you won't have honoured your own values.

I get this is painful or annoying for people in the short term, but in the long term you are helping this person or situation. If you are going to break up with someone, tell them why, honestly. If you lie to them, what does that say about you, and how does that help that person? Let's say the person you are with is very selfish, and you tell them some BS reason you are breaking up with them. How does that person realize they are selfish and decide to change? This is not to say you shouldn't be tactful, of course, but you should not hide the truth.

Honesty isn't a cultural norm, but it needs to be. Deep down, we all want the world to be a more honest place. People and situations only grow or change with honesty, so step into that space. You, those around you, we as humanity, deserve it.

Most people feel they want to live in a world that is kinder, has more love in it, where people are more honest and respectful of others. Well, that starts with us . . . with *you*. We can be the change we want to see in the world.

So when you start to take action on your 'do not do' list, however long the list is, do it from a place of honesty and integrity.

Action plan

So now I want you to consult your values list and your 'do not do' list and start to create a plan of action. Here are a few examples to help you:

You value fitness or strength and you aren't training at the moment? Why, if you value it, isn't it in your schedule? What do you need to make sure you stop doing so you have the time to do it?

If respect was on your values list, are you first and foremost respecting others? Yourself? If we want respect from others, it starts with us.

If you value wealth, what are you doing right now to build it? Do you have an investment strategy? Do you know what wealth really means, or looks like? Do you know what a 10 to 20-year plan would need to look like, because you'll need to in order to build it.

If you value courage, how are you allowing that to play out in your life? How can you start to build it up if you feel your courage is low, but you want more of it?

If you value leadership, that starts with you. I'm a leader in my business to my team and I know that starts with me. I need to successfully lead myself and my life and turn up in a big way to be able to successfully lead others.

Whatever you value, start to see what needs to change in your life so that you can start to live in total alignment with your values, and part of that process will be you needing stop doing some stuff to create room for what you value.

Remember, time is your most important life asset and it compounds. If you are doing something you don't enjoy every day for 30 minutes, or something once per week for two-and-a-half hours, that's five-and-a-half days a year you're giving to something that you don't like or enjoy doing or that adds stress to your life. Value time, fill it with the things you love to do as much as possible or have to do for your work, family and so on.

For the rest of this chapter, we need to discuss two more things: abundance and death. These may seem like a strange pair, but I'll show how they each have a role to play in your Awesome Life.

Abundance

First, abundance. The beautiful and simple thing about life is, you can feel like you are living an abundant life if your life is in alignment with your values. If you are not, you will always feel like you want more and should have more. But a life that is simple and well lived won't need too much to feel like a happy one.

Now in saying that, I want you to know you can pretty much have anything you want in life.

There are limitations of course. There are things we can't have, perhaps because of our genes, or age, or something else that physically stops the process. But when it comes to most things that matter to people (freedom, friends, money, influence), those of us fortunate enough to be born in the modern world have the ability to do far more than most people seem to realize.

So please dream and know you can have so much in your life. Sure, these things might not take six months to achieve; they might take years, but it's a worthwhile journey. I knew that I wanted to be a mainstream published author when I was young and felt I had a good knack of teaching and helping others, so I worked towards that. It took a while (it actually took longer than I thought at the time!), but over time, with commitment and intention towards the goal, I achieved it. You are reading the product of my vision, commitment, patience and hard work, which took over 10 years to achieve after the intention was set.

When it comes to abundance, please know you can live in abundance. I don't want you or anyone to hold you back from what you dream of doing. I have big goals and wants for my life and family, and so should you. Some I'll achieve next year, some will take me five to ten years, but that's OK, and I'm excited that I've embarked on the journey towards it.

So here I want you to write down a few *big* goals, and I mean BIG – goals that would make you live in abundance. That would make you feel awesome. Don't write down goals like 'be a millionaire' – ones that are too vague or not emotive and that aren't capable of being a visualized. (What does being a millionaire looks like? And what kind of millionaire anyway? One on paper? One in business assets? One where you have a million pounds or dollars in the bank?)

I want you to write down goals *that paint a picture*. Here is one of my goals:

'To have enough money to live with freedom to travel wherever I want with my family, to have a nice converted barn as our home in Suffolk, and to always have a car that works and is fun to drive.'

I can close my eyes and I can see this, even feel this.
And here's another:

'I want to get lean enough so that I feel great in clothes and have the confidence to be shirtless at the pool or beach. I want to feel strong, fit and have this empower my confidence. I want to learn about food during the process so I can maintain this goal and never put the weight back on. I want to empower myself with my body goals, to let it fuel other success and fulfilment in my life.'

And, again, I can close my eyes and I can see and feel this. It's a far more powerful a goal to work towards.

Have a go at writing down some big North Star goals in
your life. Just to get some abundant juices flowing and start
to SEE and FEEL what your future could look like:

_____

_____

_____

_____

_____

_____

_____

_____

_____

Are you feeling a bit excited? Good. Because this is just the
start.

Death

Well, it's time to talk about death and conclude Step 1: Your
approach to life.

Death is a funny thing. But it's coming for us all.

Most people you talk to are scared of death in some way, and
that's understandable: it means the end of life as we know it.
But is the mere prospect of death what we fear? I'd argue not;
it's the prospect of *not living enough* before we die. The thing

is, we are in full control of that. If you want to make the most out of life, you can.

IT'S A CHOICE.

The question is, are you going to choose to make the most of it?

I hope this book is starting to inspire that in you, and it certainly aims to give you some of the tools to do it, too. I'm 35 writing this book, and yes I would be very sad if I died; I mean – I want to live 'til I'm 100 and beyond in good health, still having fun and making an impact on the world – but if, for some reason, my time came, I would be happy, purely because to date I feel like I have given life my all, I've been 'all in' on myself, my life, and have lived it as best as I can.

An important aspect of this book is to inspire you with your own life, to show you that you deserve to live a big Awesome Life, and to also give you the skills to break through issues that stand in your way. Everyone has bouts of motivation and inspiration to change, and ultimately everyone wants to live an Awesome Life, but too few of us do, and that's because of the things that hold us back. In the process of change, it's essential to break through and confront these blocks.

A technique you can use here is to write your own obituary, or alternatively your Wikipedia entry as if you are dead. The reason exercises like this can be powerful is they can show you your capacity for dreaming up your big goals (see above), the life you can and could live, and nurture the emotion you need to break through the stuff holding you back. Now I appreciate that at this point in time you almost definitely won't know how the whole of your life will pan out, and that's OK, I'm not asking you to know that. But I am asking you to get into the habit of shaping HOW you want it to pan out, so you are constantly setting the intention of how to live your life, and also WHY you want it to be that way.

The obituary/Wikipedia exercise is something you might do every five years as you readjust what it is you want from your life. One of the key reasons people struggle with exercises like this is that they feel they have to have their career path all set out as they write. You don't. This is a habit too many people drop into because we associate too much of our identity, our sense of self, with our current job, and let our goals be defined by that job. Whatever job it is that you do, remember it is just a job. And yes, while it's important, very important in fact (because most of us wake up every day and spend a significant amount of time doing it), it's just a part of your life. It's not your life. It's not your identity. It's just *part* of what makes you *you* at this point in time. So, when you do an exercise like writing your obituary, the aim isn't to plan out a career with a few life milestones thrown in; the aim is to also set out how you intend to live your life based on a reflection or assessment of your values and dreams. It's much bigger, see, and always provisional, always a work in progress.

So when you write your obituary there might be references to your character, such as what type of person you were (yep, past tense, you're dead, remember?), what level of impact you had on the world or on the people within your community, a few key things you achieved, and how you went about it.

Here's an obituary I've written to help you see what I mean. Afterwards, we can break it down.

Ben Coomber – Obituary

Ben Coomber was a loving and present father of two who made it his mission to inspire and support his girls to be the best versions of themselves, living a life they wanted to live. Ben was also a committed, faithful and supportive husband to his wife, living close to his family so nothing in life was ever missed. Ben aimed to live a life that would inspire many, a life that was lived on his terms, in his way, by high standards. Ben was a strong character mentally and emotionally, gave support and time to others, prided himself on his own leadership that inspired movement in others, valued his health and fitness, always aimed to show up to life in a big way, and tried to get the most out of life. Throughout Ben's career he inspired change in millions, first starting in the health and fitness industry as a coach and business owner, then moving into education and policy change, all while having a successful career as an author, writing multiple best-selling books. Ben loved travel and adventure and visited most of the world, leaving this world with an empty bucket list. I know Ben would say that he lived his life well and to the full, and that he would hope that others reading this would be inspired to do the same.

I hope you can see why I wrote my obituary in the way that I did. Many Wikipedia entries you read are a list of life accomplishments, but I say again, we are not our accomplishments, we are not our work; we are people, we are human, we are emotional sentient beings, so build your sense of self and character around that. Of course, you can and should dream of doing great things with your career, but that's not who you are as a person.

The other reason it's good to not put specifics in an obituary is to give yourself the flexibility to change as life changes. Opportunities come and go, what we are interested in comes and goes, and life happens in mysterious ways, so we should always be open to change and changing. What shouldn't change is *how* you want to live your life: your sense of your character, your values and principles.

Are you ready to give it a go?

I hope so. If you're not ready right now, put down the book and come back to it when you are, as I want you to engage in this process fully.

Write your obituary below, or feel free to write it in a notebook:

_____

_____

_____

_____

_____

_____

_____

_____

_____

I expect your state of mind after writing that to be one of deep thought and reflection. What your brain should now be doing is scanning your current life and comparing it with this obituary. It should be asking: 'What am I doing right now that's not in alignment with my obituary and how I want my life to shape up.' And this is a good thing. If you are not on the right path and some things need to change, you need to set about a plan to change those things (I'll help you with this).

Feel excited about that change.

It's a change that will see you living a more Awesome Life. A life that's closer to your truth.

How to be awesome

I know I said we'd close the chapter on death, but hey, like I said, things are always provisional. I think we need one more exercise that will bring everything we've discussed in this chapter together and help you set down in strong clear words how you want to live right now, in the present. I call this final exercise, which takes the form of a short punchy list about how to approach life, 'How to be awesome'.

My own list is up on my wall in my office. It's there so that *every day* I am reminded how I aim to show up and live my life. It connects my intentions, values and ambitions together so that I am working towards how my obituary will read, combining my current life with how I want my future life to be. Let me jump straight in and show you mine. Then it's your turn to have a think, a ponder, and write yours.

HOW TO BE AWESOME

- Be honest and have integrity in all that I do.
- Bring passion and energy to EVERYTHING.
- Exercise every day by planning it into my schedule.
- Find ways to step outside my comfort zone.
- Always plan and anticipate how the future will unfold.
- Trust your intuition about people and situations.
- Love everyone that supports me, and show it.
- Contribute to the world in a positive way.
- Do good work – success will be a by-product.
- Invest time wisely, on things that move the needle.
- Health is my daily ritual, supporting all this.
- Never be afraid to say, 'I need your help.'
- Be a LEADER, to myself, the team, to my family.
- NEVER forget to have fun and live life to the full.

I have this 'How to be awesome' list; on my office wall because it's important to me to remember what I set out to achieve in my life, daily. The human brain isn't perfect – it forgets things, gets lazy at times, gets stuck in habits and routines very easily – so we need these things to remind of us what's important, what matters most to us. And if it takes a poster on your wall somewhere that you will see every day that reminds you of how to turn up and live your life, then do it. Is it a lot to ask to get the most out of yourself?

Write your own 'How to be Awesome' list. If you are not ready to write it now, come back to it when you are.

_____

_____

_____

_____

_____

_____

_____

_____

Once you've made your 'How to be awesome' list, you may find it helpful to make it known publicly, boldly and confidently stating your intention online, to inspire others to do the same and share that new energy with people close to you. Tag me in your post @bencoomber. I'd love to see it.

Key points to remember

- Work on your perspective of life, whether you feel glass half-full or half-empty right now remember you hold the glass
- Be solution focused, not problem focused.
- Take problems in your stride and grow from them, don't let them crush you or define you.
- Know your personal values and use them to steer your life and decisions.
- Make a 'do not do' list and take action on getting rid of things in your life that take time away from doing more of the things you love to do.
- Write your obituary and use it as a guide and intention of how to live your life.
- Identify some goals you think you want to work towards, and be open to changing how they look and feel as you embark on the journey.
- Be honest with yourself every step of the way.
- Live your truth.
- Choose yourself, value yourself, and know you deserve to live an Awesome Life.
- Time is your most valuable resource, one you can't get back, so value it and fill your days/weeks/months/years with as many things as possible that you want/love to do.
- Make your 'How to be awesome' list, print it out or make a poster, and read it every day till it becomes part of your DNA.

Use this note-taking section to jot down your thoughts after reading this chapter. What have you gained? How are you closer to living your Awesome Life?

_____

_____

_____

_____

_____

_____

_____

_____

_____

Water is life

Approach

Water

Environment

Sleep

Organize

Movement

Eat

Lifestyle

Inspiration

Finances

Education

'Water is the driving force of all nature'
Leonardo Da Vinci

After a thought-provoking Step 1, let's ease into a nice, practical, easily applied step: hydration. I also feel this step is a really good reflection of our priorities. The fluids we drink everyday can have a profound effect on our health and physiology, and what we drink ultimately points to what we value with our health.

If your daily fluid intake is made up of a lot of coffee, fizzy drinks, no water and a glass of wine before bedtime, do you feel that indicates or reflects wholly healthy priorities, knowing that the main fluid our body needs is water?

I'm not saying coffee, tea, soft drinks or sodas, and alcohol are bad, far from it – they all have water in them; that is their main base ingredient – but all those fluids come with other ingredients such as caffeine, sugar, flavourings, sweeteners, preservatives and alcohol that while *not* inherently bad should be taken in moderation: there is a sweet spot as to how much they should contribute to our daily fluid intake if we're focused on optimal health and performance.

If there is a large fluid focus in your daily hydration of tea, coffee, fizzy drinks, alcohol, we must question how optimal it is, and how it's contributing to your overall wellbeing.

So as with everything we need to find out what 'moderation' is and rebalance accordingly.

What could and should moderation be for you . . .

- with your alcohol intake?
- with your caffeine intake?
- with your fizzy drink intake?

Bad habits

What we drink is one of the easiest things to fall into bad habits with. It can be due to our environment, what our parents drank, what we like, how we are feeling on any given day, what someone offers us, something we have recently discovered and have fallen in love with, and all manner of external stimuli. But what is key is awareness, questioning what we are doing, and, if necessary, shifting our priorities and habits.

A good example is our caffeine intake. It's really easy to slip into the habit of having a lot of coffee, tea or energy drinks. You might experience a period when you are sleeping badly, so you start reaching for your caffeine-laced beverage of choice more, but then the habit just sticks because you like it, or simply get used to it. Or maybe you get a new job where the culture in the workplace is that someone makes a cup of tea/coffee every hour or so and you always say yes, or start making it often yourself for everyone as a way to make friends and interact, and you end up being someone that now drinks 6–8 cups a day. The habit easily creeps in, but it now might be affecting your teeth, your sleep, your energy and your long-term health.

I did this in 2021 when I was really sleep deprived, thanks to our first daughter sleeping badly while I was still suffering with long COVID. I slowly went from someone who had 1–2 moderately caffeinated drinks a day (on average), to 3 highly caffeinated drinks. I challenged it in 2021 because I was still suffering from long COVID at the time and wasn't getting any better; and with the approaching due date of our second daughter I decided to go cold turkey from all caffeine. This was probably a bad idea in retrospect, as many people get bad headaches from doing this. If you decide to challenge this habit, drop your intake slowly. I did it this way because I've done it twice before without too many symptoms, and I was already feeling awful, so felt it couldn't get any worse. I tackled my caffeine intake for two reasons:

1. I had gone caffeine-free for the arrival of our first daughter to ensure that I wouldn't have any caffeine in my system that could interfere with my sleep (you need all the sleep you can with a new-born!) It proved a successful strategy, enabling me to sleep during the day if I needed too. It made sense to do it with our next child, too, as I hate being sleep deprived. You're never a high-performing human when you're sleep deprived.

2. I also believed that, if I cut out caffeine altogether, my nervous system would be calmer and less stimulated, and this would aid in the recovery process from long COVID. There were reports that people with long COVID had issues with their autonomic nervous system[1] (ANS, the part of the central nervous system responsible for 'fight or flight'), and doing anything possible to calm it would be of benefit.

Now it's worth digging into this second reason more deeply. I had got into some bad habits, so I needed to course-correct anyway, but 2021 – the worst year I have ever experienced with my health – brought things home. Because of the symptoms of long COVID, my energy levels and brain power were extremely low and I was relying heavily on caffeine to 'make it through'. With hindsight, I realized this was creating more problems than it was solving. My body needed pure rest, my nervous system needed less stimulation, and I needed to relax my ANS, but the story I was telling myself at the time was that I needed to 'push on, focus, be there for my family and business – to step up'. So I used three very strong doses of caffeine per day to do this: a strong coffee in the morning, another mid-morning, and a big caffeine-laden can of energy drink after lunch. Each caffeine dose gave me one to two hours of focus before I felt myself crashing, getting very tired and fatigued and wanting more. And so, the cycle continued.

Was the caffeine serving me? Was it helping?

I thought so. But in hindsight, after going caffeine free, I wish I had done it sooner. Once I had cut out caffeine ahead of my second daughter arriving, I felt calmer, I felt my nervous system dampening down, I felt in tune with my energy and what my body was telling me, and I felt I was healing more quickly. And I was right: my body healed (amongst many other strategies I employed to get better, please don't think it was just because I cut out caffeine, it was more complex than that).

Now this is just one story about one kind of drink and one time in my life, but I've told you this story to illustrate a broader point . . .

QUESTION THINGS. See if what you are doing is serving you, not just in the moment, but from a broader, daily and long-term perspective. It's very easy with drinks and food to consume something we *want* in the moment, but we must consider that action in a broader sense. For example, you might *want* a second glass of wine or beer after dinner and you might enjoy it at the time, but will it serve you more broadly? Could it leave you feeling groggy and tired the next day? Does it fit with your health and fitness goals, having three bottles of beer adding up to 500 calories? It's easy to make decisions on what we want in the moment, but it's important to quickly zoom out and ask ourselves whether this decision serves our broader life, aims and goals.

Questions, questions

Question what you are doing and why. Question the habits you have and whether they are serving you. Question where you picked up a habit and how you might break it. And then do the research to find out where you need to be, or think you might need to be, and test it.

And that's often all I will ask you to do in this book. To simply question things, try something different, and test whether you get a better outcome or not.

- What would happen if you drank more water?
- What would happen if you drank less alcohol?
- What would happen if you drank fewer fizzy drinks?
- What would happen if you drank less caffeine, or even went caffeine-free for a bit to see what happens?

All manner of things might happen, of course. You could get more energy, you could feel more awake, you could lose weight, you could get fewer IBS symptoms, your skin could improve, your workout performance might kick up a gear. Maybe nothing will happen and you can pick the habit up again confident that it *is* serving you. Who knows?

It's time to start questioning what you are experiencing in your life, and to consider how changing a simple thing like what you drink on a daily basis could do to improve things. This can often start with the stories you tell yourself to reinforce *not* changing a habit.

Do you catch yourself telling yourself a story around what you drink?

- 'I NEED coffee in the morning.'
- 'I NEED a drink after dinner to help me sleep.'
- 'I COULDN'T LIVE without such-and-such drink every day.'

This isn't me saying don't drink coffee, wine, fizzy drinks, or all manner of things; this is me simply asking you to question the habit, to question whether it is serving you or not, whether the amount you are having is appropriate to your wider life goals, and then outline what might be a better approach, then adjust things accordingly.

Back in 2021 when I cut out caffeine, I noticed a few things:

1. Caffeine really 'revved' me up, and at that point in my life I didn't need revving up, I needed to rev down, to relax and heal.
2. I started to become more in tune with my natural rhythm of energy, how well I'd slept, and how I felt.
3. My resting heart rate came down 5–8 bpm.
4. I realized I was pushing myself less, which I needed to do. I had pushed myself pretty hard up until that point with business and life, and with one young child and another coming, I needed space to accommodate the lack of sleep and chaos that comes with having young kids.
5. I didn't need caffeine to perform, to be awake, to turn up to my life in a big way.

I still don't drink a lot of caffeine to this day. Because, if there is one thing that I took away from suffering with my health so much in 2021, it is that I wanted:

- to feel naturally alive and focused
- to be as calm as possible
- to never rely on something to perform
- to be fully in tune with my body and how it was working
- to not push my brain or body when it needed to rest.

So now my caffeine intake is pretty minimal. When I wake up I will have a weak coffee – about 0.7 espressos worth of caffeine

(I experimented and found that any more than 12g of ground coffee left me feeling jittery and too buzzy – so I settled on 8g of caffeinated coffee and 24g of decaffeinated coffee made in a cafetiere with 320ml of water – my DIY recipe for the perfect black coffee, using a Columbian coffee from a shop that does the same coffee bean in caffeinated and decaffeinated version). Some days I'll just have decaf, I just wake up and feel my body saying 'let's just be super calm today'. So, I listen and have none. I just have a decaf coffee and get on with my day.

It can also be our knee jerk reaction when we are tired to have caffeine. But, there are also other things we can do or use to wake ourselves up if we need it. A bit of fresh air. A walk outside. A shower. Cold water on the face (or a cold shower, which I'm a fan of). A screen break from computers. Listening to some fun music. Exercise. All these things can stimulate us, wake us up, or shift our state of being. It's also worth questioning why you feel tired in the first place. Caffeine can be great, but it can also be a band-aid solution to a problem that starts before you go to bed. A good night's sleep will leave you feeling far better than a short sleep and a big coffee.

Again, I'm not saying caffeine is bad. I'm saying we have options. And we need to question stimulants' role in our lives and whether they are wholly positive or not.

For me, the thing I love most about dropping my caffeine intake right down is the level of calmness, control and centredness I now feel. I feel that if we can get to a place in our lives where we are not beholden to something external to make us feel a certain way, where this good feeling comes from our mind, our fully functioning biology, our in-rhythm hormones, then that can only be a good thing. So, I have a weak caffeinated coffee in the morning, sometimes some caffeine if I'm going to exercise with intensity, and that's usually it (I do love coffee, so do drink more of it, I just drink decaf – and there are plenty of good decaf coffees about these days). But that works for me and where I want to be physically and mentally. It might work for you, it might not, but if you never test it you'll never know.

Track your weekly fluid intake

If I was to look at my hydration as a weekly distribution of drinks, it would look something like this:

7–10 caffeinated drinks a week
2–3 glasses of wine a week
1–2 beers
2–3 cans of kombucha (I like it, it's also good for you)
1–2 fizzy diet drinks
Sometimes a bit of kefir (good for the guts)
1–2 cups of decaf tea a day (breakfast tea, herbal tea, spiced tea, ginger tea)
electrolytes in water for when I exercise
filtered, mineralized water (for the rest of the time).

What does your weekly fluid intake look like? Write it down now and be as honest as possible (no need to hide facts here, especially from yourself):

_____

_____

_____

_____

How do you feel about what you have written? Does that look (intuitively) healthy to you? Can you see some bad habits? Can you see a few things you want or feel you should change?

Again, I'm not here to preach; I'm just here to hold a mirror up to the situation, talk about things that could be considered, consult the research on where we should be with hydration, and map out a possible path to move you forward with.

So, when it comes to the research, what do we know, and what baselines can we give ourselves?

According to the UK Eatwell Guide, 6–8 glasses of water are recommended in the UK, totalling around 1.5–2 litres (with 'a glass' being considered in these guidelines to be around 250ml). As you can probably work out, though, this generalized guideline is likely too broad to factor in the different height, weight, and 'sweatiness' of a given person. A more individualized recommendation of around 25–30ml per kilogram is often given (it's even cited in research and official guidelines, though interestingly nobody is quite sure where it came from[2]). This means that, at my current body weight of 81kg, that would be 2025–2430ml. Let's simplify that to 2–2.5 litres of fluids per day. That's one of the big 2-litre water bottles you see in the shops plus one cup of tea as a quick visual cue.

That's roughly what my body needs on a fairly normal, relatively sedentary day. If I was in hot conditions, sweating a lot, or moving about a bit, I would need more, maybe 2.5–3.5 litres per day. Then if I was doing exercise it would need more, according to the International Society of Sports Nutrition I would need approximately 500–2000ml of extra fluid per hour, depending on the intensity and my sweat rate[3].

So, keeping this simple and staying practical, what does this look like?

Your average tea/coffee cup is approximately 350ml, so that would be seven cups' worth of fluids per day if you are to hit those 2.5 litres. That's not that much and is easy to include in your daily routine by drinking water with your meals and other fixed times in the day. On some days you would need more fluids. For example, if you were to go out for a long walk and work up a little bit of a sweat, you could have a large glass of water, perhaps enriched with electrolytes when you got in, meaning water with added salts to replace those lost in sweat; if you went for a run or for a gym session, you could have 500–1000ml of water or electrolyte water while you exercised, and so on. If it was hot on a particular day, you would then make a conscious effort to drink more water on top of those usual seven cups. It really is that simple. Paying close attention to your thirst signals is a great help here; they evolved for a purpose, and if keeping water next to you while you work makes it easier to have a drink when your body tells you you need it, then that's a good change to your environment that you can make easily.

We can get more complicated with this, but for 99 per cent of you reading this it's not needed. I want to keep this stuff simple, easy to implement, and with a great effort: benefit ratio. Most people I coach easily keep good hydration habits by carrying a water bottle around with them during the day. Let's say you have a coffee in the morning (350ml), take a 1-litre bottle of water to work, have two cups of tea at work (700ml) and then go for a run in the evening and had a 500ml bottle of electrolyte water during and after, and then a peppermint tea in the evening (350ml) – that's 2900ml, 2.9L, which is perfect for active people.

That wasn't complicated and is in line with most people's habits. Winner. But let's get a little bit more geeky (for those that want it) and add a few more pointers:

- Depending on where you live and the quality of your water, it might pay to filter your water. The taste can also be more enjoyable.
- Filtered water doesn't have any minerals in it, depending on the filtration method, and minerals (electrolytes) aid in optimal hydration by allowing our cells to actually hold on to the fluid (you'll find you need to pee a little less when drinking properly mineralized water), so ideally you should drink water that's both filtered *and* mineralized if you can (at the end of this chapter, I'll give you a link to download a one-page cheat sheet on optimizing your hydration habits).
- When you exercise, you lose fluids and minerals (electrolytes/salts), so if you are exercising intensively, for around 30 minutes plus, sweat a lot when you exercise, or are exercising in hot conditions, it's good to drink water with added electrolytes to ensure optimum performance (when you sweat you lose electrolytes, so taking them in while training ensures your performance won't decline due to a lack of them). Drinking a sweet-tasting drink during exercise can also help remind you to sip regularly as the fruity sweetness acts as a pleasurable cue.
- If you are exercising intensely for 60 minutes plus, add fast-acting simple carbohydrates to your electrolyte water to maintain energy and performance (which turns your drink into a traditional sports drink) Around 6–8g per 100ml is ideal, totalling 30–60g of carbohydrate per hour during long sessions.
- Be wary of your caffeine intake. A comprehensive review of the relevant research concluded that 400mg (the recommended maximum intake in the UK) is the threshold for a risk of caffeine toxicity in healthy adults[4], though your personal tolerance may be higher or lower than this, 400mg is around 4 cups of instant coffee, 2–3 double espressos, or

2–3 500ml energy drinks. There was a time I was taking in more than this, and I felt I was on a constant caffeine roller-coaster. The devil is in the dose. Find your sweet spot with caffeine, even pre-exercise. Caffeine is good pre-exercise for improving physical performance, with typical recom-mendations being in the 3–6mg per kg of bodyweight range according to the International Society for Sports Nutrition[5]. They note that the benefits taper off quickly after 9mg/kg, and also that a number of factors, such as the menstrual cycle, other medications and genetics, can alter your ideal dose – so experiment with it and the right intake for you. You'll know you find it because you'll feel alert, you won't feel fatigued so quickly, you'll feel able to push a little harder than normal, but you won't get short of breath or jittery. 100–300mg is the range most people benefit from in my experience, probably why this is the typical dosage found in most caffeinated sports supplements.

Drinks with benefits

With the question of optimization in mind, what else might we consider changing or including in our fluid intake to reap some benefits? Potentially quite a bit. There are a variety of options that are associated with particular health benefits and are worth experimenting with to mix things up, so here I will list some types of drinks you could include:

- *Green/matcha tea* – while more research is needed, there is a sufficient evidence from human trials for a literature review to conclude that long-term consumption of green tea could be protective against type 2 diabetes and cardiovascular disease due to the catechins found within[6].

- *Herbal and fruit teas* – a walk down a supermarket aisle or a visit to an independent tea or coffee shop, or a health food shop, will show you just how many amazing options there are, from a simple peppermint brew to mango and turmeric tea. While it's difficult to make any strong claims about any particular health benefits, these are calorie-free and will often be caffeine-free so are great for any time of day. (Pro-tip: buy a high-quality herbal/fruit tea; I find cheap ones taste weak and aren't enjoyable – it pays to pay a bit more for good tea in my opinion).
- *Electrolytes* – use these during exercise if you exercise intensively, sweat a lot or exercise in the heat. It will help prolong performance by optimizing hydration.
- *Carbonated water* – this can be a nice alternative to water and can have fruit flavourings added, or you could add some fruit yourself, like some lime or mint or crushed strawberries.
- *Fizzy drinks* – there are lots of options these days – gone are the days of it just being coke on the menu, so go explore. Many are also low-calorie or sugar-free. Artificial sweeteners are safe for human consumption in small to moderate amounts, and they have never been shown to be unsafe in well-controlled human studies[7]; with that said their health effects are still not entirely clear due to a lack of well-controlled studies[7] and so while drinking a few soft drinks is almost certainly not a problem, it's probably best to stick to a can per day at most if you're particularly cautious.
- *Fruit-infused water* – you could get a water bottle with a fruit diffuser in it and add various fruits. Citrus fruits work well – just don't buy into the myth that this will cause fat loss please!

- *Decaffeinated coffee* – gone are the days of decaffeinated coffee always tasting bad; there are lots of good decaf coffees now, so go explore. Coffee drinkers actually live longer than non-coffee drinkers, research shows, but at least some of the benefits come from the antioxidants and polyphenols, rather than the caffeine[8]. I love coffee, so a good decaf means I can have it whenever I want.
- *Kombucha* – a fermented tea, often now made into a light fizzy drink with other ingredients like lemon, ginger and fruit extracts. It's super tasty and may have health benefits, though right now human data is sorely lacking[9].
- *Kefir* – a fermented drink made with cow's milk, goat's milk or non-dairy milk. It's high in various gut-friendly bacteria, and while research is really early, mostly relying on animal studies and very small trials in humans, so far the evidence seems to point to it being beneficial to our gut health and thus our wider wellbeing[10].
- *Wine* – high in polyphenols, and robust research has shown that drunk in moderation it's associated with a decrease in risk of various chronic diseases[11]; it seems that at least a little wine in our diet seems to be safe and may be of benefit (it's also dead tasty!). Pop a bottle with friends over dinner.

As you can see from that list, there are a few things you might not expect there. You might expect a health coach to say 'Don't drink wine', for example, but there is no real reason to say this for most people. Like anything in life, we need to weigh up the pros and cons and strike the right balance between it all.

Your new hydration regime

All I can do here is to encourage you to question your current routines and habits, and the stories you might be telling yourself about why you drink what you drink. Thus, as a result of reading this chapter, where do you feel you need to be with your hydration? First, carry out the following calculation to find out how much overall fluid you need per day:

My body weight is _____kg, which multiplied by the 25–30ml per kilogram recommendation is _____ .
Simplified, this is approximately _____ litres per day.

Now fill out the following table to determine your ideal weekly hydration regime:

Drink	Quantity (ml)	Frequency

Can you commit to that? Do you value committing to that? What roadblocks do you foresee on the path to implementing the above? Do you need to tell work colleagues that you are no longer drinking tea and coffee every time? Or would you rather drink a fruit tea instead when they do the drinks run? Do you need to find a different type of coffee to drink? Do you need a new 1-litre water bottle so you can easily take it to work? Do you need to buy some electrolytes to add to your exercise water bottle? If you exercise a lot, do you have a simple carbohydrate formula to add to your electrolyte mix? Do you need to find a new, healthier balance regarding the amount of alcohol you consume?

It's time to see the changes you feel you need to make. Be bold in making those changes. Know the swaps/things you need to buy. Speak to the people that will help you stick to these new hydration habits. Understand the science behind the changes and the strength of the claims – notice above that I've been honest that while some of these *might* be beneficial there isn't enough evidence to say that most of them definitely are – this is useful when weighing up whether or not you want to buy something regularly or pay significant attention to whether or not you include it.

With that being said, you can also observe the benefits you feel by making these changes – in your energy, sleep and overall mental and physical performance. Long term, this will create the buy-in you need to continue with your new regime and give you more clarity around whether or not you want to do something, especially when the data are generally positive but scarce.

What we drink might seem like a really simply thing, but it's also a really simple thing to tweak and adjust for better mental and physical performance.

If you want to download the one-page cheat for hydration, go to www.theschoolofawesome.co.uk/member and sign up for the free cheat sheets and resources that accompany this book. Once you are in, you can explore and download lots of free resources that go with this book, and find the link to this book's free but private Facebook group where we all chat, share ideas, and become even more awesome.

www.theschoolofawesome.co.uk/member

Sign up now.

Key points to remember

- It's not a lot to ask of ourselves to be well hydrated. Research shows its importance, so we should do it. Dehydration to the tune of just 1 per cent has been found in some studies to affect cognitive performance[12], with the boundary being 2–3 per cent in others (meaning that as a 70kg person, you might only need to lose 0.7kg to be affected, that's not a lot at all!)
- When it comes to choosing a source of our fluids, arguably water should be the number-one fluid we consume, though choosing some other sources from the suggestions in this chapter can provide some variety and perhaps some benefit.
- Be mindful of your alcohol intake (yes even wine with its potential benefits when consumed in moderation!) Make it an enjoyable part of your life if you want to, but don't rely on it, or use it as a crutch, and be aware of the downsides to your sleep and physical and mental performance the next day that can come when you have too much.
- Be mindful of your caffeine intake, especially its effects on your central nervous system and your sleep. Caffeine isn't bad, but the devil is in the dose; take what you need to suit your body and don't use it to replace sleep.
- When exercising, consider using electrolytes, and for long-duration exercise, electrolytes plus simple carbohydrates (ideally a blend of 2–3, such as dextrose, fructose and maltodextrin).
- Drinks like kombucha, kefir, herbal teas and wine may have some benefits for our health – as with everything, weigh up the pros and cons, especially as these can be costly (and wine, of course, contains alcohol).

- Buy a nice new water bottle to take to work if that's what you need to make your new hydration regime stick
- Buy a filtration/mineralization system for your home if you feel like you want/need to improve the quality of the daily water you drink. You'll find some on the one-page hydration cheat sheet

Use this note-taking section to jot down your thoughts after reading this chapter. What have you gained? What will you do? How are you closer to living your Awesome Life?

_____

_____

_____

_____

_____

_____

_____

_____

_____

Your environment is everything

Approach

Water

~~Environment~~

Sleep

Organize

Movement

Eat

Lifestyle

Inspiration

Finances

Education

At this point in the book and your journey, we can start to link things together and truly see how so much of life is connected and has a big influence on our thinking and actions. The environment we live in and create around us is testament to this. Do you think that:

- the food in your fridge will influence how you eat?
- how comfy your bed is will influence how well you sleep?
- how well you get on with your work colleagues will influence your daily mood?
- how much your get outside and be active will influence your daily wellbeing?
- that if your smart phone is disorganized and notifications turned on you'll always be distracted and unfocused?

Yes? Well, that's the power of our environment. If we want life to be different, it's very rare that it will just be ourselves undergoing change; things in our environment will need to change, too –either to protect ourselves from forces we don't want to influence our behaviour, or to influence our behaviour and mood positively and help us do what we need to do.

Some of these environmental changes will need to be big. For example, if you dislike your job or where you live, it will probably take some time and upheaval to change this – to apply for new positions or move home or location. And that's fine; just understand that and know the timeline you might be operating on. However, for the most part the environmental changes most of us need to shift us to a better place, to support a better life, are quite simple and easy. Some of these environmental changes might take a bit of money, too, but, more often than not, they are more about a shift in perspective, trying a few things to see what works, and sometimes a few tough conversations with people close to us.

Tough conversations

It's this last aspect or precondition of change that people often find the hardest: having tough conversations with other people. So we need to go into this in a bit more depth before looking at the various changes we can make to our environment. People have a huge influence on how we think, feel and act, so if there is someone in your life with whom you need to speak about something, you must find the courage to speak to them; it's imperative for your future happiness.

It may be that someone you know always talks to you in a derogatory tone and you dislike it; maybe your boss always overlooks your comments in meetings; maybe your partner talks over you in social situations; maybe your parents still treat you like a kid and talk down to you; maybe you have a sports teammate who talks to you like you can't play the game . . . Whatever it is – the best way to address these problems in my experience is to be 100 per cent open, honest and vulnerable. Don't aim to attack the other person, call them unkind or horrible or bad; simply outline how you are feeling and why you feel this way.

Initially, they may try to defend their actions and push back, and you may be tempted to retreat from the conversation (no one likes putting people in an awkward spot), but you MUST NOT do this. Don't let anyone try talk you out of how you are feeling if they are continually making you feel bad or unappreciated. Your feelings are important, don't shy away from that,

173

honour your happiness and your needs. By approaching the conversation by talking frankly about how you feel rather than attacking them off the bat, you can typically avoid a lot of the defensiveness.

Of course, we also have to understand our role in how we feel. We might be overreacting. We might be reacting to a situation because of something similar that has happened to us in the past. We might be interpreting the situation in a way that isn't justified, or making assumptions; in short, it might not be them, it might be us. But if someone is causing you grief or frustration, you have a duty to yourself to talk to them and stay strong in honouring how you feel and the outcome you want which is an improvement in the relationship. It's only fair.

We deserve to be happy, and we will have to broach those difficult conversations if we are to break through to a better life. The chances are, being super honest with someone will lead to a breakthrough you never thought was possible – and I'm 99.9 per cent sure you will both find some common ground or even a long-term solution that leads to both of you being happier.

Honesty is the best policy

Let me give you an example of how I would approach such a conversation, where honesty is the best policy. This example is in the workplace between a team member and their boss. I am playing the employee here – the one who needs to start a tough conversation. Chris is the boss. As you read through, try to step back and see the way the conversation is being approached, and not necessarily the specifics.

ME: *Chris, may I talk to you about something, please?*
CHRIS: *Sure. Now?*
ME: *Yes, do you mind if we go somewhere private?*
CHRIS: *Of course.*
ME: *Chris, this is a really difficult conversation for me so I'd really appreciate it if you would just let me talk and get this off my chest.*

(Saying this gives you the space to be heard. You've let them know that this is hard for you, and that there is no pleasure in this conversation for you. It will also disarm them and stop them from immediately going on the defensive. So, I would recommend trying to do this when you have difficult conversations with people. Brings out their compassionate side ahead of hearing what the issue is.)

ME: *I've been in this job for two years now and I feel I've tried my hardest to be seen and respected by you as a work colleague. I feel I communicate openly, do the work required of me to a high standard, and always deliver what is needed on time. But when we are in meetings, I feel I am always overlooked for the big and exciting projects. Sarah always gets picked to be a project lead, David quite often gets picked as a researcher, and I only ever get asked to do something if there is a problem or the slack needs picking up. I always feel I'm there to rescue the situation when something goes wrong, never get the credit for it, and am always out of the loop so have to work over my hours to play catch-up as I wasn't included from the beginning. This makes me feel devalued and frustrated, and it's impacting my work–life balance because I often have to work late to meet my commitment to the job even when I have plans with my family . . .*

CHRIS: *Oh wow, I'm sorry, but if you will just let me explain . . .?*
ME: *If you would please let me finish first, I'd appreciate it. I find conversations like this difficult, but I am saying all this because I would really like to get to the bottom of it and find a more positive way forward, because it's causing me to be very unhappy in my job, and I don't want to be.*
CHRIS: *Of course, I'm sorry. OK, carry on.*
ME: *I really enjoy many aspects of my job but don't understand why I am overlooked, especially when I am the person who quite often has to make up for others' underperformance. I don't know if this is a decision that has been made higher up or what, but you seem to be the person making the call. I feel there's an issue between us and I would really like to understand why this is the case so that I can feel more positive in my role, have a better work–life balance, and feel that one day I can push forward for a promotion. I really do love most aspects of my job, but this is a real area of friction for me, and I would like to resolve it.*

At this point, if Chris is a good boss, he should be in thinking mode. He should be feeling bad for his behaviour and trying to understand it in that moment. Most people will defend their actions to some extent, and that's ok, that's them making themselves feel a little better about their actions and perhaps they have a point of view you hadn't considered – so let them have their moment, but then afterwards they should go on to discussing potential changes in their behaviour or in the situation. If, however, someone is very status driven, with a lot of ego and narcissistic character traits (a bad boss), they will resist change and not accept any responsibility for their role in the situation – we at least then know that it's all about them and that we will have to look for another solution – by talking to a person more senior, looking to move departments or job, or looking to change how we integrate ourselves within the team.

CHRIS: *Oh wow, I'm really sorry you've been made to feel like this, it really wasn't my intention, and I didn't realize. I 100 per cent want to find a solution here as I don't want you to be unhappy in your job. You're great and a really valuable team member.*
ME: *I don't think there is a trust issue here, I don't think you would ever even ask me to be involved if it was a trust issue, so let me earn even more of your trust. Let me take the lead on the next project, outline clearly what success looks like for this project and let me prove to you I can do it. Give me the chance I feel I deserve. Let me show you how capable I am and how you can rely on me to deliver. Let me show you how I can truly perform in this role.*

You will have noticed that throughout this conversation I continued to be honest, to honour my feelings, and to work with Chris to get the outcome I wanted, however long it takes. Yes, this is a difficult conversation, but it's conversations like this that lead to a lot of future happiness.

In conversations like this, people often want the outcome to be that they prove the other person wrong; they want to *win* the conversation. Don't do this. Resist the urge. Swallow your pride and focus on the outcome you want. Don't go into conversations looking to win, to be right, to prove something. Go into a conversation looking to understand the problem, understand the other's viewpoint, to find common ground, and get to a solution. I could have pressed Chris in this conversation to understand *why* the situation was what it was, and in certain situations you would and should do that. A good example is if you are trying to resolve an issue with your partner or someone really close to you. However, in this conversation I didn't feel it was necessary, that I wouldn't get a honest answer or that Chris had true awareness of what he was doing. Also, simply shouting him down and being aggressive wouldn't have led to a good outcome. Even when you feel this is justified, it's sometimes better to play the long game and act tactfully to get a better outcome for all. I simply focused on the solution I wanted, for Chris to value me as a project lead, for him to see what I was capable of, and for the team to know I am stepping up and willing to work with them as part of the project leadership team, meaning I could push for a promotion in the future after a period of time being a project lead. If the situation continued and it didn't happen, you would revisit the conversation and ask *why*, to push harder, but sometimes you need to leave the heated debate to one side and just get to the outcome as calmly and as pragmatically as you can.

Take this approach to difficult conversations with friends, loved ones, work colleagues and people in and around your life, and you will have much more chance of a good outcome and a better future.

I know this is hard, it's uncomfortable, but it's essential for your future happiness to be able to have difficult conversations with people, especially if they are close to you and you see them a lot. Don't hide from how you feel, don't swallow it down and just get on with it. Be bold, talk to them, and just remember how I framed it above, because it works.

Optimizing your environment

Being able to broach these difficult conversations can often be key to getting your environment right – and it's to that subject we now turn. These are the key environments we must look at to optimize:

- where you live
- who you associate and surround yourself with
- your bedroom – how conducive it is to a good night's sleep
- your kitchen and the food you have in it
- your social life and the locations you frequent
- your hobbies and their locations
- your gym or fitness environment and location
- your work life and its location
- your phone and all that's on it
- and, most importantly, the thoughts in your head.

These are all environments that we live in and experience every day/week that we would want to change and optimise if they are not contributing to an Awesome Life. Let's go through each one and look at what might be an issue and what you might look to change.

WHERE YOU LIVE

Where you live – I'm thinking more of the neighbourhood here, rather than your actual home (though that can be crucial, too) – it might be noisy, hectic, not close enough to your family, too far away from a new job, or not close enough to the things you love doing. If the place where you live is a point of frustration for you, it would be a good idea to look to change it when you can. I appreciate this can be a fairly big life move, but if you would be happier in a new location, then your future happiness deserves that you work towards it.

My wife and I have just moved to be a lot closer to our family. We're now 10 minutes from all immediate family members (we were 30 minutes away before this), and with two young kids this is so nice. We're also close to a town we love with a great feel to it, and closer to the river and forest. We also upgraded house for more space, so it's been one of the best things we've done. Yes, it cost more for the location and it was a lot of effort moving, but it was worth it for our long-term happiness as a family. It wasn't something we could afford when we bought our first house, but as a couple we had it as a goal that we worked towards financially, and we are glad we did, as we're now parents and in a different phase of our life, and it's exactly what we want and need to be happier and more supported.

If you want to move, create the plan that's needed, however long-term that is. Work harder to earn more, or have a side hustle, or simply save and be patient. It will be worth it.

WHO YOU ASSOCIATE AND SURROUND YOURSELF WITH

Who you spend time with and who you call your friends is super important. Being around people shouldn't ever feel like a chore; it should be full of joy, fun and inspiration. If some of your friends cause you friction, or you have drifted apart, have the strength to spend more time with the people who you now really enjoy being around. I've always found, too, especially as someone who loves participating in sport and as a business owner, that people who are better than me at a particular sport, or further ahead of me in business, are inspiring to be around. I want to always be lifted up, to be around good people, to be inspired, so I continually seek out new or different friendships and make time for the ones I have that really excite me. I'm also not scared to move away from friendships that are not serving me anymore, and hope you can find the strength to do the same. If a friendship isn't easy and enjoyable or inspiring any more, honour that – not just for yourself but also for the other person – and start to move away from spending time in that friendship.

Surround yourself with good, inspiring, positive people. Also, if you want good friends, be a good friend. If you want to be surrounded by inspirational people, be inspirational yourself. And then go find those environments where those people are, such as sports teams, community groups and business masterminds.

YOUR BEDROOM

Sleep is something we will delve into far more in the next chapter, but here are a few key things. Where you sleep is key to an Awesome Life. Why? Because a good night's sleep underpins optimal human performance, and this is what we are pushing for. Your bedroom should be calming, comforting, relaxing, comfy and cool (in terms of temperature – I'm not here to judge your choice of décor!) Ultimately, it needs to be geared towards sleeping, which is your bedroom's primary function. If there are things in your bedroom that get in the way of a good night's sleep, you should consider changing them. If a TV in your room causes you to stay up too late watching it and not sleeping, then you should consider removing it from the bedroom altogether. If your bed is uncomfortable – the mattress lumpy, the sheets rough, the pillow old and flat – then invest in a new mattress, sheets or pillows . . .

Don't skimp here – invest. It's important. We spend a third of our lives in our bedroom: prioritise it, optimise it.

YOUR KITCHEN AND THE FOOD YOU STORE IN IT

What food is in your fridge, cupboards and freezer right now? This sounds silly, but that's the food you will eat. If you want to be healthy and high-performing, you'll need a diet that's sees you feeling good about yourself, and so it's important you get your kitchen environment right.

Are you buying food regularly enough to have fresh food in? Are you regularly batch cooking so that when you don't have time to cook, you can grab something out of the freezer for dinner, rather than resorting to takeout's or ready-meals? Do you have a plan of what you eat and why, or is your diet dictated by your stomach's wants and your mood at the time? Do you have some bad habits you need to kick? Do you need to adopt a really strict approach for a while, such as not even buying certain things in the first place?

Your diet deserves your upmost attention. The food you eat is your fuel.

This is why highlighting your kitchen and how you organize it is so invaluable, because it's actually such a simple step that has a BIG domino effect. If you're organized with your food shop, plan your week's eating, and have the healthy food there in your house, you'll eat it. You are in control of the food you buy and thus the food you eat, so your health, your energy, your weight, they're all in your control.

One area I have seen hold people back long term is their skill when it comes to cooking. You don't have to be a restaurant-standard chef, but if you're not a good cook it's hard to eat well long term, as you'll run out of ideas and slip back into convenience eating or buying pre-prepared foods. Developing your ability in the kitchen is key to long-term success. For me, this is even more important if you are a parent. It is our duty – and it's a *really* important duty in my opinion – to feed our kids well, to involve our kids in the creation of healthy food, and make the consumption of food an experience that the whole family is involved in.

In my 15 years' coaching, a common trait shared by many clients who have a problematic relationship with food is their lack of engagement with food preparation in the home during their formative years. I am grateful my mum taught me about food from a really early age, involving me in cooking, baking and food preparation. By the time I was 10, I could cook the family dinner, and these skills have paid dividends my whole life.

On average, we live 79–83 years, and most of us eat around three or more times a day. This is why food is *so* important, and it's why our relationship with it needs to be healthy. We engage with food so frequently that it's something we mustn't take for granted. And if we are parents, it's our job to teach and inspire our kids with food in a healthy and inclusive way.

What's in your kitchen will directly impact how you look, feel and perform. Avoid optimising it at your peril.

YOUR SOCIAL OR HOBBY CHOICES

Where we go and what we do to relax and unwind, such as the hobbies we do, makes a huge difference. These activities and time spent with people should never feel like a chore; if they do, they have to change. Getting respite and downtime from work and the other demands of life is fundamental to our well-being and sense of balance. If you took up golf, but now find it boring or frustrating, or maybe you want a new golf buddy to play with, then make that change; don't deliberate a second longer. If a friendship group you meet every Thursday for drinks feels like a chore now because all they do is moan and bitch or push you to drink more than you want to, then change your friendship group, or be the catalyst that forces the move away from having drinks and moaning all night to going out and doing something positive together away from alcohol.

Whatever it is that you enjoy in your life, that brings you happiness, make time for it and continually assess whether it is still doing its job. Finding time can be tough, especially if you are a parent when the demands on your schedule are so high. But even if it's just for one hour a week, it's imperative you keep doing that hobby or pastime to bring you that sense of relaxation and balance your body needs.

THE GYM OR FITNESS LOCATION YOU GO TO

The gym changed my life, so I have a strong personal bias as to its power to affect change in someone. At 18, as you know, I lost a lot of weight, got fit, and became strong and resilient, and it all started in the gym. As a coach I have always tried to inspire and push people to try something that pushes them physically. I always want people to see what they are capable of, so I encourage them to try do something that pushes their physical boundaries. They might not enjoy it, and that's fine, but I always feel it's something people should explore.

I'm not sure about you but I feel a great sense or reward and satisfaction after doing something physical. The endorphins, the sense of strength you get from training, feeling the blood flowing through the veins, the sense of completion, hitting a new personal best . . . I love it. It brings me joy on many levels, so I do think it's a great shame when people don't explore what their body is physically capable of.

If you are already active, you still need to keep on assessing what you are doing physically, in your fitness life, and its effect on you. If you are doing something you no longer find a challenge, change it up. If you want to ditch cycling because you've been doing it for years, change to something else – running or swimming, for example. If you need a new workout programme because yours isn't making you stronger or fitter anymore, then get a new programme. If the gym you go to isn't as good as it used to be because the place is being poorly run, change the location you train at. If the new instructor at the yoga studio you go to isn't as inspiring as the old one, change your class or where you go.

Whatever it is you do for fitness, make sure it is still serving you and your needs.

YOUR WORK

We've discussed this somewhat already, and will talk about it more in Steps 8, 9 and 10, so all I will say here is IT'S IMPORTANT.

Most people spend more than a third of their life working, so make it count. Make sure you enjoy it. Make sure it challenges you. Make sure you do work that uses your skills and abilities. It's not worth being in a job that doesn't progress you or your life over a prolonged period of time. Sure, we all get jobs, especially when we are younger, that we get just to earn money, but as we progress into *career mode* we should be doing work we enjoy, that we can progress in, and that challenges us in a way that isn't disheartening. If not, how are we going to stay inspired?

This is also essential if you want to earn more. Most high-paying jobs require us to be in a career path where we can progress, and it's unlikely someone will progress and earn more if they aren't in an inspired place, constantly pushing to improve and work up the career ladder. This isn't me saying work more or harder; it's me simply telling you to do a job you enjoy, that challenges you in a meaningful way, or have purpose doing.

YOUR PHONE AND ALL THAT'S ON IT

When I was young, phones were tools you used to call or text people when you were out and about. This meant they played a very minor role in our lives and took up a very small amount of our time and attention. Now, with the advent of smartphones they can literally govern our every action and all our attention. Even having your smartphone in your pocket can make you feel as though you need to be looking at something, emailing someone back, or scrolling through social media. We can order our food on it, talk to friends and family on it, do work on it, play games on it, listen to our music and watch films on it . . . we could be on it all day, every day if we wanted to. It can do so much for us, but it can also take a lot away from us.

I don't know how much your smartphone vies for your attention and what measures you have taken to control that, but assessing and reigning in your usage is an important step to make. My phone has all the apps I need on it, and none that I don't. There are no work-related apps on the first page of my phone: this stops me from getting into bad habits like checking email as soon as I open it. To do so, I have to swipe left and then open the subcategory of those apps to see my work-related apps – which forces me to think twice because it can't then be as much of an automatic behaviour. There's more intent if I have to swipe across and open up a subfolder to open them, as it's not just *there* as soon as I open up my phone. Likewise, all work-related notifications are turned off; I have to check any messaging manually. There is also nothing negative on my phone: the people I follow on social media are only positive – and if that changes, I unfollow them; the music on my phone is all stuff I love and enjoy; there are a few key podcasts on my phone that I listen to and that's it.

It can be all too easy to spend every spare 30 seconds and longer on your phone. Many of us have got into the habit of allowing our phones to fill so much space in our lives, diminishing opportunities for silence, time for observation, time for being present, time to just be, or time to just have a chat with someone you meet for five minutes – which doesn't happen when we're *always* head down on our phones. By staring at our smartphone screen, we risk missing so much of life and the world, so, when you get the chance, don't forget to be present, to enjoy silence, to enjoy being sociable with people, even strangers, and to take in and enjoy the world around you.

Our smartphone has become a significant part of our immediate environment. It can grab our attention in an instant. With a news item or social media post, it can plunge us into sadness or negativity. It can take our attention away from what really matters.

Consider what's on your phone, and where – your apps, notifications, music, books, podcasts, everything. Make your phone work *for* you; don't let your phone control you, in any way.

THE THOUGHTS IN YOUR HEAD

And as ever we finish with the big one, the thing we have to spend every waking day with – our own thoughts. As I hope I've highlighted already in this book, this is the most important environment to work on over time. And I say 'over time' for a reason, because managing your perspective, mindset and habits is a lengthy process. It can take a lifetime, so please appreciate and respect this. Let's take a minute to content ourselves with recapping what we've already covered on this subject:

- A positive outlook is going to mean your mental environment is a positive one.
- Being solution focused rather than problem focused will ensure you focus on the positive, the upside, the opportunity.
- Working on the stories you tell yourself will make it seem like the map of your life is limitless and full of opportunity and potential.

- Creating triggers in your immediate environment and routine will help keep your mindset focused on what you want it to be focused on – such as good food in the fridge, listening to a good book, spending time with positive friends, doing work you love etc, all the things above that guide how we feel day to day.

Our mindset is everything. It's what helps guide our emotions, determines our responses to challenges or stressors, dictates our current and future behaviour, moulds our happiness . . . it's literally everything. The happiest people I know are the people who have mastered life from a mental perspective. Some people can be rich and successful and still be wildly unhappy – why? Because of the way they view themselves and the world. Other people can have almost nothing and be wildly happy – why? Because of the way they view themselves and the world.

The question is: what are you going to CHOOSE?

I'll repeat: this stuff will not come overnight, but the first step in choosing a different path is knowing that we have different options. Others have lived the life we want to walk, so we know it's possible; we just have to choose to start.

So what needs to change in your environment?

Take 10–20 minutes to write down what you feel needs to change in your environment. Whether it's the people in your life, your work, your mindset, your home, what you eat, your fitness environment, what's on your phone; whatever it is write down what it is you feel needs to change, how you are going to change it, and when you are going to change it. Be as detailed as possible, so you can *see* and *feel* the solution, so the things you need to change are clear and you can act on them.

In writing the above, if you feel there are gaps in the how, that's then the time to do specific research into that. The specifics will always be individual to you, so once you hit a friction point because you don't know *how* to do something, don't deliberate or ponder on it for too long, take action. Talk to a friend who's successful in this area of their life, or read a few blogs on the topic. Get a book specifically on the area, or hire someone to help. You don't need a perfect strategy before you set out; action and momentum are key. We often sit for far too long on problems, experiencing unhappiness and frustration, waiting till things feel or get unbearable before we take action. As soon as you feel it's an issue, honour it and act to change it, fast, even if the strategy is imperfect at first.

Key points to remember

- Our environment is where we live, where we sleep, where we work, our friends, our mobile phone, and how we think. Seek to optimise all aspects of your environment so they bring you happiness and are conducive to the life you want to live.
- If you don't like where you live, create a long-term plan to move.
- If you don't like some of the people in your friendship group, work out why and act accordingly.
- Optimise your bedroom to help you get a good night's sleep.
- Ensure that your kitchen and the food you store in it are conducive to eating well.
- Create time for your social life and hobbies, but don't be afraid to shift those as soon as they become stale or no longer contribute to your wellbeing.
- If your gym workout no longer challenges you, switch it up or focus on a new type of training.
- If you don't like your job, focus on why and look to change your job role or company, or consider beginning a new career.
- Ensure your mobile phone is not distracting you, and has only things that add positively to your life.

- Work on the thoughts in your head and your mindset, and create habits and routines that will pay off.
- Getting started is the most important step. As soon as you feel something is an issue, act. Don't sit on the problem until it's making you really unhappy and miserable – fix it. Find a solution. Move forward.

Use this note-taking section to jot down your thoughts after reading this chapter. What have you gained? How are you closer to living your Awesome Life?

_____

_____

_____

_____

_____

_____

_____

_____

_____

Sleep – life's elixir

Approach

Water

Environment

Organize

Movement

Eat

Lifestyle

Inspiration

Finances

Education

> 'Lack of sleep is only bad if you have to drive, or think, or talk, or move.'
>
> **Dov Davidoff**

I don't know about you, but if I get a bad night's sleep I'm:

- grouchy and not that fun to be around
- less motivated to do pretty much anything
- likely to crave unhealthy comfort foods
- reliant on coffee all day
- more likely to focus on problems than solutions
- unlikely to exercise
- less able to push myself if I do exercise
- less likely to be affectionate with my wife
- less fun with my kids, preferring to sit around
- less willing to connect with others
- far more prone to making bad decisions at work and in life.

And guess what? None of the above is conducive to how I want to live my life. So, I choose to prioritise sleep in a big way and organize my life so I can get my full quota before I wake up at around 4:30–5am (which is when my body naturally wakes up after years of being an early riser). I'll even leave dinner early with friends if it's getting a bit late so I can get home, sort out the dog and prepare for the following day before I go to bed at 9–9.30pm.

Planning sleep

Failure to prioritise sleep is the main problem as to why the clients I coach struggle to get a good night's rest. So much of this book is about valuing the right things, prioritising them, and then taking action for long enough that it becomes routine and your new norm. Sleep is no different here.

You need to plan your sleep. If your alarm goes off at 5:30am and you know you need eight hours of sleep per night to feel good, what time do you need to be in bed? Doing that maths probably around 9–10pm, because for most people it might take 15–30 minutes to get to sleep, and getting into bed isn't the same as being asleep.

I really value waking up naturally, and I work from home running my own business, so it works for me, but I've worked to get to this place over time. I go to bed around 9pm, meditate on how I'm feeling and reflect on the day for 2–3 minutes, read for 5–15 minutes, and am asleep very soon after putting my book down, if I don't fall asleep reading it. I wake naturally around 4.30–5am, and get up 'to seize the day'. (I find my body ideally needs seven hours of sleep, so work to that.) I have always valued early mornings and what you can get done. While the world and my kids are still sleeping, I'm already getting into my stride, choosing to work or read or exercise or do something for myself. I also have kids, so it's the time I can mostly guarantee I get 100 per cent to myself. I call these my 'golden hours'. *My* time. And I use it to focus in on important work stuff, for learning, to get some aspect of my life organized, to get planned for the day if I'm out and about, or to exercise.

Because I prioritise sleep and this routine has become ingrained, I generally get good sleep most of the time. That means I have to switch off the TV or my laptop around 8.30pm so I can get ready and organized for bed. It means I have to say no sometimes to some things, evenings out, dinners and so on (although I usually ask friends if we can meet at 6pm rather than 7.30pm and 99 per cent of the time people say 'yeah sure'). Yes, it means I need to be disciplined with myself – it's easy to stay up later for all manner of reasons, but I choose not to. This is perfect for me right now in my life as I have young kids and am a business owner. When they are older, I can imagine I will shift this routine so I go to bed a touch later and get up a touch later, but for now this works for me and my family and enables me to get the most out of my life in the way that I want.

Some sleep facts

Now I'm not telling you all this to dictate when you go to bed or for how long; this is me showing you how and why I prioritise my sleep and to get the best out of myself. What you choose to do is down to you, but if you want better mental and physical performance, if you want your body to be in the best possible place it can be, you first and foremost need to value sleep and then to prioritise it.

To help you value sleep, here are a few quick facts about sleep adapted from articles published by the Cleveland Clinic (points 1–4[13]) and The Sleep Foundation (points 5–14[14, 15]):

1. It takes most adults around 10–15 minutes to fall asleep. If it takes you less than this, it might indicate sleep deprivation or general exhaustion.
2. If you are sleep deprived, your leptin level falls. Leptin is a key hunger hormone: having less of it makes you feel hungry more often.
3. Being awake for 16 hours straight decreases performance as much as if your Blood Alcohol Content was 0.05 per cent (the legal BAC limit in England, Wales and Northern Ireland is 0.08 per cent; in Scotland 0.05 per cent).
4. One of the biggest distractions to sleep is 24-hour access to internet and TV.

Sleep – life's elixir

5. REM sleep (deep sleep) should make up 20–25 per cent of your total sleep time, but few adults get this due to stress, temperature and discomfort, along with other sleep disturbances.

6. A 10 per cent increase in body fat mass can give you a six-fold increased chance of suffering from sleep apnoea.

7. 78 per cent of people are more excited about going to bed if they have fresh-smelling sheets.

8. 93 per cent of people say that a comfortable mattress is important to getting a good night's sleep.

9. Caffeine has a half-life of 5–6 hours in most adults, meaning that, if you drink coffee at 5pm, half of the caffeine is still in your blood at 10pm.

10. Drinking more than two servings of alcohol per day for men (4–5 units) and one for women (3–3 units) has been found to decrease sleep quality by 39.2 per cent.

11. Adults need 7–9 hours sleep per night, but duration isn't everything; quality is just as important, meaning a focus on getting minimal sleep disturbances is key.

12. Sleeping when it's dark is important, fitting in with your body's natural circadian rhythms which are governed by the sun and moon. (This is one reason why shift workers have poorer health outcomes over time, due to irregular sleep patterns, and why night workers have even worse health outcomes: one research study found working 10 years doing night shifts reduced life expectancy by 6.5 years.)

13. A cool bedroom is best for sleep as your body drops into deep sleep easier in a cool room. Aim for 16–20 degrees according to the Sleep Foundation, adjusting for the clothing you like to wear and the thickness of duvet you like to sleep under. Personally I love a cold room and a big snuggly duvet!

14. Light can disturb sleep. Sleep in as dark a room as possible removing all lights from the room, including small lights from your TV or plug sockets.

In the US, sales of melatonin supplements, our body's primary sleep hormone, rose from 62 million in 2003 to 378 million in 2014, a 500 per cent increase, indicating that sleep issues are on the rise, and people are looking to drugs and supplements to help. But we need to take a lifestyle first approach: it's the only long-term way to get a better night's sleep.

Sleep and anxiety

Aside from a failure to prioritise sleep, I have found one other primary reason why my clients struggle with sleep, and that's anxiety and stress. Anxiety and stress from the day, anxiety about the next day, anxiety and stress with work, friends, the kids, money . . . just life. People wake up regularly in the night, start feeling anxious about whatever is troubling them, try to problem solve, and then struggle to get back to sleep. I'm hoping that the work we've done together so far in this book will already be helping you feel less anxious about some aspects of your life and so helping here, but if you find you struggle with sleep due to anxiety and are lying awake in the night thinking about these life stressors, then this is something you must work on. It's imperative not just for a good night's sleep, but your daily emotional and physical wellbeing.

To an extent, it's a chicken-and-egg kind of thing. Anxiety will decrease the quality of your sleep, which in turn will heighten your anxiety. If this is you, try this simple three-step formula:

1. Value sleep and prioritise it, getting to bed early enough to allow time for 7–8 hours sleep per night.
2. Work on your mindset and eliminate or manage anxiety and stress in your life, using techniques such as meditation, journalling, reading and talking with others, to process and contextualise life stressors. It can also be transformative to take the step to get counselling if you need professional help with your anxiety, so I would highly recommend this if it's possible for you.
3. Set the stage for a good night's sleep with getting your sleep environment right – having a comfy bed, cool bedroom and creating a quiet space to sleep.

By implementing these tips along with the ones in the rest of this chapter, over time, you should be getting the sleep your body needs to perform at its best.

Digging deeper into anxiety

I think it's worth digging a little deeper into anxiety here, as it plays such a significant role in sleep, or rather the lack of it. Now, to be clear, I'm talking about anxiety in the colloquial sense of the word and not Generalised Anxiety Disorder which would typically benefit from being treated by a professional.

Let's start with a simple definition. In the *Oxford English Dictionary*, anxiety is defined as 'a feeling of worry, nervousness, or unease about something with an uncertain outcome'. To help give you a little perspective on the anxiety or stress you might be feeling in your life, or have felt in the past, I want to break apart this definition by looking at just one of these keywords or components: 'worry'. Consider the following:

- When it comes to worrying, what is it you are actually worrying about? Is it a legitimate worry, or something you are catastrophising in your head?
- Is it False Evidence Appearing Real?
- If you are worrying about it, is it something you can in fact control?
- Or, if not, can you let go of trying to control it and accept that's it's not a controllable factor in your life?
- Where has this worry come from? What's behind it? What's the deep-seated thing we are actually worried about?

I ask my clients this last one as often the thing we are worrying has an underlying cause. For example, if you were to worry about how a work presentation is going to go the next day, the worry might not be the actual presentation, but the fact that you want to be seen as a respected and competent work colleague to your team and are concerned about messing up. The reason it's important to identify the root cause of any stress, worry or anxiety is so that we, you, I, can deal with it in the appropriate way.

Imagine talking to your partner at 11pm while lying in bed unable to get to sleep because you are worried about that work presentation the next day. You tell your partner, and they will then likely give you a pep talk about all the usual tips that lead a great talk and presentation – good planning, knowing it inside out, turning up on time, owning the room . . . But does that help if the real reason you are worried about your work presentation is because you are wanting to come across as competent and thus be respected by your peers? Probably not. After all, you're not telling your partner the whole truth, so when they try to help, they can't because they aren't helping you solve the *actual* problem.

If you were 100 per cent honest with yourself and your partner, and were 100 per cent vulnerable and real with them by saying something like, 'I'm worried about tomorrow's presentation because I'm worried about coming across as competent in my job and being respected by my boss Sally and my line manager Kevin – I really want them to see what I'm capable of so that in the future I can push for a promotion', this is totally different. Sharing that real reason with your partner (or family member or friend or peer) opens the door to a true and honest conversation that can lead to a solution.

Because you have been honest about the real cause of your anxiety, your partner's advice will likely be more targeted to the problem, and actually help you feel less anxious about the situation. They might say, 'Yeah, I can see why that would worry you, but this is what I see. You are great at your job, you have prepared well for this presentation with the time that you have been given, you know your subject area, you've been given praise by them before so you know they have a certain amount of respect and admiration for you, but if you really want to come across as competent and win their respect tomorrow this is what I would do. Start the day in a calm way, get into a good flow state and feel happy. To help with this I will take care of the kids in the morning so that you can focus on what you need to do. When you get to work, go through your slides just so you are 100 per cent aware of the flow and cadence of your presentation. Don't overanalyse the details or try remembering too much; just feel the flow so you are aware of how you are approaching each slide, and let the slide, your knowledge and your preparation do the rest. Before you start the presentation make an effort to say hello to Sally and Kevin before you start, make that connection and show them your excitement for the presentation, this will make you feel less nervous by connecting with them before hand as a peer, rather than a subordinate trying to impress. Then just take your time, don't rush, stand tall, smile, enjoy it, and leave time at the end for questions so you can expand on any key areas, focusing eye contact on Sally and Kevin to again connect with them as much as possible. Then, after your talk, approach them and ask them what they thought, and if they had any further questions, reiterating one or two key things you feel really passionate about, and that you're excited to catch up over the follow days about outcomes and a plan of action.

This advice from your partner is now far more helpful than before – why? Because it's speaking to the real problem, and it gives tactful tips on how to make the best of the situation and make the presentation go well from the perspective of the problem wanting to be solved.

Now a key aspect of this example is something we've discussed earlier in the book: being vulnerable about the root cause of the anxiety, being honest in explaining it, and being completely open to the advice that follows. After receiving this advice I would personally grab a notebook and write down the advice and ideas. First, this will give substance and feel to the advice, capturing it in the moment; second, it will give you a record to read later rather than relying on your memory of the conversation; and lastly – but importantly – it will allow you to put the thoughts to bed and allow you to get a good night's sleep by settling that anxiety you felt about the presentation.

This is the power of being vulnerable, of talking about the real causes of our stress, of getting support with solutions. And importantly, boldly taking action.

Now I appreciate this was a very specific example, but I hope you can zoom out and see how you can use this technique in your life in talking to others about problems, stresses and anxieties you have, especially if these issues are going to keep you up at night with these things rattling around your brain.

If you don't have someone you can speak to about your stressors before bed or at any time for that matter, you can write it down instead. Writing this stuff down gives you the opportunity both to make what you are thinking and feeling real and find solutions all in one go. This is called journalling, and there are many good resources out there which will show you how to use the technique to help with your mindset and anxieties. Examples of some stressors you might be experiencing as anxieties that are worth discussing with a friend, partner, family member or professional might be:

- money and supporting your family
- your health and feeling unwell
- pressure at work
- a specific situation with a friend or work colleague and how it will play out
- an upcoming event you are nervous about.

Whatever feels like a stress or anxiety for you in your life, be open and honest, and talk to someone about it, or journal your thoughts on it. Then, develop solutions and or coping mechanisms.

Bedtime reading and meditation

Talking things through might not be a cure-all, and this is where we would still employ techniques to help with getting a handle on our anxieties so we can get a good night's sleep and have more stress-free days. This is one reason I read before I sleep. I read something that calms me, gives me perspective, and helps me continue to think in the way that I want to think. It's a key reason I read Stoic philosophy before going to sleep. I find it's the perfect antidote to a better mindset and a broad perspective on life. If you would like to follow suit, I highly recommend reading a few pages of Ryan Holiday's *The Daily Stoic* as your bedtime reading. A few chapters of this book and I am calmer, have more perspective, and feel happy and ready to sleep. It's also a book you can re-read again and again for this purpose. You always take something away from reading a few pages.

Another tool I recommend is meditation. When I was younger, I spent a lot of time meditating. I'd do it on a daily basis, first thing in the morning and last thing at night, but now I only do it two to three times per week when I feel I need to get more centred, gain perspective, and give my body and mind a true rest by minimising all inputs and outputs. Meditation is a powerful de-stressor. Have you ever met someone with a daily spiritual or religious practice who appears stressed? I haven't. Perhaps that's because they have a daily commitment to a ritual where they work to become aware of how they are feeling, work on being more mindful, have an affirmation of gratitude for what is positive in their life, and constantly remind themselves of what is important in life.

That was why I first started. I wanted to make sense of life. I wanted to understand my thoughts and my brain. I wanted to make sense of the anxieties I was feeling and bring more truth and clarity to my inner ramblings. Over time, the aim is to become calmer, more balanced, have a greater level of self-awareness, and bring clarity to problems I'm experiencing by honouring why they are there and dealing with them.

Most people, in my experience, struggle with meditation and this is often because they assume that the art of meditation is all about clearing your mind. Good luck with that – it's pretty impossible to do. The mind is an alive and aware beast and is always off exploring thoughts, emotions and experiences, however much you try to stop it from doing so.

The art of meditation is about giving your thoughts and emotions space and air time – so you can appreciate them and understand them better. The aim is to become fully connected with what your mind is seeing and feeling and what your body is experiencing.

So what's the easiest way to start learning to do this? In my opinion: guided meditation.

Let someone with experience and the right energy lead you. I have a few go-to audio sequences that are valuable to me for a meditation session. They are 10 minutes long. I find a nice quiet space, I press play, and I let the audio do the work. Because you are listening and giving your energy and focus to something that is actively guiding you, you automatically shift your attention away from your monkey mind and thoughts and focus on the words of the guide. Over time, this guided practice becomes a subconscious behaviour: even without the presence of the guided meditation, over time you learn to become more aware, calmer, and more in tune with your thoughts rather than fighting them or trying to control them. Over time you will find, like I did, that you need to meditate less and less often as you become someone who is more balanced and stress-free, almost in a meditative state on a day-to-day basis.

So, here's my personal recipe for an anxiety-free life that might help you get that precious good night's sleep. Feel free to adapt it to suit your own needs.

- Set aside 10 minutes twice a day for guided meditation – once in the morning and once at night.
- Set aside another 10 minutes per day to read some Stoic philosophy (or any other book that calms you or helps you get perspective on many of life's stresses). Prioritise getting to bed 20 minutes earlier to do this.

If it takes you 30 minutes to get to sleep, on average, and you did 10 minutes' guided meditation, spent 10 minutes reading, and you got to sleep in 10 minutes, isn't that 30 minutes well spent? It's the same 30 minutes it took you to get to sleep beforehand!

You'll be calmer, have a better outlook and perspective on life, and will be asleep at the end of that 30-minute window. Then, over time, I bet you find you can do 5 minutes of each and end up getting to sleep faster because your body and mind is better at calming down and getting rid of any anxieties that you might have previously battled with before bed.

Your new sleep routine

It's now your turn to create your new routine. What do you feel you need to change to get a better night's sleep? The time you go to bed? Your routine? What you do before you get in bed? What you do when you're in bed? Your caffeine intake? What you eat before bed? How comfy your bed is?

Reflect on this chapter and all you've learned, and commit to a new routine that you're going to implement. (Tip: if you need to bring your bedtime forward, do it slowly, let your body clock adjust, if you're used to going to sleep at midnight and you go to bed at 10pm you'll lie awake for ages, slowly bring your bed time forward 10 minutes each day and slowly let yourself re-adjust.)

_____

_____

_____

_____

_____

_____

_____

_____

_____

_____

Key points to remember

- Value and prioritise sleep.
- Do your sleep maths: if you know you need to get up at a certain time, work backwards and be in bed with enough time to wind down and be asleep to get your full 7–8 hours sleep per night.
- If you have very young kids like me, it's even more important to get to bed early, because if they wake you several times in the night then you're instantly on the back foot.
- Find techniques that calm your mind before bed, such as talking, reading, journalling or doing a guided meditation.
- If your bed isn't comfy, invest in a new one, or new sheets, or a new pillow, or blackout curtains. We spend a third of our life in bed, so it's a wise investment.
- Keep your room cool: a cool room helps you drop into deep and REM sleep (the two stages of sleep most associated with recovery, a reduction in tiredness the following day, and memory formation).
- Your body knows how to sleep. Don't rely on gadgets or pills to get there. Instead, optimise your mindset, routine and physiology. If you need supplements or medications

to sleep, that's fine short term, but try long term to reduce and eliminate these using natural sleep techniques

- If anxieties or stressors keep you up at night, talk them through or write them down. Don't let them sit and rattle around your brain. Get counselling if this becomes an ongoing issue.
- If you don't get enough sleep at night for whatever reason, try a power nap during the day – ideally for 20–30 minutes or 60–90 minutes (the middle zone of sleep, 30–60 minutes, could leave you feeling groggy).
- And again – I can't stress this enough – prioritise sleep. Make it a priority over TV, going out late regularly, scrolling through social media . . .

Use this note-taking section to jot down your thoughts after reading this chapter. What have you gained? How are you closer to living your Awesome Life?

_____

_____

_____

_____

_____

_____

_____

_____

_____

Get organized

Approach

Water

Environment

Sleep

Organize

Movement

Eat

Lifestyle

Inspiration

Finances

Education

> 'Organization isn't about perfection; it's about efficiency, reducing stress and clutter, saving time and money, and improving your overall quality of life.'
>
> Christina Scalise

Getting organized may sound like a really obvious step in the process towards building your Awesome Life, but in my experience as a coach, most people, while they know in theory that they should have a plan and be organized, don't have one. Let's take food as a simple example: everyone knows a few sensible facts about good nutrition, but few have a plan that ensures they eat well, consistently. This is despite the fact that planning your meals is a very simple but powerful step towards getting healthier. By streamlining the process of working out what you're going to eat, planning the food shop, preparing the food daily or every few days, and then eating it, hey presto, you're fuelled with nutritious food that will provide steady energy and support your immune system.

Once someone has the motivation to do something, creates a plan, and executes on it, as long as it's a good plan it will work; it's that bloody simple.

First things first

So, what is it you need to get organized with?

Maybe a lot, maybe a little, but either way you'll need to start creating plans (which may evolve over time as you learn better techniques and try things out) and, importantly, start executing them.

So, the question for now might be: what do you get organized with first?

My suggestion is to start getting organized and planning for the biggest friction point in your life, or for the thing that will lead to the most positive impact in your life. For many people reading this, I think, this will be health and fitness goals, or sleep, because our physical and mental health determines so many of the other outcomes we seek in our lives. If your body and mind were to perform better, if you were to maintain a good standard of physical health, if you were full of energy every day, how much more awesome would you feel, and how much more awesome would your life quickly be?

What does being organized with your health and fitness look like?

We've just spent some time in Step 4 discussing sleep. Did you take action on getting more organized with your sleep? If so, good. If not, why not?

Getting sleep organized is a huge step in the right direction as that is going to underpin so much of your daily performance and energy. The energy and vitality to live an Awesome Life. So being organized with your sleep might simply be having a revised and simplified routine. As an example, it might simply be:

1. Turn all tech off at 9pm.
2. Get the next day organized and tidy the house.
3. Shower.
4. Get in bed at 9.30pm.
5. Do a 10-minute meditation or breathing exercises or catch up with your partner over a 10-minute chat.
6. Read for 10 minutes.
7. Lights off around 10pm.
8. Alarm set for 6am.

This is simple and effective, so, where possible, do it daily. Prioritize your routine.

What might being organized look like with your nutrition? A plan might look like this:

---

1. Sit down on Thursday evening (with your partner) and plan the food shop.
2. Decide what will be batch-cooked, decide on any supplies that need to be stocked up on and decide on one new recipe to cook this week.
3. Check to see if you are eating out or away any time this week and tweak your weekly shop accordingly.
4. On Friday, do the online food order or go to the supermarket.
5. On Saturday and Tuesday batch-cook two meals.
6. After dinner, prepare overnight oats for the next day's breakfast, so all you have to do is microwave your breakfast when you get up.

We'll be looking at food in a lot more depth in Step 7, but for now this shows just how easy it is to plan a simple routine around food and what being organized around what you eat might look like.

Wider planning

Zooming out now, what other areas of your life need a plan and need you to be organized so you get a better outcome?

Where is your life going? What is it you want to achieve? Where do you want to be in in one, three and five years' time – if you know that is (you don't have to know, btw)? Do you have a plan to achieve it? Are you organized in a way that will get you there?

There are key things in my life that keep me organized, focused and on track. Here are some of them:

1. My weekly digital diary of work/commitments/social life/ holidays that syncs between my smartphone, desktop computer and laptop

2. A monthly and quarterly plan of my work that works alongside our family planner so my wife and I are both aware of each other's commitments

3. A notebook for ideas and musings, both a small one for my thoughts, and a bigger one for me to draw out ideas on blank paper

4. A printout of my gym's opening times and the times of the adult lane swim sessions in the pool

5. If I'm training in the gym currently, I'll keep a running record of my training in my iPhone notes, and mark a calendar in my shed gym of when and what I did so I can loosely keep track. I prefer this over my phone so I can see my pattern of training at a glance

6. On my smartphone I keep a lists of local places to do stuff, places we like to eat out at, and potential holiday destinations and a host of other things so we always have a record of things for when we need ideas

7. A whiteboard weekly planner in our kitchen for our family meals with what to order on the weekly food shop, factoring in everyone's needs/wants

8. Automatic payments set up with my bank to put money into investments every month

9. Reminders in my digital diary to check certain things every year or every few months – simple things like sweeping the chimney, ordering new water filters, reviewing outgoings – things you can easily forget in the day-to-day routine. Put it in a digital diary and you never forget

10. A visual dream board in my office attached to a five-year timeline – which I review once a quarter to see whether I am on track and if I am happy and aligned with that plan still, and then, importantly, whether I need to change the actions that I am taking to achieve those goals

11. And sleep ... But you know how important that is by now!

Those 10 key tracking tools and routines keep the majority of my life and my family's life on track (of course, my wife has her own plans, too, which we ensure we sync on and adjust where needed). There are also a few more tools I use to manage my business and all its key functions, but that's the key stuff on a broader, personal, family and life level. This is where a smartphone can be really valuable, with all its apps and tools to keep life organized and under control. Is there really an excuse now to *not* be organized with so much tech helping us out? Just be clear, as we've already discussed around how you want your phone to be a part of your life – notifications can help or hurt you depending on how big a role they play.

So what needs to be more organized in your life?

Use this list to help you focus on the areas in your life where planning and getting organized could really move you closer to your Awesome Life:

Your sleep?
Your nutrition?
Your finances?
Your family life?
Your next holiday?
Your fitness routine?
Your investment strategy?
Your mind?
Your life plan?

You might be sitting there and saying, 'All of them!' If that's the case, then that's fine, all good. Don't be stressed by it, don't feel overwhelmed, don't think, 'My life is so disorganized. I don't know where to start, so what's the point in starting at all?'; instead, think, 'I love this. I'm literally a blank canvass. I'm excited about looking at my life goals, and coming up with a plan to achieve them. Where's that notebook?'

Remember, see the positives, see the opportunity, know you hold the glass.

I know these are BIG questions, but this book is about getting BIG results in your life, so those big hard questions are going to be needed. Let's see and seize those opportunities. Get your notepad and pen out, and start making some BIG AWESOME PLANS. Get organized, now, GO!

Reflect on what you need to be more organized with now, and also write down how you're going to get more organized. Then act on that!

_____

_____

_____

_____

_____

_____

Are you feeling better for having written all that down? Good. Now put down this book for a while, put off reading Chapter 6 for now, and go take action on getting life and your BIG PLANS more organized, because Chapters 6 and 7 are big ones and I want you to be ready for them!

Key points to remember

- Being organized is such a simple bit of advice but is often overlooked.
- Be organized with your weekly food shop so you can eat well.
- Be organized with your work and home life so they work in harmony, and you get the most out of both.
- Know your gym or fitness schedule and how it fits into your routine.

- Be organized with all things in your home life so you don't drop the ball, and regularly sync with your partner or parents or house mates so you consider everyone's needs.
- Use technology to simplify areas of your life and get back time (not always so you can do more).
- Plan fun, adventure and holidays into your year and on a regular basis. All work and no play . . . Meh, boring.
- Keep simple things like your diary up to date.
- Add reminders into your smartphone for the big things that come round less often and so easily get forgotten.
- Why be organized? To get more out of life!

Use this note-taking section to jot down your thoughts after reading this chapter. What have you gained? How are you closer to living your Awesome Life?

_____

_____

_____

_____

_____

_____

_____

_____

_____

_____

Movement is medicine

Approach

Water

Environment

Sleep

Organize

~~Movement~~

Eat

Lifestyle

Inspiration

Finances

Education

'Movement is the song of the body.'

Vanda Scaravelli

I don't know how you feel about movement, but I feel movement is life. And it's not too much of a stretch to say that movement is medicine, too – hence this step's name. There have
been times in my life, and I'm sure the same can be said for
you, where I've not been able to move like I want to. Remember
a similar time in your life? Perhaps it was an injury or you'd
been unwell, or life just got too busy, or you had young kids . . .
I am coming out of the most prolonged period of minimal
movement in my whole life. I'm now getting back to more
walking and some light swimming after having long COVID
for 14 months. Not exercising beyond 5000–8000 steps per
day has been unheard of for me as someone who has always
been active, played sport, lifted weights, and generally not
ever been held back by much, unless injured, in exercising
how I wish.

It made me reappreciate the value of movement, not necessarily the big stuff like taking part in a rugby match, or a half
marathon, just simple things – like taking my daughter on a
long walk, playing in the park for an hour, then carrying her on
my shoulders home for tea. I couldn't even do that, and I
missed it. And it made me really appreciate how my level of
fitness enabled me to live a limitless life. I had never been held
back before, and I never, if possible, want to be in that position
again.

Movement allows you to explore life in a limitless way. It
allows you to do a half-day of gardening without thinking
twice about it. It allows you to go off on a random trek for the
day and be out in nature. It allows you to lift and shift things
about at home with vigour. It gives so much to life.

There are so many simple movements I love doing that bring a ton of value to my life. I can imagine you feel the same?

- I LOVE a good long walk in nature, especially somewhere new.
- I LOVE being able to move freely and without pain.
- I LOVE having the strength to chop and carry wood for our home fire.
- I LOVE being strong and fit enough to carry both my kids some distance.
- I LOVE having a good base level of fitness so I can always, pretty easily, get involved with any sport I want to.

Now I'm not about to tell you to go to the gym, far from it. Sure, if you have a goal that will be easier to or relevant to achieve by going to the gym, cool, join a gym, but no one needs a gym to be fit, whether that is cardiovascular fitness, strength ability or endurance. Most of what we want to achieve can be done with no equipment, or minimal equipment; all it takes is a desire and a goal.

Setting fitness goals

Being goal-based with your fitness can be really helpful in channelling your energy. Even if the goal is to never feel sore or be able to do anything around the house and garden, it's still a goal and focuses your efforts on the right things that will help you achieve it.

For example, I love being muscular and strong. I always have, and I think I always will, so I will look to build and maintain it. Not in an extreme way: I don't want to walk around looking like a competitive bodybuilder or a prop rugby player (I also don't have the genes for that!), but I love the feeling of being strong, I love the look of having a certain amount of muscle; it makes me feel good about myself and my ability as a human. You might not have this goal, but what goal do you have about how you want to look and feel?

Whatever that is, movement and fitness can provide for that.

- *Want to move well?* Awesome, make sure stretching or yoga or a similar flexibility practice is in your weekly routine.
- *Want to be fast?* Awesome, train for speed or do a sport that develops or at least maintains your speed.
- *Want to be stronger?* Awesome, lift heavy things, whether that's in the gym with weights, or in your garden with lots of random bits of heavy things you've found and accumulated.
- *Want to be a healthy weight and move in a healthy way?* Awesome, maybe you just aim to walk 10,000–15,000 steps every day and spend 5–10 minutes stretching and foam-rolling in your lunch break to keep those niggles at bay

I'm not here to dictate what it is you should do; I'm here to fly the flag for movement and all its benefits, and to say that you should have some movement in your life, ideally attached to a goal you want to achieve if you want that life to be Awesome. Whether it's just walking or doing 15 hours of training a week to compete in an Iron Man race, visualise what it is you want your body to be able to do, or how you want it to perform, or how you want it to look, and create your goals off the back of that, followed by a plan to achieve it. A lot of people exercise just to burn calories, but this is a bad starting point. If you always exercise to 'burn fat' you're likely never enjoying it, and exercise won't become an enjoyable part of life that you have a healthy and consistent relationship with. Plus, how many more calories are you burning from a workout you hate doing vs a workout you might love doing? The reality is that a large majority of the work required to lose body fat is done by what you eat. That's where the true gains and losses are made. Sure, exercise helps, but it can quickly be undone with an evening raid of the fridge. So, my suggestion? Exercise and move in a way that you enjoy, and in line with how want your body to look, feel and perform – and let your diet do the heavy 'fat loss' lifting.

Some motivation from science

To drop some research evidence into the mix, here are some facts about movement and exercise – with the difference being that exercise is planned and structured movement, ideally with an aim or goal in mind.

1. Exercise improves mood and can help prevent and even contribute to the treatment of anxiety and depression[16].
2. Resistance exercise strengthens your bones and muscles, slowing down the effects of ageing[17].
3. Exercise can improve sleep quality and may reduce sleep latency (the time from being in bed to being asleep) though results here are a little more mixed[18].
4. Exercising outdoors (especially in green spaces) is associated with improvements in mental and physical wellbeing

over and above those seen with indoor exercise[19]. Personally I love training outdoors as it feels like it improves overall wellbeing and helps me feel connected with nature and the world more generally.

5. Exercise improves glucose tolerance, helping reduce the chances of getting type 2 diabetes, and also helps in the management of it by helping insulin receptors work better, and helping cells take up glucose in the absence of insulin more efficiently[20].

6. Exercise helps reduce chronic levels of C-reactive protein (CRP), interleukin 6 (IL-6), and various other markers used to measure the level of inflammation in your body[21].

7. Cardiovascular exercise helps improve the health of, predictably enough, your cardiovascular system. Because of this direct effect and more indirect effects (like improving the health of mitochondria, a part of your cells responsible for making energy out of nutrients), it reduces your risk of cardiovascular disease[22].

8. It has been hypothesised, and there is some evidence to support the idea[23], that exercise reduces telomere attrition. Telomeres can be thought of like 'buffers' at the end of your DNA which are gradually destroyed as your cells get copied, leading to many of the effects of ageing. This means that, if true, exercise can slow ageing!

9. Overall because of its effects on arterial hypertension (blood pressure), diabetes type 2 risk, dyslipidaemia (issues with blood lipids), coronary heart disease, stroke, and cancer risk, regular exercise was found in one 2012 literature review[24] to correlate with a 30–35 per cent reduction in all-cause mortality risk.

Changing goals

Over time, the level, quality, and kind of exercise in your life is likely to change, and that's completely normal. As goals change, what you do will change, and this will happen at key periods and stages in your life. For example, fitness for me when I was 25 was a huge part of my life. I played rugby on a weekend, trained twice a week, and lifted weights three times a week. I'd often play tennis or swim and do other sports if given the opportunity too. So a typical week of exercise was very structured for me and looked like this:

Monday – gym/weights
Tuesday – rugby training
Wednesday – gym/weights
Thursday – weights pre-rugby, extra skills practice, rugby training
Friday – rest/stretch
Saturday – game day
Sunday – rest/swim/hike/tennis/cricket.

These days it's very different. I don't play rugby, and at the time of writing this book I don't lift weights. I simply try look after myself. I don't even have a set schedule but I still exercise in some way daily, whether it's a long walk, a cycle, a swim, or an hour of gardening – I simply keep it fluid in terms of timing and type of exercise to keep family life my priority. I know that when this phase of my life changes (with me getting more sleep and life being a touch less chaotic with my kids being older) and I can put more exercise structure and intensity into my life, I will pick up a sport again or pick a challenge like a cycle sportive (a non-competitive long-distance cycling event) to focus my training, alongside lifting weights again, and where possible, it would benefit you to do the same. Have a goal, plan how to fit that into your routine, enrol in a challenge or join a gym or find a class, and hold yourself accountable to achieving that goal. And when that goal is achieved, shift focus, plan the new goal, and get after that new target.

So many argue over the best method for getting fit, and that's no surprise as methods can be many, but it's the result we are after and the truth is that the method is, for most of us, less important than the broad principles. What's important is to move, daily, to simply do something, even if it's a good walk or some gardening. Your body is a tool, a tool you must nurture, stimulate and use if you want it to continue to perform at its best. If your body isn't used and stimulated, it will lose efficiency and ability, and you don't want that, do you?

I'm lucky, I have a really good example of this in my life: my granddad. When I was growing up, my grandad always said to me, 'If you don't use it, you lose it'. He'd then go on to tell me how many press-ups and sit-ups he did every day, and he knew how good he was feeling that day by how many he did. At the time my grandad would have been around 60, and at that age he was still keeping fit by walking lots and doing his press-ups and sit-ups every day. Sure, many might argue this wasn't loads, but how many 60-year-olds do you know who have stayed committed to a simple fitness routine like that?

The most important thing behind this for me is the mindset my grandad had. The mindset to get up and do it every day, first thing in the morning where possible, and to combine it with the mantra of 'use it or lose it'. I'm very grateful to have had that influence in my life, and I hope my grandad can inspire you to keep moving as you age and not make the excuses everyone does like 'oh I'm too old for that'.

Use it so you don't lose it.

Making exercise manageable

Whatever fitness you do, make it manageable. There's a lot in this book that you will want to do, and most can be slotted into your existing lifestyle by tweaking and amending what you already do. When it comes to fitness, though, it's going to take cold hard time. So, make it easy. You might already give a lot of time to exercise, and if so, awesome, high-five. If not, the best thing you can do is make it easy. Things are easy to shoehorn into your schedule when motivation is high. Look at how many people make time to go to the gym every day after work in the New Year, only to be going twice a week, if at all, come April – they now don't have time . . .

A good example of this is with early years' parenting. This period of parenting is always challenging and goalposts are always changing, like, daily. The kids aren't at school yet, and sleep is a variable. So fitting fitness in as a parent with young kids can be really tough. It's where my wife and I are right now, so we just try do what we can when we can – it's that simple. We get out and walk in nature a lot as we live rurally. My wife grabs 20–30 minutes two to three times a week for a run, sometimes taking our all-terrain buggy with the baby, and is planning to do some personal training sessions soon to help her get back to fitness and strength post-partum. I mentioned what I am doing currently previously, and what I plan to do when things change. It's the best we can do right now as busy, often tired, parents. And you know what, it's fine: it's all we need right now to stay fit and well.

Fitness doesn't have to be the gym. Fitness doesn't have to be a one-hour workout. Fitness doesn't have to be the latest thing being done by influencers on Instagram. It can be whatever you want it to be.

If you look at the 'blue zones' across the world – the places globally where people live the longest – these people aren't hitting the gym four times per week in their nineties. They are simply active. They walk, they lift and carry things about, they move a lot outdoors; they simply continue to use their bodies as much as they can while eating well, and so live into a ripe old age. I tell you this to give you comfort and the flexibility and freedom to create your fitness life to be what you want it to be.

I've coached hundreds of people who felt fitness had to be a certain thing. That they had to join a gym and go five times per week to achieve their goals. That they wouldn't be good enough or wouldn't get the results they wanted if they didn't do things a certain way. The reality is the most important thing for all of us is to just move. To be active on a daily basis. To walk. To lift and carry things. To use the tool that you have been gifted, your body. If you do things on top of this, such as going to the gym, playing sport, hitting the road bike for two hours, going to a HIIT class, going for a swim in a lake ... then that's of extra benefit and will serve your body – and your mind – well. But the baseline is to just be active, on a daily basis.

I want you to be inspired to exercise in some way, but I also want you to know there are no real rules apart from one. The only rule is to move and to use your body. After that, it's a case of 'What do you want to do?, What are you motivated to do?, What do you want your body to be able to do?, How do you want it to look?'

What this book is not here to do, in this discussion of move-ment and fitness, is give you a plan, this book is here to give you enough perspective to work out what *the best plan is for you*. For you to be inspired to make fitness work for you, wher-ever you are in your life right now, whatever your current situ-ation, and depending on the goals you have and the time you have available.

Loving your body

We also need to approach exercise from a place of love and respect for our body, out of a desire to do the right thing by our body, to look after it. This makes motivating ourselves so much easier and makes the actual work much more enjoyable. Too many people engage in fitness practices out of fear – fear they won't be able to lose weight, fear of losing a certain element of fitness, fear of not fitting in in some way, fear of getting fat. But this is misplaced. Taking action on your health, body and mind through fear is a losing prospect. Approach it from a place of love – love for your body – and the rewards will be so much greater.

As we'll see in Step 7, this applies to your relationship with food as well. Just as we should eat for the love of our bodies (and, of course, for the love of food), so we should exercise for love of our bodies, too – exercising, not to punish the body or constantly try to burn calories, but to sharpen it like a tool that you want to keep healthy, fit and strong.

What I want you to realise is that your body is a beautiful, powerful, capable thing. Yes, I want you to try push yourself. I do want you to see what you are capable of and find out what your body could do. But I also want you to ensure that you develop a healthy relationship with moving and value the really simple things, like walking, as much as possible, looking after your joints and mobility, and maintaining your strength and muscle mass. You might have a physical limitation, such as a disability that limits you doing many of the things the fitness industry is good at promoting, and thus all we, you, I can do is optimise and utilise what we have.

You get one body . . . how are you going to choose to use it?

Don't compare yourself with others

As a final note before I ask you to make a plan, please don't compare yourself with others, or even with yourself at a different stage in your life. Compare yourself with yourself *now*. It's very easy to be defeatist and say, 'There's no point in doing X because I can't be as good as my friend' or 'There's no point doing Y because I won't be as good as I used to be'. That helps no one – your goal is simply to look after and optimise what you have now, to prolong your health and body's ability to do things.

Let's take me as an example here. I know I can't do some stuff others can. Ever since I can remember, I've been unable to straighten my right arm; there's some bone-related issue and my arm is 18 degrees shortened at the elbow. This means I can't do things that put too much pressure on my right arm when straightened. I've always wanted to nail a really heavy snatch in the gym and do handstand walks, or to turn my hand to some gymnastics moves, but I can't; my arm simply can't take the pressure. But I don't moan. I don't compare myself to others. I just do what I can do because there's so much else I can do. I focus on myself, on what I can do, and simply aim to optimise and improve what I've got.

Likewise, if I went back and played rugby, I know I wouldn't be as fast or as sharp as I used to be – I'm 35, not 25 – but that's not the point. If I were to go back to playing rugby, it would be to keep fit, to challenge myself, and to have fun simply playing the game – not to compete with the memory of how I used to play, wishing I had the body of my 25-year-old self again.

Set your fitness goals

If, at this point, you are still unsure what's best for you, I'll simply outline what I feel is beneficial for most people, for the human body as we know it, that might shape a weekly approach to exercise. This is loosely based on the WHO recommendations and, if you can stick to it, you'd be in a great place.

1. Walk 8000–15,000 steps a day, ideally outside, ideally with some of that being fast enough to raise your heart rate a little, at least a couple of times a week if you can.
2. Lift weights twice week or take a resistance training class. This should target all of your major muscle groups at least once per week.
3. Stretch for 10 minutes a few times per week on key tight/stiff/sore areas.
4. Do something fun or recreational one to three times a week, such as playing tennis or squash, swimming or kayaking . . . This one is probably the hardest to fit in for many, so maybe start once or twice per month and work up to it if your schedule allows.

That for me would be a good general guide to looking after general fitness and strength as you age in a semi-structured way, while keeping it varied, fun, and interesting. It will keep your strength up from the weight training and help you keep your muscle mass or to maybe build some if you feel you need or want to, it will keep you moving, keep you mobile, and keep you having fun while stimulating your cardiovascular system in multiple ways.

What you do on top of that is completely up to you and goal dependant; swim, run, lift weights more, dance, play sport, bungee-jump . . . whatever it is that sets you on fire or whatever goal you want to chase. CHASE IT!

If you are struggling with something currently, have pain, or feel there is a consideration you need to make before you exercise, please do see your Doctor first, or the appropriate health care professional.

Now take a moment to write down some new goals, or new commitments for your fitness and the movement you want in your life. (A gentle reminder if you aren't doing much at the moment, start small and build up. Don't write goals down that might be a stretch to achieve. Start small, and build up to longer/harder/more demanding things, always.)

_____

_____

_____

_____

_____

Key points to remember

- Movement gives life momentum. Do it daily, even if it's a walk.
- You don't need to go to the gym to be fit – you can do all manner of things – but what's key is to be active, to walk lots, and try to get outside as much as possible.
- If you want to build muscle, lift weights/do resistance training.
- If you want a more muscular physique – with you having more muscle than you currently have, then the only way to do that is through regular and progressive resistance training. This is where joining a gym, getting a programme, and learning about this area would be key.
- If you have built muscle and just want to maintain it, know that maintaining it requires a lot less effort than building it. You might hit the gym 3–5 times a week to build muscle, but only 1–2 days a week to maintain it.
- Make fitness a simple part of your life. If you have only 10 minutes for something, cool, do that; it's *far* better than nothing.
- Know the benefits of weight training for slowing down the physical effects of ageing from strength, muscle, and bone density loss
- Value your flexibility and know the key stretches that keep you feeling and moving well. Do them regularly.
- If you have never been through a phase in life where you have tried to push your body and seen what it's capable of, do. I think it's a waste to never find out.
- See the value in fun and recreation-style activities, like hiking, playing soft sports, and generally moving with others, in both a competitive and non-competitive way.

- Outside of the things we know to be of benefit, exercise for the goal or outcome you want. Specificity is key.
- Exercise reduces the chances of lifestyle-related diseases such as type 2 diabetes, stroke and osteoarthritis. Value it to help you age well.
- Get the balance right and make exercise an enjoyable part of your lifestyle.
- Exercise for a love of your body, not out of hate for your body and how it looks.

Use this note-taking section to jot down your thoughts after reading this chapter. What have you gained? How are you closer to living your Awesome Life?

_____

_____

_____

_____

_____

_____

_____

_____

You are what you eat

Approach

Water

Environment

Sleep

Organize

Movement

Eat

Lifestyle

Inspiration

Finances

Education

'Let food be thy medicine and medicine be thy food.'

Hippocrates

If there is one goal I want to achieve as a result of this chapter, it's that you feel you can have (or at least work towards having) a good relationship with food after reading it. Nutrition is one of the areas that I am most qualified in, and I've spent a large chunk of my career working around it. I've focused so much of my work in nutrition because of the power it's had in my own life as well as that of so many of my clients. Exercise gets a lot of attention and focus in the world of health and fitness, and while it's important, I don't feel it's as important as what we eat:

- It can affect our energy levels.
- It can increase or decrease our chances of lifestyle-related diseases.
- It can, short term, give us symptoms like bloating or fatigue.
- It can alter the health of our hair, skin and nails.
- It has the power to make us lose or gain weight.

It affects a lot. But I don't want this to alarm you; I want this to excite you. Most people I work with don't need to change a huge amount when it comes to what they eat. So much of nutrition is about being organized, valuing what you eat, and what it can do for your body, knowing what and how to cook, how to structure a meal and why, and being relaxed about it when you want to eat what you want at a restaurant or other social situation and enjoy yourself.

No secrets

And the best thing about nutrition? It's actually simple. Now that doesn't mean it's always easy, I appreciate and honour that, but it is simple. The people selling diets and systems online want to you to believe nutrition is difficult and that there's some magic, secret plan out there for you if you pay £39.99. But there are no secrets. Trust me.

There are, however, a few things we have to get right:

1. Value eating well and what it can give to your body.
2. Be organized with your weekly food shop, and make time to cook and prepare what's needed (or be willing to buy a lot of pre-prepared healthy food!).
3. Know how to cook a good array of healthy foods, not just for yourself but also for your family and friends.
4. Approach nutrition in a relaxed way – something I often frame to my clients (as do many other nutrition coaches I know) as the 80/20 rule: 80 per cent of the time eat well, eat good healthy, natural foods; 20 per cent of the time eat what you want, while being mindful of moderating how many calories you might consume with this 20 per cent.

I use the word 'moderation' in this last 'rule' because moderation is a must if you want to maintain your weight or at least don't want to be fighting your weight down week on week. Many people, for example, struggle with the weekends, eating sensibly during the week only to go all out at the weekend. By all means enjoy the weekend, relax, enjoy food with friends and family, but if you always choose to go to town on that takeaway menu, expect to be frustrated come Monday when you have put on one or two pounds and feel you need to work harder than you want to in the week to balance it out, again. If we moderate the 20 per cent a little better, then we might not be chasing our tail (weight) all the time.

This is why I opened this chapter with my number one goal regarding nutrition – having a good, healthy relationship with food – because, when you do, food becomes fun, enjoyable, and serves both our overall physical health and mental wellbeing. A lot of this comes down to good old-fashioned education. If you get to know fact from fiction when it comes to nutrition, you'll be empowered to make the right choices. And this is why I'll aim to make this chapter as simple as humanly possible to implement. Just because I am a nutritionist and know a lot about food, it doesn't mean this chapter is going to be *War and Peace on Food*!

So, let's jump into the science of food and explore what we know to be true, a little of what's in the grey area of not-quite-known, and what's outright fiction.

'Which diet is best?'

This is a *very* common question, and I get why. First, let's try to shake off the word 'diet' because it mostly indicates a short-term approach to eating to lose weight, to then go back to how we were eating before, often putting the weight back on again. So, let's ditch the diet mentality and find a way to eat that works for you long term, and optimises the vessel you have been born into, that beautiful and unique human body of yours. We'll start by looking at a common goal: fat loss.

When it comes to fat loss, all diets work in the same way. They aim to create a situation where you end up eating fewer calories than your body uses on a daily basis, causing weight loss because your body is forced to make up the 'calorie deficit' with stored energy, ideally from fat. So, whether you go on the 5:2 diet, go keto, eat the Zone Diet®, go low fat or paleo, or go to a slimming club, the result in terms of fat loss is the same: you eat less and you burn body fat.

Do some diets make you lose weight quicker or more than others? Yes, but there are several nuanced reasons for this. Some diets are higher in protein, which reduces muscle loss, so if your diet is low in protein you might get more weight loss from muscle mass loss. If you eat a higher protein diet you're also likely to eat fewer calories due to the filling nature of protein-containing foods, too (notice a lot of fad diets that promise fat loss without calorie-counting ask you to eat a lot of protein!) You might lose more water weight and glycogen (stored carbohydrate, a good thing used for exercise) initially if you are on a low-carb diet, and thus see more weight loss on the scales. Some diets are easier than others to stick to.

But despite these very small variations in diets, over a six-month period of following whatever diet, the outcome will largely be the same: all diets will lead to pretty much the same outcome given a long enough time period – you'll lose fat if you stick to it, and you won't if you don't.

So if we know this, the next question shouldn't still be: 'OK, I hear you, but which diet is best?' It should be: 'What does the human body need to get from nutrition?'

What is a healthy diet?

Coming back to the research and what is broadly associated with the best health outcomes (at least in terms of metabolic disorders like type 2 diabetes[25] and cardiovascular disease[26], and various cancers[27]), a fairly clean picture emerges. When diets are compared, we generally see that a Mediterranean approach to nutrition seems best. So let's look at what food the Mediterranean diet generally contains.

The Mediterranean-style diet is based around what was likely to be eaten around the coastal areas of the Mediterranean prior to global trading. It's typically considered to be based around:

- bread, rice, pasta and other whole grains
- pulses
- vegetables
- fruit
- nuts and seeds
- olive oil and olives as the main source of fat
- small amounts of whole-fat dairy
- moderate amounts of fish
- small amounts of white and minimal red meat
- herbs and spices
- wine, specifically red wine

That would be the bulk of the diet, or at least 80 per cent of it. And alongside this, there would be a relaxed approach to living: people would get outside a lot and be in the sun, be active in a normal everyday kind of way (not hitting the gym, but just being active), and value family and connection.

It's a very relaxed, balanced, healthy way of life in the Med. Maybe it's one of the reasons it's such a popular holiday destination. But that doesn't mean we can't do the same if we live somewhere different. The benefits of this style of eating are very well supported.

Remember, provided we have the resources to hand we can make our diet pretty much however we want. I'm not saying your diet should look exactly like the above. You might choose, for example, to eat vegan and thus cut out the animal products, or know you are intolerant to cows' dairy and so choose to avoid that. You might choose a higher protein approach to support a larger amount of exercise. That's fine. All I am trying to do here is look at arguably the most well-established answer to the question 'What should we eat?'.

The best approach here is possibly to look not at *The Mediterranean Diet* but to look at what underpins it: Lots of plants, lots of variety, plenty of monounsaturated fats (from fish, olive oil and nuts/seeds), and some amount of moderation when it comes to red meat. These are principles we can use without turning them into restrictive *rules.*

I'm not here to tell you what to eat. You are your own person and it's you who chooses what your diet consists of, but I'd like to think that we can start to firm up on what your food intake should look like for the best health outcomes, whether you choose to eat plant-based, keto, low fat, or just kind of normal and balanced. So, let's all agree: the diet we should eat should probably consist of *80 per cent-plus real, whole, natural foods* – wherever you live, whatever culture you have been born into, regardless of what foods you are used to eating, if having a healthy body is a priority.

How many calories does your body need? Doing the maths

Now we've shaken hands on this, we can look at what your *particular* body needs, and to help, I'll use myself as an example. I currently, at the time of writing this, weigh 82kg and have roughly been this weight for a long time, so I know and understand my needs well as I've been eating for my body weight for over 10 years.

How To Live An Awesome Life

We can make very rough calorie calculations from a person's body weight. So I am 82kg. We then take this and multiply it by 22 if you're a woman, and by 24 if you're a man (the difference is due to the greater proportion of muscle mass in men than women). So . . .

$$82 \times 24 = 1,968 \text{ calories}$$

This is the amount of calories my body would need if I were to lie in bed all day and do nothing. We call this our Basal Metabolic Rate (BMR) (for more accurate calculations, you can use the detailed calculator linked to at the end of this section). On top of this we then need to add calories according to the amount of activity we do daily, averaged out across the week. We do this using what we call an activity multiplier. These multipliers are as follows:

You are generally sedentary day to day and work a fairly
  sedentary job   × 1.2
You actively try move in your day, maybe hitting 10,000 steps
  per day   × 1.375
You actively hit 10,000 steps per day and exercise three hours
  a week   × 1.55
You are highly active, working out most days for an hour-plus
                                                             × 1.725
You are highly active engaging in prolonged endurance activ-
  ities most days   × 1.9

Looking at these activity multipliers, we can see it's like feeding an engine. Our bodies need fuel, and it's our job to feed it adequately so we have energy and vitality and a stable weight.

In my day-to-day life right now I walk on average 10,000 steps per day and do 2–3 hours of cardio base training a week. So the 1.55 multiplier is the perfect starting point for me. I say 'starting point' for an important reason: none of this will ever be 100 per cent accurate. It's based on averages, so treat it as that – a starting point – and tweak it over time based on the results you experience. So if you started on 3100 calories but didn't lose weight over a 2–3-week period, you know the calculation is a bit off and you can then decide to drop another 10 per cent or so and see if that then allows you to lose weight. So for me the calculation is:

$$1968 \times 1.55 = 3050 \text{ calories}$$

What we then do is make this a *flexible window*. Your body will never burn X number of calories every day, so add and subtract around 100 calories either way. Based on how you feel, how much you move and a few other micro physiological factors, your body will burn calories within a calorie window – so, in my case, likely 2950–3150 calories per day. This works right up until you engage in far more activity than normal, then in my case it would be higher than 3150 calories. Let's say you go on a three-hour hike at the weekend: you might then burn an extra 1000 calories and thus need to eat extra that day, for example. However, if you move a very similar amount day to day or at least week to week with daily fluctuations, you can be safe in the knowledge that you are likely burning calories in a small range such as the above and can focus on being within that most days.

This focus on a window of calories gives flexibility and doesn't create so much anxiety around what we eat, which is something we definitely do not want. I also don't want you to feel like I am sending you off to count calories every day for the rest of your life; I'm not, because that's not stress-free living and eating.

What I am ensuring we talk about is what the human body needs, how it works, and how we get it to thrive. Once you've established a calorie window that works for your body's weight and activity levels, have spent a bit of time counting calories to learn what's in your food (which we'll cover shortly), then you can more or less leave the calorie counting alone safe in the knowledge that you know what you need to eat for your body's needs – unless you have a specific goal you want to focus on and optimize, in which case you might pick up dietary tracking again. Why? Because tracking data increases the chances of a more dependable outcome . . . you achieving your goal.

This is especially important when you are looking to lose body fat, which is a goal many have. All the above information and calculations have been focused on a calorie intake that simply aims to cater for your body's daily needs. So, if you do the above calculation and it turns out you need around 2800-3000 calories per day, that's for weight maintenance. If you want to lose bodyfat a good starting calorie deficit to aim for is around 15–25 per cent. Any more (over 25 per cent) and you might find you get hungry a lot and find dieting a chore, any less (5–10 per cent) and you might find the results slow and disheartening. You can eat in a larger or smaller deficit within this range, but bear in mind that the lower you go, the hungrier you'll get in return for faster progress. One useful tactic is to set a target that runs the full range, so if you calculate you need around 2500kcal per day, you could aim for between 2125 (15 per cent) and 1875 (25 per cent) calories, then eat to hunger on the day.

You can use a larger calorie deficit if you wish (over 25 per cent), just bear in mind the pitfalls of this, including significant hunger and potential muscle loss if you're not training very hard with weights (something that increases hunger and can reduce overall health).

If you were looking to gain weight (muscle), add approximately 10 per cent more calories per day to your diet to fuel the extra calories needed to build muscle.

I have written this all out for you so you can learn and understand this as much as possible in a simple way, but should you wish to get a fast track hand here and be guided through it a little more by video, here is an online calorie calculator I built to help people: https://awesomesupplements. co.uk/pages/calorie-calculator

Macronutrients

Above we've covered our weight and our calorie needs, now let's look at our macronutrient needs. Macronutrients are protein, fats and carbohydrate. We need a certain amount every day to thrive, and although we often look at most foods either as being a protein source, a fat source, or a carbohydrate source, everything you eat mostly has a combination of all three, just in varying proportions.

Protein is generally the benchmark we work from because we know the body has an essential need for it. The UK government recommends 0.75g per kilo of body weight per day. This is the level we need to hit as a minimum to ensure that our bodies suffer no negative effects. However, personally I don't deal in adequacy but in optimality. So, what *is* optimal?

This is a difficult question to answer fully, but typical intake recommendations range from around 1-1.2g of protein per kilogram of bodyweight[28] for the general population with low activity levels, to 1.6–2.2g per kilogram for resistance trained athletes who need protein to help muscle growth. Synthesizing this, if we were to take the activity brackets we used to work out our calorie needs, this would also be a half-decent guide for our protein needs as well:

- You are generally sedentary day to day and work a fairly sedentary job   0.8g/kg
- You actively try move in your day, maybe hitting 10,000 steps per day   1–1.2.g/kg
- You actively hit 10,000 steps per day and work out three hours a week   1.4–1.8 g/kg
- You are highly active, working out most days for an hour-plus   1.6–2 g/kg

This simple approach will see you get enough protein for your goals, basic physiological needs, and help you feel full, which many people struggle with especially when dieting.

In short, I recommend a moderate to high protein diet for most people who are active, as it generally fits most people's goals. Most people want to:

- lose/maintain lower body fat
- build lean muscle/tone up
- improve sports/gym performance and recovery.

This isn't an exact target, but a loose one, again keeping things flexible and stress free. Treat it like an 'ideal' rather than a daily must. If you drop a few grams short every now and then it won't be the end of the world, but if you can make a habit of hitting these (maybe slightly higher than usual) intakes, you'll come out well on the other side.

> Rules and principles keep us grounded: they guide us, but knowing how and where to be flexible gives us the freedom we want and need.

So we have our calorie needs for our body weight, we have our calorie needs for our daily activity levels, and we have an optimal range of protein to eat. But what about fat and carbohydrate? If you used the calorie calculator link above it would have told you about some rough targets for protein, carbohydrate and fat, but I want to make things simple and easy for you, while still being effective – if not more effective, and definitely more enjoyable. I would personally recommend calculating your calorie intake and tracking that for your goals (fat loss or muscle building), ensure you are eating enough protein for your goal and to stay full after meals within that calorie goal, and to then be flexible with your carbohydrate and fat intake based on your preference for how you like to eat (higher carb and lower fat, or lower carb and higher fat) and how food makes you feel. For example, some might have a high-carb meal and feel sleepy, if that's you make it low or moderate carb within your calorie needs for that meal and you'll hopefully find that ratio energizes you more.

Now just so you are aware of the calories contained in each macronutrient:

- Protein – 4 calories per gram
- Carbohydrate – 4 calories per gram
- Fat – 9 calories per gram
- Alcohol – 7 calories per gram.

I threw in alcohol as it's good to know: so if you were to drink a pint of beer, you would really just say, 'That's 230 calories', and be done with it. Again, let's keep things simple, because they should and need to be simple to work long term (alcohol also catches a lot of people out, especially at the weekend, it's an easy way for the calories to rack up).

The reason I am making this simple is both so you can easily follow it, but also because getting overly geeky with your macro-nutrient intake won't change the result unless you are an athlete and looking to drill down into the detail – at which point you should work with a sports nutritionist on this anyway. Tracking your overall calorie intake, knowing where your daily protein intake is roughly at, and then being flexible with your carbohydrate and fat intake will ensure you are accurate enough to get the result you want, but relaxed enough to enjoy your food and not make your diet a maths lesson. And once you become experienced with doing this, you can stop counting calories with your new nutrition knowledge guiding your forward, staying at a healthy weight, which we shall now cover.

Tracking calories

The easiest way to get on top of all this is to use a calorie tracking app. If the technology is there, why not use it? What I don't like people doing, though, is using technology to replace using your brain. It's important we engage with the process and learn from it. So when you track your diet, pay attention and learn from what you're doing! For example, if I put a tofu Thai green curry into a calorie tracking app and it spits out the protein, carbs, fat and total calories of that meal, I can then see what how many grams of each macronutrient that meal roughly contains, how that looks visually on my plate, and how much of my total calorie needs it meets, and then, crucially, use that knowledge long term (take a mental picture) so you don't have to spend every day counting calories – which isn't the goal here. That way in the future you can cook yourself a similar meal and know that if you eat roughly the same portion size you won't be too far off what you need. Yes, you won't be 100 per cent accurate, but likely accurate enough to track your diet with enough accuracy to maintain your weight. Counting calories for a period of time also allows you to see how all the little things add up, a beer here or their, a packet of crisps, a cup of tea with two sugars and two biscuits, a big dollop of mayo with dinner, adding avocado to your salad, these little things can catch up with you when they add up over the course of a day – and counting calories for a while brings your awareness to the calorie value of the things you eat, big and small. Writing this book now I don't count calories anymore unless I'm struggling to lose weight (if this is the case, I'll simply count my overall calorie intake to check I'm roughly eating around 3000 calories), as through the process of doing it a lot over the years I now know how to eat in a freestyle manner by visually looking at food and knowing what portions sizes are right for me, when to indulge a bit, and when to say no, which I can then just take a mental note of as I go throughout my days eating. Sometimes keeping a mental log of what you eat can be as simple as observing 'Ooh I'm going out for a big dinner tonight so I'll have a light lunch and try be as active as I can today.'

When I teach nutrition, which has been a big part of my career to date, it can be useful to think of tracking calories in four levels, each of which has its own place:

- Level 1: Freestyle your nutrition and eat freely.
- Level 2: Track your overall calorie intake.
- Level 3: Track your overall calorie intake and your percentage or amount of protein per day.
- Level 4: Track your overall calorie intake and all three macronutrients.

The above levels lead to you tracking differing amounts of data daily, and thus have varying levels of diet accuracy. In my experience, different people use each level for different aims. As an example, my usual approach with clients is to have them at level 3 for a month, or longer, depending on how quickly they are learning or depending on their goal, then, when they are aware of what X amount of protein looks like in a meal, how to achieve balance, and then what X number of calories looks like per day (their total daily calorie need) split across X number of meals/snacks, they then drop down to level 1 or 2. The good thing with spending time at level 3 or 4 is that you learn and can then drop down to level 1 or 2 knowing you have the skills to manage your weight and nutrition more confidently and competently. Dropping back to level 1 and freestyling (as I personally do with my nutrition now, unless I'm training for a specific goal and want to enhance the certainty of the outcome by tracking more data), you should now know what X number of calories looks like, what X amount of protein looks like, and having got into the swing of things it's now totally different from you doing level 1 the way you were before – uninformed, unaware, winging it. You are now aware and empowered from your time at levels 3 and 4. Level 4 tracking is then only something I tend to do with people with highly specific goals, such as athletes (whether professional or recreational), people wanting to engage in body building, or I sometimes use it to train people to understand what a certain percentage of carbohydrate and/or fat looks like in their diet, so we use it as a tool to get more specificity, or a better understanding of macronutrients.

I really don't want you to sit there thinking that I am asking you to track what you eat for life. I'm merely saying that learning about nutrition is an important life skill, and learning the basics about nutrition, the calories in the foods you eat, and how to structure a diet to reach your goals is important. You're not going to be able to learn how many calories are in common meals and foods you eat without tracking what you eat for a period of time and learning from the process. So I am asking you, at minimum, to learn the basics, track what you eat for a while, learn from that process, and then let that empower you when you come to freestyle your nutrition in the future – which should be the long term goal.

That's the place that I want you to get to. The only other time you would track what you eat at levels 2–4 is if you are working towards a specific goal and wanted to get a guaranteed outcome by tracking the numbers more closely. For example, if you were training for a marathon and you wanted to fuel yourself optimally and make your best stab at it, you would track how you are training, what you are eating at level 3 or 4, and probably a few other variables to ensure you maximize the outcome. You might also just jump from level 1 to 2 when on a diet, as just tracking the total amount of calories you eat every day is a sure-fire way to guarantee fat loss happens. Level 1 is freestyling, level 2 is tracking total daily calorie needs, so if you're unsure if you're eating in a calorie deficit every day you can guarantee the results at level 2, without worrying too much about your daily protein, fat or carbohydrate consumption – as being in a calorie deficit is the #1 most important thing for fat loss. Being at level 3 might just make it easier as keeping your protein up will keep you fuller for longer – which is super helpful when on a diet, but it's 100 per cent not necessary. Level 2 would suffice in terms of accuracy for the outcome.

Listening to your body's feedback

After we've taken the step of tracking calories, seeing how our nutrition stacks up, seeing what a 400/600/800/1000/12,000-calorie meal looks like, we can start to change things based on feedback we are getting from our body. Let's say you keep getting hungry or tired mid-morning. OK, why is this? Is the breakfast you're eating simply too small? Would a bigger breakfast see you through for longer? Maybe you like a small breakfast and just need to implement a mid-morning snack? Maybe you didn't eat enough the day before and your body is asking for more today to catch up? Maybe you are just hungry a lot at the moment because you are dieting? Maybe you had a meal that was too low in protein and fat and the high-carb nature of your breakfast saw your blood sugar shoot up and down a bit too quickly, and now you're hungry? Maybe it was too high fat a breakfast and you like a high-carb breakfast and it's left you feeling a little sluggish and you want to eat to try get the energy? Maybe you didn't sleep well last night and that's made you feel hungry?

Whatever you feel the answer is, just try something else and track the result. Keep tweaking things to find what works and optimizes your energy, your appetite, your exercise performance/how you feel when you exercise and, ultimately, your results. It's also important to notice if there are any foods causing an issue. If you have a food intolerance, consider fixing the issue over time, working with a gut health specialist if you think there is a prominent, wider issue. It can make a difference. I used to be intolerant to cows dairy and gluten when I was younger. Cows dairy used to give me eczema and make my asthma worse, and gluten used to make my ADHD much worse and would make me really drowsy after eating it. But I worked on my gut health, committed to doing it strictly for a good amount of time, and I've been fine eating gluten and dairy ever since.

Eating foods your body has an issue with isn't a good thing. If you value your health, you'll pay attention to what foods are causing an issue and look to remove them and fix the underlying issue, if there is one. This is an important step in seeking optimal health; otherwise your body is going through cycles of having increased levels of inflammation and exacerbating whatever symptoms you are experiencing. Please value your health, listen to the signs, and play around with what's causing an issue. Your long-term health deserves it.

If you are unsure of the effects a food might be having on you, then just cut it out for a few weeks as a little experiment and see how you feel. Is it really much of a hardship to remove dairy or gluten or alcohol or nightshades or whatever food (group) you feel is an issue to see if it has a positive effect on your health? Don't be scared to do little 30-day micro-experiments, adding something in or taking something away from your diet and seeing how it affects you. We are all a work in progress. Constantly go through 30-day experiments on yourself to see if certain things can optimize how you feel and perform. You can't write something off as 'not working' or 'useless' if you only did it for a few days, can you?

Back to food. Once we know how many calories we need, what we are aiming for when it comes to our protein, carb and fat intake, and we have started to play around with a calorie tracking app and analysing what we currently eat, we can move on. But before we do, I'd like to do a quick exercise:

Download a calorie tracking app right now, maybe MyFitnessPal or similar, and start to track what you eat for a week. Simply write down below what you see, learn and experience doing it. There is no time like the present to give this a go and start learning more about what you currently eat, before you have even decided to change anything:

_____

_____

_____

_____

_____

_____

_____

_____

_____

We don't eat calories, we eat food

Now, knowing that, ideally, we want to be eating at least 80 per cent natural wholefoods. This might mean you need to add to your recipe repertoire. You might know a good handful of healthy recipes but need some new ones to keep things varied and interesting. The good thing is that once you double your recipe repertoire, you'll likely be onto a winner and have more than enough recipes to cycle between and choose from. Hopefully, this inspires you to cook more and enjoy cooking new things, and over time your recipe repertoire will build. Ultimately, healthy food is amazing; we just need to be good at cooking it and to keep mixing things up.

One of the digital notes I keep on my phone is a list of breakfasts, lunches, snacks and dinners I like. I do this because, when I come to sit down to do the weekly food shop, I can scan through, think, 'Ah, I'd love to have X, Y and Z this week', and then organize adding that stuff to the food order (if the wife agrees, of course!) If you have a list of stuff you love, all you have to do is refer to it when building the weekly shop. And, as you keep adding to the list over time, things becomes easier and easier. One of the things my wife and I also do every week is to take turns to cook something new. We grab a recipe book, have a flick through, and simply give it a go that week on an evening when we know we'll have the time. This allows us to mix things up and keep adding to our recipe repertoire as a family. This whole approach allows us to be organized, continue to keep things fresh, and easily stay on top of our health and good eating, as a family.

To help you develop your own weekly list of meals, here's that digital list of meals I keep for reference on my smartphone – I'm not saying these are the best meals or the ones you should eat, they are just to give you an idea:

BREAKFAST

Home-made muesli with goat's milk or half yoghurt, half milk
Four eggs on sourdough toast with a piece of fruit or berries
Protein bar with a fruit smoothie
Bacon sandwich with a piece of fruit
Four scrambled eggs with onions, spinach and pesto
Oats with mashed banana, coconut, flax seeds and plant protein powder
Leftovers from the night before
Protein pancakes with fruit and yogurt on top
Feta cheese omelette with fried tomatoes and mushrooms
Bubble and squeak (from the weekend's roast veg) with four fried eggs
A protein bar with peanut butter on sourdough, plus a piece of fruit
Blueberries, homemade nut, seed and dried fruit mix, bran flakes, milk, protein bar

LUNCH

Sandwich or toastie (with deep filling), often with soup or fruit
Eggs and sourdough with smoked salmon, with fruit
Leftovers from night before (curry, chilli, cottage pie, pasta, etc.)
Jacket potato with filling (tuna/prawns/chilli)
Moroccan-style chickpea and couscous salad
Chunky mixed salad, often with feta cheese or chicken
Homemade chunky soup
Mini mezze of veg sticks, hummus, crusty bread, some halloumi cheese
Spicy chickpeas, onions and wilted spinach
Mexican eggs
Scrabbled eggs with rice, avocado, tomatoes and soy sauce

SNACKS

Protein bar
Fruit smoothie
A small portion of leftovers
Peanut butter oat bar
Half a sandwich
Veg sticks and hummus
Fruit with a handful of nuts
Homemade flapjack/granola bar
Protein shake with a piece of fruit
Berries with yoghurt
Scotch egg (my favourite snack!)

DINNERS

Baked salmon with lemon and roasted vegetables
Jacket potato with a topping and salad

Tofu/prawn/chicken Thai curry

Spanish one-pot chicken (chicken, rice, tomatoes, veg)

Homemade KFC chicken with corn, jacket potato and BBQ beans

Sausages, mash and peas

Cottage pie and braised cabbage

Mexican tacos/fajitas

Sweet-and-sour chicken

Hot-and-sour noodle soup with tofu or chicken thigh

Chicken or tofu mushroom ramen

Fishcakes and salad

Vegan sausages with roasted vegetables

Baked white fish with vegetable ragout

Marinated chicken thighs with sweet potato chips and salad

Meat and cheese board with crusty bread, pickles and veg sticks

Burgers with sweet potato chips and salad

Any Asian curry with rice/noodles, love them all

Roast dinner with *all* the trimmings

All the above meals are mostly homemade and have a lot of variety and influence from other cultures and their cooking. We occasionally get a takeaway, usually Indian, Turkish or Thai food, getting a good mix to share. And we *love* cooking a roast dinner with our family on Sunday, my favourite meal of the week.

I'd like to think none of the above sounds weird or different or challenging. It's pretty normal food cooked well using quality ingredients (local where possible), with plenty of vegetables, a core protein source, and a balance of carbohydrates and fats. They're dishes *all* the family love, too.

You might read the above and think something along the lines of, 'But I'm vegan!' Cool. Make up your list according to what your needs are! Whatever you choose, understand your body's needs, know what you like or want to eat or good meals that match your goal – such as leaner meals when trying to lose body fat, get organized, get cooking, all while making sure that food is an enjoyable, sociable, stress-free part of your life. Does this sound achievable? Like something you and the whole family can get behind? I hope so.

Key points to remember

- Value what nutrition can do for your health, energy and body composition.
- Eat good food 80–90 per cent of the time. Don't go so overboard with the remaining 10–20 per cent of non-optimal food but don't stress if you eat a big pizza sometimes. Everything in moderation, including moderation.
- The Mediterranean diet isn't just good, the traditional Mediterranean lifestyle is arguably one of the best for longevity and health, too. This is not only because of it's a fresh, natural approach to nutrition, but also because of the relaxed and connected way of living that often goes with it.
- Most people living in the world's 'blue zones' (of which Sicily in the Mediterranean has one) have a few things in common: an active lifestyle, low-stress approach, great community connections, and a diet consisting of a lot of wholefoods and an absence (or minimal amount) of highly processed foods.
- Try to eat a wide variety of foods to help your gut health. One study in 2018 found that those reporting that they ate over 30 plant foods per week had the healthiest and most diverse population of gut bacteria[29]. You may not need to go quite this high to gain benefit, but it does demonstrate that the more diverse the diet, potentially the more diverse

the microbiome. This wasn't explained in this chapter, I thought I would throw this in quick at the end!

- All diets work the same way: they cause you to eat fewer calories than your body needs daily, so if you want to lose body fat – eat fewer calories (around 15 per cent fewer calories is a good target to aim for), in a good, healthy, balanced way.
- Learn to cook well. Eating good food is so much easier when you know how to cook.
- Value good nutrition, not just for yourself but for your family.
- Understand your calorie need and track it for a while so you get a good understanding of what you should be eating. Adjust it for your goals, such as fat loss, maintenance, or muscle building / sports or gym performance.
- Understand the role of protein, carbs and fats in your diet and what a good balance between these looks like.
- Know what level (1–4) you need to be at to learn what you need to learn about food. Then try to settle back into level 1 or 2 and confidently manage your nutrition day to day.
- If you suspect you are having a bad reaction to a certain food, cut it out for 30 days and see how you feel. Then either remove the food longer term or work on your gut health/the underlying issue – working with a highly recommended, specialist, qualified practitioner in this area.
- Get to place where you and the family are all enjoying food and it's a healthy part of your life.

Want to learn more about nutrition?

Nutrition is the topic I have the most information on 'out there' as it's the field I've worked in for the longest. There are lots of additional resources and cheat sheets at www.theschoolofawesome.co.uk/member, my podcast 'Ben Coomber Radio' which I have run for over nine years with over 20 million downloads to date has a lot of nutrition-focused shows – a show you can find wherever you listen to podcasts, and my nutrition education company The BTN Academy is the place to go if you want to study nutrition in a more formal way https://btn.academy/ we even offer a free nutrition short course available to all on the website.

Use this note-taking section to jot down your thoughts after reading this chapter. What have you gained? How are you closer to living your Awesome Life?

_____

_____

_____

_____

_____

_____

_____

_____

_____

Live the lifestyle

Approach

Water

Environment

Sleep

Organize

Movement

Eat

Inspiration

Finances

Education

> 'Life is the most difficult exam. Many people fail because they try to copy others, not realising that everyone has a different question paper.'
>
> **Marvin Walters**

At this point in the book, it's time to up the excitement. It's time to ask yourself: 'How do I want to truly live my life?'

If you could create your perfect life, what would it look like?

- What would you be doing?
- What job would you have?
- How much would you work?
- How would you split your time?
- What would you do at the weekend?
- Where would you go on holiday?
- What would you say yes to, and what would you say no to?

I bet you know what I am about to say: you can have it all.

The important questions are: first, are you going to believe it's possible, and second, are you going to take action to achieve it?

Many people have what you want. They have had the vision to create it and created a plan to achieve it (I say 'a' plan, not 'the' plan, as there are many ways to achieve a goal). They have built up the courage and confidence to go take action, consistently showed up – even when it gets tough to keep going, and have surrounded themselves with the right kind of people to help make it happen. They have continued to believe it's possible . . . and, in the end, got there.

This chapter will aim to achieve two things:

1. to set out a vision for how you want your lifestyle to be
2. to live the lifestyle that will take you there.

As ever, I am not going to tell you how you should live your life; only you can do that. All I can do is share some stories, show you what's possible, and guide you through the process of achieving your goals.

Your perfect day

Let's start with a quick exercise. Write below what your *perfect day* would look like. Don't overthink it; just write what you would do if you could wake up tomorrow wherever and do whatever. Go on, write it now . . .

_____

_____

_____

_____

_____

_____

_____

_____

_____

Now reading that back to yourself you're probably dreaming of waking up and having your perfect day tomorrow, and so you should take a moment to dream, BUT:

1. Not many of us really want every day to be the same.
2. We all have real-world responsibilities to attend to.
3. Most of us, at least for a while, need to do some kind of work.

Most people who do this exercise describe a day that's as if they are on holiday. Thus, their perfect day often looks something like this:

1. Wake up to a nice sunny day in Mexico.
2. Go for a walk on the beach, then for a swim/surf/do some yoga.
3. Have [insert favourite breakfast] with [insert favourite person or family members].
4. Leave to go to [insert a really cool activity, like swimming with turtles].
5. Have a Mexican buffet lunch in the mountains with ice-cold beers.
6. In the afternoon go [insert another fun/thrilling activity, like climbing up a Mayan pyramid].
7. Go for a sunset swim/walk on the beach.
8. Have amazing sex.
9. Go out for an incredible five-course dinner.
10. Dance the night away on cocktails and wish it would never end.

This is amazing, but it isn't often our reality. Yet something like it can be; we just need to tweak our perspective on things and break down what it is about this perfect day that you want more of in your life.

So, if I was to break apart that perfect day into each step and draw from it what I think people want (and, to be honest, what

I want in my life), we can start to find the underlying desire that may be there, allowing us to work out what we *really* want from life. This is important because it's hard to make a plan when you don't really know the destination.

Wake up to a nice sunny day in Mexico.

We all love good weather. We all love sunny exotic locations. Most of us love to travel. We all dream of what new and exciting places will be like. Most of us like a sense of adventure.

So, what I think we want more of in our lives as a result of this statement is: more travel, more time for fun, more time to explore the world, to experience more good weather, and, of course, to have the money to do it.

Go for a walk on the beach, then for a swim/surf/ do some yoga.

Most of us want to have the time to be in nature, to be immersed in beauty, to have the time to wander carefree, to be active, to have time for leisure activities, and to do it all in lovely places.

So, what I think we want more of in our lives as a result of this statement is: to be or be close to lovely places to explore, and to have the time to do it.

Have [insert favourite breakfast] with [insert favourite person or family members].

Most of us want to eat well, to eat healthily, be cooked for like we are in a hotel, and to enjoy this with people we love.

So, what I think we want more of in our lives as a result of this statement is: good food, good people, and the time to enjoy it.

Leave to go to [insert a really cool activity, like swimming with turtles].

Most of us want to experience life and all it has to offer, to do cool things, to have good memories, to explore the world, to tick things off the bucket list.

So what I think we want more of in our lives as a result of this statement: adventure, travel, freedom, and to have the money to do it.

Have a Mexican buffet lunch in the mountains with ice-cold beers

Again, we all want good food, in great locations, with good people.

So, what I think we want more of in our lives as a result of this statement is: good food and people, variety, culinary adventures, new experiences.

In the afternoon go [insert another fun/thrilling activity, like climbing up a Mayan pyramid].

The same can be said here as for the morning activity: we want fun, adventure, and the freedom to experience life.

Go for a sunset swim/walk on the beach

We often want to end our day in a calm way, to feel that we are winding down from the day's adventures, have peace in our hearts, and be with people we love.

So, what I think we want more of in our lives as a result of this statement is: freedom and peace; to see great sunsets, to be in nature, to feel the breeze of the sea on our faces.

Have amazing sex

Need I say more?

Go out for an incredible five-course dinner

Again, we all want to experience life through good food, ideally shared with people; it's an amazing part of life.

Dance the night away on cocktails and wish it would never end

We all want to laugh, to dance carefree like no one is watching, to perhaps lose yourself in the haze of a few drinks, to be with good people, to have real fun and feel like it will never end.

So, what I think we want more of in our lives as a result of this comment is: carefree fun, to express ourselves, to have the option to have a few drinks without anything to worry about, to have no concept of time or responsibilities.

Now this perfect day does happen: it happens when we go on holiday, where we live it up and go big on life. If we want our life to be more like a holiday, however, it probably means we are far from being happy with where our day-to-day life is right now. What we really want is our real, everyday lives to be perfect. So, the real trick isn't to turn your everyday life into perfection, but to bring some of that perfection into your everyday life. What if every week or month you had more walks on the beach, or ate out more, or did more fun leisure activities, or went and danced carefree more, or played more golf or tennis, or saw your family more, or swam more?

Whatever your idea of perfection, is it really that far away? Couldn't we get more of this perfection if we were more organized, planned ahead, said no to things we don't want to do and YES to more of what we want to do, or maybe just packed a bit more into our day? I think we can, let's break apart life and see what we can optimize . . .

Getting more out of your time and work

If we work on average 40 hours per week, which most of us do, allowing maybe 5 hours for commuting, what are you doing with the other 47 hours in your week when you are not working and not sleeping? If you have kids, then you are probably spending a good chunk of it with them. But don't use that as an excuse to stop doing this exercise. If you want more of all that perfection in your life, what over time has to change for you to facilitate that?

- Do you have to work less? Or work closer so there is less of a commute? Or have a job that is more flexible with its working hours?
- Do you simply have to be more organized? Plan further in advance? Think of the things you want to do and plan it into your diary?
- Do you have to get up earlier, or go to bed earlier, or both?
- Do you need more money, or to change how you spend it?
- Do you need to shift your mindset to what's possible?
- Do you need to move house so you are closer to the things you want to do?
- Do you need to say no to stuff you don't care for anymore to create more time in your day?
- Do you need to get the kids involved in the stuff you love so you can do it with them?

- Do you need to get a bit more childcare or swap responsibilities around so you can get more time to do some of this stuff?
- Do you need to get more disciplined with yourself and your screen time?

My point here is that so much of that perfection is more achievable than most think. What if we were all spending our time doing the stuff we enjoy doing, including work?

Most people's idea of the perfect day doesn't include work – it rarely does – but for now, for 99 per cent of us, real life has to include some work, so if you were to work on that perfect day, what would you be doing, and why? Write it down below.

_____

_____

_____

Is there any reason you can't work towards doing that job? You would be living a better, more fulfilling life if you were in that line of work, right? What's stopping you from doing it? Write it down.

_____

_____

_____

Is that really stopping you from doing it? Can you make a one-, three- or five-year plan to get into that line of work or

---

into that position? Could there be a job that's a half-way house between what you do now, and what you ideally want to do? Could it even just be time for a change, a new challenge?

I bet you can make a change with your work, for it to be more positive and rewarding. The question is: are you going to be brave and bold enough to do it, even if you need to spend an hour a week slowly getting yourself into that position to make the career jump?

Work makes up a huge part of most people's adult life, so personally I can't for the life of me fathom why people do jobs they dislike. I get it. We get comfortable, change can be tough and tiresome, we can get used to having a good income in a job we don't like and don't want to give up the pay check, or we don't feel we deserve better.

But we do. You do. I do. We all deserve to do work we enjoy and that brings us purpose, just like we all deserve to be living a good, fulfilling, happy life.

The question is, are you going to join me in creating it?

My perfect day

As I write this book this is how I am living my life:

- I work roughly 25–35 hours per week, roughly 9–4 Monday, Tuesday, Thursday and Friday, with a few early mornings if I'm up before the kids with extra time for a spot of work. Sometimes I'll do shorter days and move it around a bit, but I keep it flexible to work around family life, the weather, and things that crop up, all while being around for key business meetings.

- I look after my eldest daughter on a Wednesday for half the day and we try have as much fun as possible – going swimming, going for walks, and just exploring life together (with me working part of the day, often when she naps).
- We eat out most weekends or have family over and cook big meals and have big laughs.
- We go on three to five family holidays a year, and I travel for work on occasion when good opportunities come up.
- I exercise/make time for myself four times per week, 4–5pm, and get a 'me time' slot at the weekend, too, as my wife knows I need alone time to recharge my mental and emotional batteries.
- I cook a new recipe most weeks.
- I read lots in my free time, often when I wake up early, but always before bed – a mixture of books, audiobooks when I'm out walking, or email newsletters.
- We get out and walk us much as possible, whether it's a 30-minute local walk, or a two- to three-hour trip out at the weekend.
- I do work I love, work that challenges me, that I feel has an impact on others.
- I have the money to have the freedom I currently wish to have – which was an early goal in my career.

What I'm getting at is we can all get more of that perfection in our weekly/monthly lives with planning, forethought and commitment to the goals we have.

- Could you make a little more time to walk in nature more?
- Could you make more of your weekends?

- Could you spend less on X, so you can spend more on good food or going on adventures?
- Could you swap jobs, or work from home, or change your working hours?
- Do you really want to commit to that new spend – let's say a new car – when really what you want more from in life is fun, adventure and travel?

I don't know what it is you want more of specifically, but when I coach people, they tend to say they want a bit more fun, adventure and excitement in their lives, that things have got mundane, that it's all about work, adult responsibilities, family, sleep, repeat, and that they feel meh, stuck, uninspired, flat.

So, let's fix that. Let's stop with the excuses, stop spending money on stuff we don't want or need, and start pouring our attention, money and time into the things we *really* want to do in life.

One of the best things I ever did in my life was go 'all in' to this career path of helping others with their goals, and then start my own business. I always wanted to do work with purpose and meaning and to feel like I was having an impact. And I have always, since a young age, valued freedom. And owning my own business – to an extent – gives me that. I wanted to do things on my terms, in my way, and to constantly explore my curiosity with work. So, I started my own business and have never looked back since.

It's not for everyone. Being a business owner can be really tough at times as it's ultimately all on you, but if you feel you have it in you to be an entrepreneur, you have to scratch that itch or you will forever regret it.

One of my companies is called the BTN Academy, and is a nutrition education company. We train hundreds of people every year to be nutrition coaches. And lots of the students that graduate go on to set up small side businesses where they coach people outside their normal job, at evenings and week-ends. This works for them, and it gives them a taste of what working for yourself could be like. And that's a good thing.

- So, if you're interested in coaching others, maybe try doing a bit part time?
- If you're into sports, what about teaching on two evenings a week?
- If you're into painting, what about doing more and selling it online on Etsy?
- If you're good at maths and spotting trends, what about investing and trading in your spare time?
- If you're really into cooking, what about creating a recipe book and trying to sell it, or get a publishing deal like I did?
- If you are a good photographer, why not do ten weddings each summer as a side hustle?

Who knows what it is you want and could try to do. My only point here is this . . .

TRY IT.

What have you got to lose?

Life phases and planning

When discussing living your dream life and painting a picture of your future, I've made it sound a bit easy, right? As if we just tweak a few things and hey presto, it's sorted, we're living the dream. For some of you reading this book it could be easy, for some it might take a lot longer, and that's fine. Don't be put off just because some of the changes might take some time – that's not a reason not to do something. Life is long, whatever you are thinking of doing or want, it's *so* worth it, even if you're 50, because you've likely still got more than 20 years ahead of you as yet. Also know that what you want from life will change as you age, what I wanted at 20 and then 30 and then when I had kids were very different, but I still planned for what I wanted, executed on it, and was always glad I did the work to put myself in the position I wanted to be in.

Now as a side note, it is no lie that all this change is harder with kids: they are an unknown entity, there is far more chaos in my life now than before, and time is less easy to control. But again that's not to say it's not possible with kids – it 100 per cent is – but you just have to be more patient and go at a pace your life allows, even if it's slower than most want (which I very much struggled to adjust to in the early days, but am much better at now, and it is easier once your kids grow up and they are out of the baby and toddler phases).

When it comes to planning, when did it start for me?

Around the age of 20 is when I really started to plan my life. I started to envisage how I wanted every stage to be, anticipate what those phases in my life would need, and do the work to make it happen. At age 21 I went to university and knew it was a time in my life that could be fun, rewarding and full of opportunity. So, I created the perfect environment to capitalize on that. I made the most of my time at university, getting up early but partying 'til late whenever I wanted. I put my hand up for every opportunity that came our way on the uni course I was on. I studied hard to learn and get good grades. I always had several part-time jobs so I was never short on money to do things. I worked abroad during the summers so I could get away, travel and experience the world while earning money at the same time. I just went 'all in' on university life.

As I then transitioned to work life full-time after getting my degree, I was already planning what I wanted the next five years to be like. I wanted to climb to the top of the ladder in my field. So, I started to map out what I would need to do to achieve this. I had started my second business by this point and was working hard to network and meet people in my industry. I started to 'put myself out there' online so I could build awareness and a brand around what I did. I started to speak at industry events. I started a podcast. I hustled my way to the top. I did this because I knew it would create the freedom and stability to have a strong business and personal brand, but I also wanted to prove to myself I could do it, and I enjoyed doing it.

At 30 I started to enter the next phase of life planning – the family phase. I knew I wanted kids in my mid-thirties, so started to make plans with my finances and my time so that when I reached that point and had kids, I would be in the exact position I wanted to be. And I sit here in that position now. As you saw above, I work four days a week now, have enough financial stability that we have a nice home, can go on holiday a lot, everyone has what they want and need, and my wife can choose not to work and just be a mum, which is what she always wanted.

The next phase of my life is to create a bit more time and financial freedom, to build our dream home, to take my work to the next level with this book, to execute a few cool new ideas I have in the world of education, and to travel and go on adventures with my family. I'm dreaming, I'm planning and, importantly, I'm taking action.

If you have a vision for your life then plan for the outcome, but importantly, take action on the plan. You too can have what you want. I did, and I do. And it didn't happen by accident. All of it was planned for and had the right work put into it. And I feel grateful and proud of myself for doing it. I feel honoured to be able to write this book and try inspire others to do the same. Don't be scared to dream big too. I think it's motivating to dream big. It gets you hungry to achieve things and I love pushing myself to see what's possible. It's fun. It's me and you playing the great game of life.

Where are you in life?

- What life phase are you now entering?
- What plans do you want or need to create for yourself?
- How long will it realistically take?
- What resources don't you have, that you need to find?
- What do you not know that you need to find out how to do?
- And, importantly, are you willing to do the work?

I hope so, because you deserve it, and that's the whole purpose of this book, for you to create your most Awesome Life.

I hope at this point I've got you thinking, dreaming and scheming. If so, good. Write down your thoughts. Don't let them escape you . . .

_____

_____

_____

Key points to remember

- Ask yourself how you truly want to live your life, and know it can happen if you find the way and do the work.
- The perfect day every day doesn't exist, but how you imagine your perfect day can be scattered throughout your weeks, months and years far more than it is now.
- Maybe it's time to change your job, or your working hours, or how flexible your work is, so you can do more of what you love.
- Say no to all the stuff you don't want to truly do, and say yes to more of the stuff you love to do.
- Plan the stages of your life and how you want them to play out. And work to bring things in to line so you can live that phase of your life just as you envisage.

Use this note-taking section to jot down your thoughts after reading this chapter. What have you gained? How are you closer to living your Awesome Life?

_____

_____

_____

_____

_____

_____

_____

_____

_____

A spark of inspiration

Approach

Water

Environment

Sleep

Organize

Movement

Eat

Lifestyle

~~Inspiration~~

Finances

Education

> 'People inspire you or they drain you – pick them wisely.'
>
> Hans F. Hansen

In life you never know where inspiration is going to come from, so instead of waiting for it, go find it.

This is a secret of highly successful and fulfilled people – they don't wait for inspiration, they don't wait for bolts of lightning, they don't sit there wishing things would be different; they make things different, they get inspired, they seek it out and constantly try things – and you need to do the same. We all get caught in the habit loop of life, struggling to jolt ourselves out of a rut. We periodically get beaten down by bad life experiences such as illness, a pandemic or a job loss and feel as though getting back to our old self seems unreachable.

But that's just another crappy story we tell ourselves. Life can be awesome again, but it takes sparks of inspiration, and not just one or two, but continually, often daily.

Think of the power of music to make you feel good and put a beat in your step . . .

Think of the power of a good friend who gives you sage pieces of advice to spur you on . . .

Think of the power of a good workout to make your body feel strong and alive again . . .

Think of the power of an awesome book to give you strategies to live better . . .

Think of the power of a good holiday to reset you, give you space and perspective, and re-charge you . . .

Think of the power of a motivational seminar to get you refocused again on what's important in your life . . .

Think of the power of a fitness challenge to focus your energy into reaching a new level of fitness and maybe supporting a good cause in the process . . .

Think of the power of simply getting a good night's sleep and eating well . . .

We can CHOOSE to empower and inspire ourselves, but seeking out the environments, messages and stimuli that will give us this spark, over and over, is key. It won't happen by accident.

The inspiration chain reaction

Many people assume that you are either 'an inspired person', someone who has been blessed with inspiration from the Gods, or has had some kind of experience that enables you to focus time, energy and passion into certain things, or you're not, that inspiration just isn't something you're destined to have.

Sure, the 'inspiration falls out of nowhere' thing happens to some: some people are born into really inspirational environments or have very inspirational parents; others have had things happen to them in life that have inspired them to do great work or help great causes. But for the rest of us – that's you and me – we need to regularly find things that inspire us.

And that OK, that's normal, and we need and must to do it purposefully. Inspiration doesn't just happen, just like we can't rely on motivation to get us to do many things we must do in life – because it's fleeting. We must work at it, like anything in life. It's a practised behaviour.

My own inspired journey started with me choosing to radically change my body, the way I looked and the way I felt about myself. This body transformation saw me go from obese, unhealthy and unhappy, to fit, confident and athletic. A new me, an inspired, motivated and capable me. This is what big challenges can start for us: they can start a chain reaction in us that inspires us to push for more, to think bigger, and see what we are truly capable of.

Let's look at my own inspired journey a little more closely, to see how this chain reaction might happen for you. When I started my fat loss journey there were times I could feel my energy waning. There are always bumps and challenges in any journey, and after a few dips I decided to make myself accountable to a *big* goal to mark the end of this part of my journey. I signed up for the Tough Mudder UK event, which in 2004 was one of the hardest adventure races in the UK. It was 18 miles up hills, over obstacles, down giant slides, carrying logs through rivers, going through underground pipes filled with water and more. I signed up because I knew I had to continue on my journey, and that, if I got over that finish line, I would show myself just how strong, fit and capable I had become. I ran the race in just under five hours and crossed the finish line in bits, having sprained both ankles twice on the run (but I was never not going to finish even if I crawled over the line).

That event inspired me to do more, to *be* more. It had showed me what I was capable of.

My time didn't matter. Anyone else running that race that day didn't matter to me. I was there for myself, to run my race, to show myself what I could do. That day was an inspiration for me, and I've sought days, events and experiences like that ever since:

- I've attended many educational and motivational events on fitness, health, mindset, business and life, some in the UK, some abroad.
- I've mastered cold therapy out in nature with ice baths
- I've done charity challenges that see me hit a fitness milestone for a good cause.
- I've joined business masterminds, groups of people who have been successful/trying to be more successful, to get

insight and support into the next level I am striving for in business.

- I've travelled the world to far-flung places to experience different cultures, often on my own, just to see how people there do the things I do.
- I've attended therapy to see how and where I can optimize myself and release demons I might have.
- I have gone on retreats aimed at uncovering layers of my potential.
- I've done wild things like skydiving and riding on plane wings.

Pair this with weekly doses of inspiration from books, people, videos, podcasts, workouts, good food, sleep, walks in nature, and there's more than enough to keep those sparks of inspiration coming – but now and again I do need a big reset to get focused for myself, what I want for my life, and to get perspective. Because of this I often take, even as a parent now, a holiday on my own for a week to get this for myself. I and my wife know it helps me continue to be the best version of myself. I also use it as a writing holiday to write things such as this book. And throughout the year I take days off to be by myself to get mini-breaks to recharge – as at heart I'm an introvert and need time alone to recharge my state of mental and emotional health. This also doesn't have to be expensive, the last trip away I took cost £3–400 as I went and stayed with a friend in Portugal, so it only cost me my travel and spending money while I was there. Days out and away could just be for a long hike, some swimming, and lunch out, travel and adventure doesn't have to cost a lot.

Inspiration lows . . . and how to get out of them

It is totally human to read this book, feel inspired and motivated for three months, and then have a bad patch and feel that inspiration slip. What's the antidote? To get re-inspired, of course. Maybe you come back to this book and read through all the goals you wrote down. Maybe you pick up a different book. Maybe you meet up with a good friend who always supports you. Maybe you join a new fitness club. Maybe you set yourself a challenge. Maybe you find a good motivational video on YouTube. Maybe you just need a few days off as work and life has been a bit intense recently. Maybe you got ill, stopped working out and you just need to get back into the swing of it again. Maybe you need a *big* reset and need to go on holiday or on a retreat to get re-inspired.

Who knows what you need; it doesn't matter. Just go get your fix, get inspired and keep getting inspired. And in the future plan those sparks into your year so your inspiration tank doesn't drop so low that you experience a lack of progress for too long.

After a sustained period battling with long COVID, I'm sitting here right now feeling like my own inspiration tank is around 70 per cent. It was at an all-time low recently, but a holiday alone in Portugal to write the first draft of this book has begun to fill me up again. Much better, but I feel I need more. I know I am not at 100 per cent and I want to get back there. So this is my action plan:

1. Slowly build back up my fitness now I am well again.
2. Meet up with like-minded business friends again.
3. Take the next step in my business I've been itching to take and hire the people my business needs to take another layer of responsibilities off me.

4. To plan a big crazy thing! It's been too long . . . I'm thinking of paragliding!

It's a mini plan which I think will work, and if it doesn't, or I feel I need to add something else in, I will.

Whatever it is you feel you need to do to be inspired, do it. And if you don't know, just try stuff. Saying you don't know what will inspire you isn't an excuse; sure it's a reason, but the more you try things, the more you work out what it is that works for you and what doesn't.

During the COVID-19 pandemic of 2020–21 when I was recovering from long Covid, I started researching and doing cold therapy after being recommended it by a respected practitioner friend. It involves controlling your breath and state of mind in very cold water for one to five minutes, and aside from it having a profound effect on my health and recovery from long COVID, it has also had a profound effect on my mental health and state of mind. I found that being submerged in that cold water, with my nervous system going wild, sharpened my mind and stopped any negativity I had in a flash. It was profound. I loved it. Sure, it wasn't easy getting into my swim shorts and jumping into an ice bath in my garden when it was 2 degrees outside in the middle of winter, but it was SO worth it. The after-effects, the way I felt, the impact on my health . . . just WOW! And to this day I still have a blast of a cold shower most days (a 60-second blast after my normal shower), as I love the feeling it brings, the strength it gives me, and the benefits research is now starting to uncover with cold water therapy.

The lesson here, just TRY things. What are others doing that they find cool, motivating and inspiring? Just give it a go, see if the same works for you. If it doesn't, cool, at least you can say you've tried.

Fixing problems with the 10:1 technique

When we feel uninspired it can often be because there are problems in our life. I'm a big, quick, radical problem solver. As soon as a problem arises, I'm there on it. I don't want it to steal any more of my happiness than it needs to.

This where I use the 10:1 technique: both to fix problems in my life or to find out about a topic to take a certain area of my life forward. It's a simple method to jump-start change or knowledge in your life. This is what you do:

Step 1 Watch 10 YouTube videos on a topic.
Step 2 Read one book on the topic.

The 10 YouTube videos start the process of enquiry, understanding and thinking around a topic. That volume of videos often allows you to find a person you resonate with to help with Step 2, because if one particular person on one of those videos connects with you, and they have a book, hey presto you've found your book for step 2. The book you then read takes you on the journey to properly understand a topic, to give you a framework you can follow, and takes your understanding to the level needed to properly take informed and empowered action.

So, for example, I used this technique during the pandemic lockdown to learn how to invest my money. For my whole adult life I've been very loose with money. Money has always been something that I've earned simply to live my best life. Before then I had never had personal savings and never had more than a few thousand pounds in my personal bank account. But at 35, with two kids, a house, and a desire to improve our family's wealth and security I used the 10:1 process to learn about investing.

So, I put into YouTube 'How to start investing money' and 10 videos later I had some pretty awesome ideas on what to invest in, as well as the basic knowledge to know what I was looking for, how to achieve it, and what to expect. One of the videos I watched was by Rob Moore and his character resonated with me. I liked his energy, and I liked his no BS approach to the realities of money. So, I bought his audiobook *Money* and started to learn more about investing and taking control of my finances. This whole process probably took me about 15 hours. I was then very inspired by what I had learned and started talking to a few money-savvy friends I knew for some advice, and even reached out to a friend in a business mastermind I was in , Jason Graystone, and we ended up collaborating in business and I learned more again from him. I then got to work straightaway and during 2020 made some great investments that saw me grow my money 28 per cent in a year. That's a pretty decent return on those original 15 hours.

Now you do, of course, need a good BS detector when using the 10:1 technique: you don't want to be spending too much time watching videos online of people who are full of hot air and then reading a bad book as a result, so have your critical thinking hat on or speak to a friend who you know to be good in this area for a starting point on who's good to learn from. For example, if you did want to know more about investing (staying with that subject area), and feel you aren't getting the information you want online, text or phone a friend you know with a lot of money. Ask them: 'Hey, X, I'm wanting to get more serious about my money, investing and my family's wealth. I've always seen you as someone who knows a bit about this. Are you able to point me in the direction of a good book or somewhere you learned about this so I can get more serious about this and take control of my money?' And they will likely tell you a good place to start. Never ask them to teach you the whole lot – what's in it for them, after all? Ask for something small, a nudge in the right direction, and start to do the work yourself. And if they do offer to help you learn more, great, but don't expect that of someone, simply ask for help with where to start your journey.

What could you use the 10:1 technique to master in your life?

Is it time to reset?

Sometimes in life you're not sure what the problem is, or there are so many problems you don't know where to start. When this happens, I have only one piece of advice: go on holiday and/or take a break.

Yes, you might feel like you can't take the time off work, or that the timing isn't right, or you don't have money to go away, or some other reason. But when you are turning up to life at 40 per cent, you feel rubbish, stuck and totally uninspired, so get away, disconnect, reset. It doesn't have to be an expensive trip, or to be carefully planned; the important thing is to get some space and freedom to think, to relax, and have a little fun.

How do most of us feel after a holiday?

Reset, re-inspired and ready to go again.

So do it. Get away. Get a reset. See it as an investment in yourself.

I've done this throughout my life. I really value travel and how it feeds the soul. But one particular time stands out for me. It was 2021, during the COVID-19 pandemic. As you know, I was at an all-time low. My health was in a rotten place. I felt overwhelmed with work. I felt the burden of being a parent for the first time. I had this book to write and felt I couldn't break the back of it. I just felt stuck and hadn't been away for a reset in two years (something that was built into my work life pre-pandemic with lots of work travel).

So, I told my wife what I needed: to get away, to reset, to decompress, to get the space to figure things out and write this book. At the time we were still in the throes of the pandemic and we had a 14-month-old baby, but she still generously gave me her blessing: 'Do what you need to do,' she told me. So five days later I flew to Portugal to stay with a friend who I knew would help, someone who was feeling similar to me, who would be just the right dose of fun, who would help me deconstruct what I was thinking and feeling. I would also get the space to get to grips with this book. And I knew we'd have a ton of fun together too (and we did, thanks James).

And it was transformative. In a week I got a jump-start on my recovery with my health. I wrote 30,000 words of this book. We had a ton of fun. I caught up on sleep. And I got time to think, explore how I was feeling, and create a new plan for when I returned home.

It was only one week and cost me about £500, but it was worth 10 times that in how it changed my outlook and motivation.

So, if you feel you need a reset, don't be afraid to do it. If you have a job and kids and a partner, just sit them down and tell them what you need, honestly, And if you have good supportive people around you, they will understand, they will support this process for you.

You might not need a week away, maybe just a week off from work would do it . . . who knows? All I'm trying to pitch to you is the power of a reset. The power of a different environment. The power of different people. The power of travel and movement. The power of not having to think about work and so much STUFF all the time – because it can get on top of us from time to time.

So please don't be afraid of a hard reset. It's not weak to need that. It's a strength to know what you need to be yourself and to give it to yourself.

Inspiring yourself

What you will also notice is that over time you start to inspire yourself with your actions, habits and routines, and this should also be a goal. It shows you are developing your inner confidence in yourself and what you are doing in your life is inspiring you to do more, to continue. This is the Holy Grail.

So many of the steps in this book (and so much of your future) hinge on your confidence to step into a big life. To seek and have what it is you want. Now this isn't something you snap your fingers and get; no motivational YouTube video can give you confidence overnight. Like anything, it is a practised skill. But you must start. It's imperative to start with yourself, to accept who you are unapologetically, and lean into what it is you truly want for your life. Good things happen when you simply be yourself, you optimize yourself, and you push forward with your innate desires for life. Then, you grow as you start. So many say, 'I wish I was confident and could do X'. But you don't just get confident at something, you build confidence at things. And sometimes it does take a fair chunk of time. But it's worth it, and starts with you choosing to be yourself, chase what it is you want, and start one small step to being *that* person.

What would make you a more confident runner?

Likely going for a 10-minute jog, then the next day going for 12 minutes, then 15 minutes, then 18 minutes, and then hey presto 6 months later you can run a half marathon and would likely say to yourself, 'Yeah, I'm an alright runner, did a half marathon in a pretty decent time'. After another 6–12 months you might have then completed a marathon in a time you are happy with and would say to yourself, 'Yeah, I'm a confident runner'. You got there because you practised the skill, the thing, and over time your ability and performance grew, transforming you into a confident runner. But it started with just a 10-minute jog around the block.

What do you want to be more confident at? What do you want to feel stronger to do?

Start small and practise it. You might even need to break down the skill and practise it in chunks, so that when you fit it together your confidence comes from the amalgamation of skills that end up in the final performance.

Over time, you *being good* at the things you do and are interested in can help you develop an inner confidence. For me, however, this has to go hand in hand with your body and mind. The best platform I could have ever given myself to be a strong and confident person is the platform of a strong body and mind. I got fit, I lost the weight I was unhappy with, I developed skills that allowed me to better manage my health, I started to sleep better, I got rid of health issued I had or found ways to manage them better, which all made me a more confident person. I felt good in myself, and that radiated a certain amount of confidence. Then I built on that.

That's why I want you to transform yourself.

That's why I want you to want to be fit. To be healthy. To be well slept. Because it will support and start SO much of this journey to living an AWESOME Life, and trust me, being a confident badass of a person will unlock so much of life that you think is unavailable to you.

But without belief, nothing will be achieved.

As much as you feel something isn't possible at first, you have to believe it is. When you believe it, you keep looking for answers. You keep trying things. You find better ways.

I know you can find someone on the internet that has conquered the thing you feel you can't do. There is a success story out there for any of life's journeys. Through belief, trying, failing, and finding better ways, we eventually get there.

Sure, there are certain limits to this. We are not standing here saying 'I believe I can fly', when structurally it's not possible for humans to do this by themselves. We're using this in a normal life context, saying things like:

I believe I can find true happiness
I believe I can find a job I love
I believe I can get really fit and healthy
I believe I can build true wealth for myself and my family
I believe I can one day speak in public in front of 100 people

You might not feel it now, but believing is the first step, because it makes you put one foot in front of the other to find answers and ways of achieving it.

Writing this book is another perfect example. When I was at school, I was a D and E grade English student and got heavily critiqued for the way I wrote. One teacher took time to help me, Mrs Pearson (thank you), and that, coupled with my belief that I could write better, allowed me to later in life pick up blogging. Sure, I was a rubbish blogger at first, but through the weekly practice of writing a blog I became better, my writing became noticed and appreciated, and 12 years later I write this book with a publishing deal. All that from being a 'no hope', D/E student.

I believed. And yes, I was crap when I started, but aren't we all pretty pants the first time we start something? If it's worth doing at all, it's worth doing badly for a while.

We fail. We learn. We practise. We reflect. And we get better. It's as simple as that.

I want you in one year's time to glow with a new level of confidence. I want this book to start the process of you believing you can do more and be more, but you have to BELIEVE it's possible. Without belief, there is no hope.

I believe I can keep doing great things and make a great account of my life, and you should too. But, if you just can't feel this or get to this place, to even start to fathom it, there will be a reason, and it's important we don't ignore it, but again aim to deal with it. This is where it will be important to get help, to talk, and deal with the past that's holding you back.

Deal with your trauma

If you are really struggling to take this step to believing in yourself, it's possibly because of past trauma and/or some pretty negative influences in your life. Some stuff might have happened in your past that has left an imprint on you. A tragic accident. A death. Being oppressed by a teacher or friend or parent. Being exposed to unkind people. Being abused. Whatever it is, whatever you feel deep down holds you back, please have the confidence to take the step to go and talk to someone about it.

Therapy could release the true you if you feel you are being held back. If you feel you can't read these words and start to believe in yourself a little more, you need help with doing so.

An example always sticks in my mind, and I apologize for how simple I am making this sound and how graphic this example is, but I need this example to be quite extreme. I know a guy through my work who as a kid was sexually abused by a male family member for a prolonged period of time. Now this sort of behaviour is horrible, and I feel for anyone who has been exposed to any form of abuse, verbal or physical, especially if it's sexual. But through taking the brave step of getting therapy, of talking to someone, of going on a self-development journey, he has totally transformed his life.

An experience like this in life could, and likely would – because we're human – leave a scar on us, but only if the wound is left to heal by itself in an unsupported environment. In situations like this, it's really important we get professional help. We speak to people who can help us through these challenges. This guy I know is now a great coach, an inspiration to many, and no longer allows this experience to govern or control his life – which it did for many years. He no longer feels a victim or feels abused; he is empowered, knows his value, and has self-worth. I feel if people like this can do it, you and I can to.

I've had therapy at several points in my life.

I've had it to get context, perspective and closure on my parental upbringing and how my parents getting divorced and my dad not being around much affected me. I've had therapy to help me get perspective on stepping up in my professional life to achieve bigger and better things. I had therapy when I was suffering from long COVID and needed outside support (as there were also a lot of other life challenges at the time).

And I'll get therapy again if I need it or simply want to talk to a professional about things.

If you feel you need to talk to someone, please have the strength to break through and reach out. I value this so much that I have made it an internal process in my company if I feel I can help my team members by them talking to someone externally. I have then paid for sessions, or the start of sessions, to give them the nudge to talk to someone. And it's been transformative to everyone I have done this with. Why?

Because you unlock unknown elements of yourself and regain so much personal power by removing old scars and pain.

Don't let past experiences hold you back. Talk to someone to get the perspective, understanding and closure you need. This could be a friend, but it's best to work with a qualified professional with this stuff, one that you connect with and feel confident with.

Getting inspired will cost you, but it's worth every penny

The reality is some of this will cost you, but ask yourself, is it worth it?

Is spending, let's say £1–200 a month, worth you being a better version of yourself?

This book cost you money. Buying better food will cost you money. Having holidays a few times a year will cost you money. Talking to someone will cost you money. Having a coach will cost you money. Buying a few key (Awesome) supplements will cost you money.

But is it worth it?

For me it's worth every penny.

Sure, you might not have much money right now, and that's fine, even if you committed £10 a month to being a better version of yourself by reading a book a month, or subscribing to X subscription that might empower you with a key tool is something pretty transformative.

I can imagine you are starting to think it's worth it, but you need more convincing. The only way to convince yourself it's worth it is to start trying, to then see the benefits. If you got a session with a coach and it improves your life/training/performance/health, then it's worth it. And then you are bought into doing more and spending more on yourself and your AWESOMENESS.

Step 10 of this book talks about money and your finances, as this is a very important piece of the puzzle that works in a harmonious way to get more from life. If you could become more AWESOME, what are the chances you can earn more, to then spend more on *yourself*, and over time become the most AWESOME version of yourself?

Hopefully you're starting to see how all this works together. You become better. You earn more. You can do more. Because you can do more you become even more confident and bad ass. You then earn more again. You then start investing in your long-term wealth. You can then do more again and have fun in the process. And this AWESOME cycle of AWESOMENESS just keeps going and going and you become the success you always dreamed of.

But you've got to start the journey, believe in the journey and be brave enough to start and then continually commit to the work.

There is no short cut here.

Right, now it's time for you to reflect on your inspiration tank. How full, or empty, is it right now? And depending on that and what you feel the issues are, what simple solutions can you put in place to try to fill your tank up some more? I don't want to tell you what to write or dictate any particular process here, so I have left the below blank. All I will ask you to do is take the time to think (please don't start Step 10 yet, this process is important), and openly and honestly write down some thoughts on what you want to change or what you want to start to commit to as a result of reading this chapter. Again, even if you start small, with one thing, it's a start, and it will build over time as your confidence and awareness grows:

_____

_____

_____

_____

_____

_____

_____

_____

_____

_____

Key points to remember

- Don't wait for inspiration to hit you – go find it!
- Make time and money available to try things that you think will inspire you.
- Inspiration breeds inspiration. Get the ball rolling by plunging in at the deep end. As you go on this inspired journey you'll start to inspire yourself with your actions.
- Radically problem solve and use the 10:1 technique where you need to go down the rabbit hole on a problem.
- If you're unsure what the problem is, if it all feels a bit overwhelming and you feel stuck, be brave and have a hard reset. Go away or get time off work and just rest and have fun. It will give you the space you need to figure things out, and the time to talk to others to help you unpick things.
- Value your body and mind and go on the journey to optimizing it. This will inspire you more as you become more confident and capable as a person as a result of getting fit and healthy.
- Start inspiring yourself today – don't delay. And if you're unsure how, just try stuff!

Use this note-taking section to jot down your thoughts after reading this chapter. What have you gained? How are you closer to living your Awesome Life?

_____

_____

_____

_____

_____

_____

_____

_____

_____

_____

Finances, money and wealth

Approach

Water

Environment

Sleep

Organize

Movement

Eat

Lifestyle

Inspiration

Finances

Education

> 'Money is a tool. Used properly it makes something beautiful; used wrong, it makes a mess.'
>
> Bradley Vinson

As I've matured, both as a person and a coach who's dealt with different problems over the years, I've found there is another key relationship people often struggle with (the first is what a lot of this book focuses on, the relationship we have with ourselves) . . . and that is a relationship with money.

I personally struggle to understand it. Culturally, I get how it has happened, why people are so cagey with discussions around money, often because they don't earn a lot and possibly feel ashamed – like it's a reflection on them as a person, but it's a relationship I feel many people need a perspective shift on. The reality is that whether we like it or not, the world operates on money; it's a currency of exchange. That's all it is when we boil it down. Money was invented to use as a sign of exchange. Back in the day we used to exchange a pig for a basket of wheat, or a new chair for the shoeing of a horse, but as culture and society developed, we needed a better system to allow for delayed bartering, and thus money was created. We shouldn't feel uncomfortable talking about something so integral to how our civilization operates.

Now am not I saying you should all be about the money, but you should 100 per cent understand money and work to get more of it because it will help you live your most Awesome Life.

Not having to worry

One of my goals when I started my business was to 'never have to worry about buying something'. I never wanted to have to worry about buying a new pair of shoes, or having to fix my car, or buy a new one. I wanted to be able to afford a nice house, to hire a coach if I wanted one, to be able to go on nice holidays, have a membership to a good gym, or go on a little adventure for a day skydiving or something mad. All those things I didn't want to have to think twice about, so I could always live my best life. It's not about the money, it's about the lifestyle that it can facilitate.

The reason I had set this goal for myself is because when my parents got divorced at age 11, we never had much money. Buying a new pair of trainers was a big decision. We never went on holiday. We could never afford the food we wanted or to eat out that much. Now, my mum did an incredible job providing for us on a low wage, and I am forever grateful for that, but I never wanted that for myself as I grew up and brought my own children into the world.

That life experience drove to earn enough that I never had to think twice about living the life I wanted to live, with the freedom I wanted. I wanted to know I could just whip out the credit card and boom, we're off, it's mine, let's go. This is another reason I decided to go self-employed, and even before that I always had two or three jobs at once so I could afford whatever I wanted to afford (I've had more than one job ever since I was 18). This desire, combined with my desire for freedom, saw me go into business and set off on my own.

Mind you, business is tough; I won't lie. During the first few years your earnings can be terrible, and you have to work a job at the same time as you build the business, which I did for around four years. But with vision and commitment and focus, the tide turns; it did for me anyway. Since the four-year mark in my business I've made good money and reached that goal I had: to never think twice about spending money on everyday things and life's simple pleasures.

Now please know this is my story – one story of 8 billion others in the world. What matters is your story, your values and goals. I am merely using my journey, my experience, my insight to help you define what you want your future to be like. There are certainly things that you will want to work towards having, and that will take a certain amount of financial flexibility, but do know, please, that so much of life's happiness comes from everything else money can't buy you. Most of life's happiness is found in:

- a deep and connected relationship with your partner/ family/friends
- good health and fitness
- time spent with your friends and family
- having fun doing the things you love
- a good long walk in nature
- cooking and experiencing good food.

So many of the good things in life take no or minimal money; you just need to get yourself into the right position – mentally, emotionally and physically – to enjoy those things. But to get to that sweet spot, you need a comfortable income. So all I'm saying is . . .

Earn the amount of money you need to create the freedom and things in your life you want.

It's that simple.

Why £50,000?

A famous 2010 study found that emotional wellbeing (often reported as 'happiness' when this study comes up) peaked in US citizens when their income was around $75,000 at the time[30]. This is often translated, according to differences in cost of living and rough exchange rates to be about £50,000 per year. Beyond this point, emotional wellbeing (at least according to that study) didn't increase as income did.

Now you might be reading this right now thinking, 'It would make me a damn sight happier earning £100,000 per year', but let's zoom out for a second and look at why this might not be the case.

If you earn £50,000 per year your monthly spending might look like this:

Income per month (after 20 per cent tax) = £3,333.00

(The above could be less if you contribute to a student loan, pay into a pension, or have other costs pre-salary)

Rent/mortgage: £700
Bills/Council Tax: £350
Car plus fuel: £320
Food: £400
Eating out/fun stuff: £400
Kids' stuff: £400 (if you have kids)

You can calculate your salary minus costs at: https://www.thesalarycalculator.co.uk/salary.php

Now you can change the above to fit your situation, or potential situation if you made some changes, but the above adds up to £2,470. That leaves £763 per month as money to use/spend.

You can see how that level of available disposable income creates a lot of life flexibility. Nice holidays. Nice things. Money to invest. Money to save up. Money to do whatever you please with.

And this is why I think we see that statistically we don't observe people becoming any happier after this salary bracket, because at this level, and before it, probably closer to £40,000 per year, people can do and buy the majority of things they want and need to live a good life.

Now this isn't me saying don't earn more or don't aspire to build more wealth. If that's what you want, then go for that. But you often hear people say things like, 'I wish I was a millionaire', as if that's the income in life that buys ultimate freedom, or at least a really good slice of it. But in reality, for most of us, that freedom is much, much closer and achievable than you think. The only thing that might be stopping you is your relationship with money, so let's look at that more closely.

Assessing your relationship with money

I'm now going to ask you to answer a few questions. Be as honest as you can, so you can really begin to understand your relationship with money, how it plays a role in your life, and how you use it.

Do you feel your relationship with money is healthy? If not, why not?

_____

_____

_____

Reading back the story you tell yourself about money, is it based on fact, or how you were brough up, or how society tells you to treat money?

_____

_____

_____

Do you want to change to have a healthier relationship with money? If so, how do you want to re-frame this relationship?

_____

_____

_____

Do you realize and appreciate that money is just a currency of exchange, and that the amount you earn is a direct sign of the value you create in the world, or that the market will pay for the service you provide in your job?

_____

_____

_____

Do you feel the amount you earn right now is limiting your ability to lead the life you want to lead, bearing in mind the above example, and what we have spoken about in this book so far?

_____

_____

_____

Did you use to subscribe to the idea that you need to be a millionaire to be free of financial worry, and has your perspective taken a shift?

_____

_____

_____

What could be a good career and financial goal for you for the next three years?

_____

_____

And five years?

_____

_____

And 10 years?

_____

_____

What has to change for you to achieve these goals?

_____

_____

What do you need to change with your career path to enable you to reach your financial/life goals?

_____

_____

To press my main point home, this is *not* me limiting you to pushing yourself to earn more and continuing to build your wealth; this is me simply outlining what is possible and the level at which things really change for most people, and then dangling the carrot in front of you should you wish to chase for more. I've lived a very comfortable life earning over £50,000 for some time now. It's a great level of financial income, but I am personally pushing way beyond that, because I believe I can and because I have new goals for myself and my family. It's also possible to have more money for the things you want by changing how you spend your money. Many people have expensive cars on finance but one of their values is fun and adventure, no point spending £400 per month on a fancy car, or having the latest fashion and changing wardrobes, both limiting what you can spend going on adventures. That's not a value-aligned life decision for most. So, while we can aim to earn more, and build our wealth, we also have to ensure we use the money we do earn for what makes us truly happy.

Building wealth

I won't speak too much on building wealth as there are far better people out there to listen to on the topic, and I have also only been building my personal wealth seriously since 2020. However, I have been building my business wealth, equity and leverage for 12 years now – which does feed into my personal wealth. As I write this, my business should turnover £2 million in 2022, which is a good asset to have in wealth building.

My mum always told me as kid: 'Spend a little, save a little, and you'll always have money there when you need it.' This was great advice and I wish I had listened to it when I was younger, but I didn't. I lived the first 14 years of my business and adult life fast and loose with a money abundance mindset. And it worked (for me at least), but I do still wish I had done things better and listened to my mum more. What position would I be in if I had always saved 10 per cent of my personal income over the last 14 years?

Here's a quick crude example. Say I put £1000 into an index investment fund to start myself off with investing, and then put just £150 in every month. If I had started doing this as a working adult, just saving £150 a month and never touching it, after 14 years I would have doubled my money if it was a good index fund and I was getting, say, an 8 per cent return.

That means over 14 years I would have paid in £25,200, and the interest earned would have seen my investment grow to £49,257.

Pretty cool. Imagine if your investment had done better, or you could invest more every month? It would compound even more. When I got into investing in 2020, I took some well-calculated risks. I knew the investment market would explode in 2020 due to how much the world would change during the pandemic. When the world changes a lot, BIG returns can be had, because key markets win (at the expense of other key markets losing). In the global pandemic, which industries won? Home delivery. Technology. Home fitness. Green energy. And the people who make it their life's work to know what investments to invest in will win. So why not go harder on investing when you know the world is tipping towards a new balance? That was my mindset anyway.

So, I did my research and found what I felt was one of the highest-performing index/growth funds (Blue Whale, if you want to check them out and do some research, as this is not financial advice) and put in all the money I was happy to invest. I then took out a loan at 3.4 per cent and put that in, too. I knew that, if I could get around 10 per cent return in this fund (which is what they had previously returned over the previous four years), it would be worth me taking the loan out to have the extra money to invest. It would still see me net a 6.6 per cent return, and even if it didn't, I would still have the income to pay the loan's monthly repayments, so I felt it was a calculated low-risk move (again, this is not financial advice, and this would leave some uncomfortable, but I was happy with the risk because I could pay the loan off should I need to).

I then committed £500 per month into the fund to keep it compounding, and seeing as we were all at home doing not a lot and not spending a lot during the pandemic, it was the perfect time to invest. Over the course of 2020–21, around 15 months, I grew my investment 28 per cent, I then used half towards a new house, kept some in to of course keep adding to and keep it compounding (I invest a minimum of £300 per month into this fund), and then decided to take some out and put into a few riskier investments I had spent time researching.

Most people invest in a savings account, but there you barely get a return. You want to aim to get 5–10 per cent return on your investments. If you're not, put in some research time because there are many options out there, such as investing in HMO properties which on average return 17 per cent, but do require more upfront capital. Why get a measly 0.75 per cent return when you can get more? Again, this isn't financial advice, this is merely what I did with some free time and money I had to build my wealth more. Please do your research – either way it's important to make the money you do have work for you.

Passive investments

I'm not a big fan of this term. Only because no investment is ever truly passive. I think it makes us have unrealistic expectations with investing. Every investment you or I make takes time. We have to research it, understand it, know the process, manage it on an ongoing basis, and ensure that it's working. Sure, some investments might take a minimal amount of time. You might research a good index fund, start throwing 10 per cent of what you earn into it every month, and look at it once per year to see how well it's doing. That's a pretty low amount of time invested, but most of us don't do that. The human brain is often hardwired for more. If you make a good investment, you generally then think, 'How can I make or do more?', and rightly so. Then we spend our 'lying in bed' moments and 'chilling out' moments researching on our phones other things we can do or try. This all takes time and energy, so while you might earn passively once you have put the money in, it all takes time and energy to set it all up.

All investments have generalized market return rates as well. If you stick money in your current bank account you're going to get an average market return of 0.25–0.75 per cent, which is terrible. It's widely known that money left in your normal bank account loses value over time. Inflation generally goes up 2–2.5 per cent year on year. If you are getting 0.5 per cent from your bank, but the cost of living is going up 2.5 per cent a year, your money is losing its value sat in your bank account. That's why it's a good idea to put spare money into investments. Leaving it in your bank account is a pretty terrible idea, unless it's a pot of emergency money you want in a flash – as investments can often take a few weeks to get your money out of, or sometimes longer.

A friend and finance wizard, Jason Graystone, who I mentioned earlier, took me to one side before I started investing and told me to put aside an emergency life fund. This pot of money is three months of emergency money. This three months of cash sits in a bank account where you can't see it daily (to ensure you don't think about it and get an urge to spend it) and is enough to cover your mortgage, bills, food and so on in the event that anything in life goes wrong. This can also be used if you get a home disaster or just need a lump of money. So, before I started investing, I saved up £7,500 and put it into an account where we never touch it. I also did the same in my business, in a business savings account there is three months' worth of salaries and expenses, so if we have a downturn, I can keep everything running for three months while we get our act together and fix things.

Back to average market returns. You could put your money into an index fund and get 5–10 per cent return (on average), you could invest in property owning rental homes or HMOs. If you're not, put in some research time because there are many options out there, such as investing in HMO properties (houses let to multiple occupants) which on average return 17 per cent. These are two fairly sound and safe investments (remember no investment is without risk, and I'm not a financial advisor, so make sure you do your own research). Or you could explore higher return investments, which of course come with more risk, like cryptocurrency or individual stocks and shares or trading.

There are many things you can invest in to build your wealth over time, so it's important to do your research. Some things might take you ages to learn about before you can invest. For example, if there is almost too much to learn and do to build a HMO property then is it worth the 17 per cent return you will get compared to the 10 per cent you might get in an index fund, which might not take you too long to research and start investing in?

My point here? Look at the bigger picture. Invest in yourself, your personal wealth, your family's wealth, your businesses wealth if you have one, and have your eye on compound gains over time. Trying to build wealth over time gives us more security and freedom, and that's something we all want. The wealth to enjoy our lives in the way that we want to.

Imagine if I worked hard and smart, invested all my extra money for 10 years, and had a business that was turning over £2 million and I sold it? With those two investments combined I would never have to work again should I choose to (as long as the money was put to work in good investments that continued to pay out over time).

If you had £1 million and put it into an investment that returned 10 per cent, do you think you could live off £100,000? If you live off £30,000 now, in theory you could never work again if you could get £300,000? Maybe you could work hard and invest wisely? Maybe you could build a business and sell it? Maybe you could build a business and then have someone else take over, take a salary of £30,000 and stop work?

Who knows? But know this: investing is paramount to wealth building and to creating the freedom many want more of. Knowing money and how to leverage it is a life skill you want. Financial literacy is important to everyone, and I wish I had had this spelled out to me more when I was younger.

Living within your means

Most people live within their means, so if you earn £20,000, you live within that with your food, bills, rent etc. If you then earn £30,000, you do the same, spending more on rent, food, bills, etc. Then at £40,000, you do the same again, buying a bigger house, nicer car, buy better food etc. This is all well and good, but what if you want to build wealth?

If you do, you'll have to stop expanding your spending and commit to putting it into investing. What would happen in 10 years' time if you kept your outgoings to £23,000 per year, but were earning £35,000, and all your spare money was going into good investments?

Most people don't have any savings above a few thousand pounds, and it's often because we always increase our spending to our salary. But what if you had an investment strategy? What if you were thinking longer term about your money rather than buying a more expensive car on finance?

I value investing so much right now in my life that I am driving a 2007 Audi A4 estate that cost me £2000. It costs me around £100 a month to run in tax, insurance and fuel (because I don't drive that much), and hasn't needed any work yet (touch wood). I could spend £500 per month on a lovely Range Rover or a new electric car which everyone is doing, but I'd rather put that £400 I would then be spending on a car (which 99 per cent of the time sits on my drive looking pretty) into investments to build my family's wealth, and either allow that to continue to compound over time, or use it for things like a house extension which would overall improve our quality of life more than a fancy car.

That's me being really clear on my financial priorities and playing the long game. It's all too easy to make it a priority (also, because it's fun buying new nice things) to just spend more, a new car, new clothes, more expensive holidays etc, and while we should do this, it's us enjoying and experiencing life. Ask yourself where the limit is, and what your financial priorities are looking long term, not short term.

How much of your money should be going towards bills, food, living, having fun, but then investing in the future? And the money you do invest in the future, is that in good investments? Are you getting at least 5 per cent, if not 10 per cent, and can you get more? If not, do the research, change the investments, because money sitting in your bank isn't doing you any long-term good.

How do you think that 50-year-old person you know with lots of money came to have lots of money? They worked in a good job or built a business and over the years learned about putting their money to work. They learnt the best investments to put their money into, played the long game, took a few risks, knew the right people, never stopped learning, and moved with the times (and were probably a bit frugal in other areas of their spending too).

And it's what I am now doing. I'm 35 and by the time I am 40 my aim is that my family is financially free. Why is this now a goal for me? Because FREEDOM is my number one life value. And freedom to not have to work or worry about money is one of the ultimate forms of freedom. I won't stop work; I love it and have SO much I want to give to the world. But to have that as a goal is awesome, to know we won't ever have to worry ever about money is a great thing (as long as the investments I make stay fairly secure and diversified, nothing is a guaranteed cert in life).

So, what's your next step?

As a starting point, do you know what you spend every month and are you happy with how you spend that money? Are you making the wisest decisions right now with your money? Are you buying stuff you don't really need and thus taking away from money you could be investing in your future? Are you willing to do the research to invest your money better?

Most people spend what they earn, and that's that. They have no real long-term money strategy and, if you want my opinion, that's not going to see anyone get wealthy as they age, and there will be times when big bills or issues come along and they'll cause lots of stress because you have no safety net to dip into. So, get moneywise and start building a long-term strategy.

Take 10 minutes now to download some thoughts on what you should do next and why:

_____

_____

Money take-aways

Just so we are super clear, I want to revisit what we have just gone over. Money is not the be all and end all, but it is important. It makes the world go round and, yes, many of the things in life that make us happy cost nothing, but to live a rich and rewarding life it's good to have a certain amount of money. You can then have the house you want, holidays you want, to eat good food, and, ultimately, have freedom and flexibility from having a good income. So put yourself in a good position to earn well, over time. This might mean you have to change careers, work a second job, or start a business and take things into your own hands. But in saying that, do check your spending so you are not spending money on things that are not in full alignment with your values and what you ultimately want to spend money on. After that, create an investment strategy. I invest 20 per cent of everything I earn. I started at 8 per cent, but over time spent less on things like cars, and am now investing more and more so I can increase my rate of wealth building. Whatever money you think you can spare, invest it, ideally at least 10 per cent per month. And, know you can and should push yourself to earn more by adding more value to the world, pushing for a promotion, changing careers, starting a business, or by building a side hustle.

Investing in your most invaluable asset . . . YOU.

So, let's discuss your career, your goals, and what's next for you. If you are earning a low salary right now, and you want that to change, what needs to change? Do you feel you want to change your job/career path? Do you currently enjoy your work? If not, what can you do that would give you a greater sense of purpose, that uses your skills better, and that challenges you? Maybe you don't want a new job, but a change in job situation or working environment to better fit the lifestyle you want to lead? Have you ever had a desire to start a business and now is the time to scratch that itch?

There are many questions you could ask yourself here, so let's simply spend 15 minutes asking and answering some. Your answers can steer you in knowing what actions to take next to build a more Awesome Life for yourself, by finding out which of the above questions need to be delved into more. All I ask is you answer these questions honestly, with a solution and opportunity-focused mindset, not a problem and stay safe mindset:

If you feel you want to change jobs/career path, what in life do you enjoy doing?

_____

_____

What are you good at? What skills do you think you have?

_____

_____

If you were to ask other people what you're good at, what do you think they would say?

_____

_____

Now ask three people you trust to answer that question honestly and write their answers here.

Person 1:

_____

_____

Person 2:

_____

_____

Person 3:

_____

_____

What are you most passionate about?

_____

_____

If the perfect job existed, what would it be?

_____

Do you know if that job actually exists? Or could it exist if you created it?

_____

Can you write down five other jobs you think would make you happier and more fulfilled, that utilize your skills more, or you'd relish the challenge?

_____

_____

What would make you happier in your current job if you could change ANYTHING?

_____

_____

Have you ever sat down with your boss, had a heart-to-heart, and asked if things can change?

_____

_____

How much do you want to aspire to earn, and why?

_____

_____

Can you earn that in your current line of work/career path? How do you know this to be true?

_____

_____

Are there certain conditions you would want for your work life – for example travel, working from home, a company car, flexibility around when you work? Write down your ideal wants for your job:

_____

_____

What kind of people do you want to work with?

_____

_____

Have you ever wanted to start your own business? If so, do you know what doing?

_____

_____

If so, what's held you back in the past?

_____

_____

What could you do to overcome those barriers?

_____

_____

If you could change something about the world, what would it be?

_____

_____

Are there jobs that you could do/create which would help you make those changes you want to see in the world?

_____

_____

Would you be open to doing two jobs – either working the jobs both part-time, or having a side hustle on top of your full-time job? If so, what would that look like?

_____

_____

Are there things you aren't good at or dislike about work and would want to minimize in any future line of work?

_____

_____

Are you willing to have the conversation with any future employer about this if it's important to your future happiness?

_____

Do you want to work till retirement, or would you love to retire early?

_____

If you wanted to retire early, what would have to happen for you to do that? (Please don't just say 'win the lottery' because you know that's just a near-100 per cent impossible goal.)

_____

_____

Are you willing to work a job that you kind of like that's very well paid, that still leans on your skills, for, say, 10 years, so that you can invest and build your wealth, and then after that period of your life pivot into a job that you'd love to do but is low paid? (Lots of people do this but you need to have a clear strategy of what, why and how.)

_____

On the basis on your answers above write down a list of jobs or businesses that you feel could be well suited to your skills, or that you feel you would enjoy exploring, or would love to try, and see how these things feel to you as future options:

_____

_____

_____

Whatever you have written above is all completely possible. With the advent of the internet, NOTHING is off limits anymore. We know people who do the weirdest, craziest and 'out there' jobs and earn well from it. We know millionaire gamers, YouTubers who make money from opening boxes thanks to video ad revenue and endorsements, and people who collect plastic out of the ocean as part of a non-profit. We know people who make furniture at home and sell it on Etsy, and people who make a living out of coaching others online. And we also know people who work as a whole array of traditional jobs and are happy, fulfilled and earn well by working their way up the ladder or by becoming more valuable by building their reputation and demand. We are ultimately limited only by our minds, our willingness and openness to change, and our confidence to do it.

Any change that you want to make starts with what you believe to be possible.

How To Live An Awesome Life

Sure, the changes you want to make might not be possible in a month or six months, or several years, but that's OK. A career for most of us will be 40–45 years long, and that's a long-ass time. So even if you are 45 and have 15 years left of your career, it's STILL worth changing, unless you want to be bored and unhappy and unchallenged for the rest of your working life?

I really hope a lot of young people read this book. I've achieved a lot in my nearly two decades of being an adult, but so much of what I've done and experienced could have been bigger and better, and certainly a lot quicker. Don't be like me – use this book as a bible for life success and go crush life, all of it, from today!

As a final summary, write down what bold changes you're going to make from today. What wheels are you going to set in motion, or at least start to explore and think about?

_____

_____

_____

_____

_____

_____

_____

_____

Key points to remember

- Most people have a warped relationship with money. Money isn't bad, or evil; it's just a way to value things.
- Don't hate on the system or complain about taxes; just accept the game of money and life and play the game – like every successful person out there. Complaining leads to bitterness and inaction. Accept and take bold ACTION.
- Having a well-paid job or thriving business affords us the flexibility to live an Awesome Life.
- If you dislike your job, it's time to start thinking about your next move. What would really light your fire?
- Do what you are good at, where your skills as a human are put to good use, whatever they might be.
- In the internet age no job is off limits – you can literally do anything and make a job or career out of it.
- Don't have the goal of becoming a millionaire. Start with having the goal of earning around £50,000 per year, which buys the freedom most want. Once you reach that goal, reassess, and if you want more, cool, crack on and earn big.
- Once you've reached a good level of financial stability, reassess how you spend your time, your goals in life, and what's next.
- Commit to investing 10 per cent of your monthly income into building your wealth – and over time build your investment knowledge.
- Retiring early could be closer than you think. If I sold my business today and secured investments that paid out at just 6 per cent, that's enough for me to live off.
- Any change you want to make starts with what you believe to be possible.

Education is power

Approach

Water

Environment

Sleep

Organize

Movement

Eat

Lifestyle

Inspiration

Finances

Education

'The great aim of education is not knowledge, but action.'
Herbert Spencer

This book cannot provide you with everything. My aim was to provide you with a Swiss Army Knife that allows you to start to get the most out of your life, to help you become a solid generalist who has a real grasp of what it takes to optimize the key areas that matter, to live an Awesome Life.

Now is the time for you to identify what's next, where you need more advanced learning, and for you to go find those next steps. Of course, you probably don't want to do that right now. After reading this book there is likely a fair amount of planning and taking action you want and need to do, so only take the next steps when you are ready, you don't want to get overwhelmed. If you pick up another book straight away after this one, you'll have less time to take action because you'd be too busy learning again. Go through cycles: learn, create a plan, take action, then repeat.

Only learn more when you've done taking action based on what you've previously learned. Or only when you have capacity. After all, the brain can only focus on so much at any given time, and if you let too much new information in, you might be at risk of forgetting or losing focus on the stuff you are wanting to change currently.

When you are ready for more, take action. Pull the pin.

I'd like to think that from reading this book so far, you can really see the power of education and how it can affect your life trajectory. The thing is, so many of us got put off education at school because we were learning about stuff we didn't want to learn and in a way that didn't connect with us, then we go on to start learning in jobs we don't like, or learn things we had to learn just because life asked us to. Sometimes, though, learning – learning we're fired up about or that has a real impact on our lives – can be liberating and transformational. I never liked reading much at school, but I'm glad I picked up that book that was recommended to me at the start of my fat loss journey, the book that helped me lose 5.5 stone in 8 months and started a chain reaction in me to become a life-long learner, that's led to me writing this book for you 17 years later.

Now that's the power of a book. That's the power of *learning the right stuff*. And I hope this book has been powerful for you.

Educating yourself – fast and slow

Now a key thing to consider in the process of getting educated around a topic is the speed in which you want the information and the level of understanding you want around a topic. If you read a book or two on a topic, or enrol on a course, it can take a long time to learn that topic and understand it, but the upside is you understand it more thoroughly. If, on the other hand, you hire a coach to show you all their trade secrets and top insights in an area, you'll get access to the highlights and the best tips, enabling you to take action faster, but the downside is you understand the topic less. Perhaps there is a middle ground: getting a coach (find the best coach you possibly can, or afford, trust me – it's worth it), to get going in a particular area, so you can take action, *then* pick up a book or take a course. Start surface-level, take action, then go deeper and get to understand the topic properly, long term. You could even ask the coach you work with to recommend their top book on the topic, so you get access to a top resource straight out of the gate and shorten your journey to mastery.

In saying this I don't take your time for granted. I know how much of a precious resource it is, especially when you have kids and you've only got a free 30 minutes at 9pm at the end of an already long, hard day. So, it's imperative we get to the right sources of information as quickly as possible, implement what we can as efficiently as possible, and create more time for living life.

My top 14 books

I continue to learn every day, even if it's a tiny bit – sometimes just a few pages before bed – because I love the feeling of evolution. I love to learn, to grow, to evolve, and to become better. Perhaps it is an addiction, but it's one that is paying off, and could pay off for you, too. I've read hundreds of books, but this is the cream of my crop – my top books for when you're ready and want to plunge deeper into a particular area.

Mindset by Carol Dweck
A brilliant overview of the mind, how it works, how we live our lives, the changes we want to see, and how we can achieve more with key mindset and perspective shifts. Dweck is a master in her field, and this is a top mindset book.

The 7 Habits of Highly Successful People by Stephen R. Covey
This is probably in a lot of people's top 10 list of books, even though it was written some time ago now. As an all-round self-development book, this is pretty much unsurpassed.

The Daily Stoic by Ryan Holiday

Holiday is one of my all-time favourite writers. In 365 short chapters, he updates Stoic philosophy for modern times. Whether you want to be calmer, have a better perspective on life, be wiser, or more at peace with yourself, I highly recommend this as a bedtime read or something to start the day with. All his other books are top class too.

Enough, Already by Heather Jayne Wynn

If you are struggling with your self-worth, you let the world dictate your behaviour too much, and feel lost in your own identity, this offers advice that feels very personal but which also has a strong scientific underpinning. A female perspective on finding yourself and your way in life.

The Almanack of Naval Ravikant edited by Eric Jorgenson

This is an incredible book centred around two core areas: wealth and happiness. Written in very short chunks, it's super easy to pick up and put down. Ravikant, the well-known US entrepreneur, has an incredible way with words, distilling so much wisdom in short, snappy. Sentences. This book will make you think A LOT.

The Book You Wish Your Parents Had Read by Philippa Perry

If you want to be a better parent, this is my current number one book on the topic. It provides amazing insights into how our kids think and how we can work with them to help them grow, rather than creating a life where you are always fighting what is happening.

Loving What Is by Byron Katie

If you feel you need to love yourself more, to understand yourself more, to be more connected to your inner self, this is the book for you. It asks hard questions and gets you to do the work.

Daring Greatly by Brené Brown

If you want more courage, if you want to harness your inner power, if you want to get rid of any pressure you feel is hanging around your neck, whether that be from your past, culture, society, expectation, anything, this is the perfect read. Brown is a great author who has helped so many dare to live their life more greatly.

Why Zebras Don't Get Ulcers by Robert Sapolski

If you want to understand stress, better manage your stress and generally reduce your levels of stress, then this is a good, simple read. It covers the biological underpinnings of stress, shows how our modern world can run counter to that biology and gives advice on how to reset your stress.

Eat What You Like and Lose Weight for Life by Graeme Tomlinson

If you want to understand how calories work, get a great insight into the food you eat and what calories visually look like on the plate, this is a straightforward, no-BS look at nutrition and what you eat.

Eat Well, Move Better and Feel Awesome by The Lean Machines

John and Leon have always done a great job of simplifying fitness and nutrition. This book is simple, easy to follow, and even easier to implement. If you want an all-round book on eating better and moving better this is perfect. Plus it's got some lovely recipes, too.

The World's Fittest Book by Ross Edgley

If you do want to get a bit hardcore, to push your body, to start to really see what it's capable of, then Ross's book is a winner. He's hardcore, pushes his body, and loves science, but is also a great Stoic. I've known Ross for years and he's an inspiring character. You can't go wrong with this book if you want to explore what the body is capable of.

Money by Rob Moore

A great overview of the history of money, how we use it and view it, how to have a better relationship with it, how to work to have more of it, how to invest wisely, and much more. A great bible for building up your understanding of money and building wealth. There are some great stories, too.

The Untethered Soul: The Journey Beyond Yourself by Michael Alan Singer

This is the book my therapist recommended to me, even if it took me three attempts to read it (I had to be ready for it, to really listen and let the message in). It's deep and powerful and looks at how to let go of all that's in your life and let it happen. It will help you become calmer, more centred, and more at peace with yourself and life. Highly recommended if you are ready for deep work on yourself.

Reading can be powerful, so choose your next book wisely.

Do – but don't – get addicted

This personal development stuff can become an addiction. I've felt it and have had to have a word with myself at key points in my life. Yes, we always want to be learning, growing and evolving as people, but we need to make sure the volume of learning we undertake is in proportion to our needs. In my twenties I probably spent a good three to five hours a day learning – learning my trade as a coach, studying business, listening to others' advice and experience on podcasts, digesting newsletters from my favourite people . . . but I needed to. That was what I wanted and needed at the time to get to where I am today.

Now, though, it's about 30 minutes a day, sometimes a little more. And that's enough. I had realized that sometimes I was learning for the sake of it, that it had become a habit, and sometimes I wasn't even enjoying it. It was going in one ear and out the other. I also felt I needed time to make sense of everything I had already learned, to give myself more time to implement it, and then decide where my learning wanted to take me next. So, I changed my learning habits accordingly.

This is why I want your learning to be targeted and relevant to where you are in life and what you want to master. It's also OK to *not* be learning, to *not* have a book on the go, to *not* be listening to audiobooks, to just be, to just enjoy life. There are many other ways to learn in life, especially if you are self-aware and mindful of your surroundings. After all, if we have our eyes wide open in life, if we are always taking things in, making sense of things, learning from people and experiences, then we will be developing on many levels. Books and courses, coaches and podcasts, are extras: handy tools to grab when you need something specific to meet a particular need – like delving into your DIY bag at home for your weekend's job list. Occasionally we may need to renovate the whole house, but usually we just have a bit of pottering about to do. Learn according to your needs.

Key points to remember

- Value the power of a good book, a top-class coach, or course to take your knowledge to the next level.
- When planning your next steps, try to be specific as to what it is you really want to learn.
- Consider how fast and thorough you need your leaning to be. A book or course will be slower but allow you to master a topic better; a coach will see you implement things quicker, but you won't get the depth of understanding you would from a course or book.
- Don't get so addicted to personal development that you are just doing it for its own sake. Know what you want to learn, and when and why.
- If you've got your eyes wide open, you'll also learn from the world around you and your experiences.

Let's take action – that's all that's left to do

I hope you don't see this as the end of the relationship between you and this book. A good book is something you go back to again and again. Maybe some chapters spoke to you more than others and you want to go back and review them. Maybe things change in your life and other parts of the book become more relevant to you as your situation, needs and goals change. I'd like to think of this book always being there on your shelf, close to hand, there when you need more advice, more food for thought.

I hope, too, that you go back and review the things you wrote, maybe having a go at writing more on some things or giving completely different answers as your thoughts become clearer. Keep on using, too, some of the techniques and processes I've talked about on how to be more awesome. More of which I cover at www.theschoolofawesome.co.uk/member – so make sure you're in!

Remember, the truth sets you free, but you have to courageously seek it, which isn't easy, so please be open and vulnerable to it. Then take action. Your future awaits.

No one likes a talker who's not a doer, so do yourself the honour of taking action and start to live a truly Awesome Life, not just now, but for the rest of your life.

You deserve it.

I deserve it.

We all deserve it.

No one should steal our potential, but most importantly don't steal it from yourself.

We often blame others, things, experiences, but it's only ourselves who really holds us back.

Free yourself from the past, stop blaming others, start to get to the truth, start to find out what it is you want to change, then make a plan, get the right advice from experienced people, and GO TAKE ACTION towards living your most Awesome Life.

'Life isn't about finding yourself, life is about creating yourself.'

George Bernard Shaw

If you want to stay up to date with me and continue to learn with me, follow me on social media @bencoomber

Ensure you are on my email newsletter by going to www.bencoomber.com

And don't forget the free resources you can get that accompany some of the steps at

www.theschoolofawesome.co.uk/member

References

Part 1

1   Kirkpatrick, C., Bolick, J., Kris-Etherton, P., Sikand, G., Aspry, K., Soffer, D., Willard, K. and Maki, K., 2019. Review of current evidence and clinical recommendations on the effects of low-carbohydrate and very-low-carbohydrate (including ketogenic) diets for the management of body weight and other cardiometabolic risk factors: A scientific statement from the National Lipid Association Nutrition and Lifestyle Task Force. *Journal of Clinical Lipidology*, 13(5), pp.689–711.e1.
2   D'Andrea Meira, I., Romão, T., Pires do Prado, H., Krüger, L., Pires, M. and da Conceição, P., 2019. Ketogenic Diet and Epilepsy: What We Know So Far. *Frontiers in Neuroscience*, 13.

Part 2

1   Buoite Stella, A., Furlanis, G., Frezza, N., Valentinotti, R., Ajcevic, M. and Manganotti, P., 2021. Autonomic dysfunction in post-COVID patients with and witfhout neurological symptoms: a prospective multidomain observational study. *Journal of Neurology*, 269(2), pp.587–596.
2   Vivanti, A., 2012. Origins for the estimations of water requirements in adults. European *Journal of Clinical Nutrition*, 66(12), pp.1282–1289.
3   Kerksick, C., Wilborn, C., Roberts, M., Smith-Ryan, A., Kleiner, S., Jäger, R., Collins, R., Cooke, M., Davis, J., Galvan, E., Greenwood, M., Lowery, L., Wildman, R., Antonio, J. and Kreider, R., 2018. ISSN exercise & sports nutrition review update: research & recommendations. *Journal of the International Society of Sports Nutrition*, 15(1).
4   Temple, J., Bernard, C., Lipshultz, S., Czachor, J., Westphal, J. and Mestre, M., 2017. The Safety of Ingested Caffeine: A Comprehensive Review. *Frontiers in Psychiatry*, 8.

5   Goldstein, E., Ziegenfuss, T., Kalman, D., Kreider, R., Campbell, B., Wilborn, C., Taylor, L., Willoughby, D., Stout, J., Graves, B., Wildman, R., Ivy, J., Spano, M., Smith, A. and Antonio, J., 2010. International society of sports nutrition position stand: caffeine and performance. *Journal of the International Society of Sports Nutrition*, 7(1).

6   Chacko, S., Thambi, P., Kuttan, R. and Nishigaki, I., 2010. Beneficial effects of green tea: A literature review. *Chinese Medicine*, 5(1), p.13.

7   Sharma, A., Amarnath, S., Thulasimani, M. and Ramaswamy, S., 2016. Artificial sweeteners as a sugar substitute: Are they really safe?. *Indian Journal of Pharmacology*, 48(3), p.237.

8   Colombo, R. and Papetti, A., 2020. Decaffeinated coffee and its benefits on health: focus on systemic disorders. *Critical Reviews in Food Science and Nutrition*, 61(15), pp.2506–2522.

9   Kapp, J. and Sumner, W., 2019. Kombucha: a systematic review of the empirical evidence of human health benefit. *Annals of Epidemiology*, 30, pp.66–70.

10 Kim, D., Jeong, D., Kim, H. and Seo, K., 2018. Modern perspectives on the health benefits of kefir in next generation sequencing era: Improvement of the host gut microbiota. *Critical Reviews in Food Science and Nutrition*, 59(11), pp.1782–1793.

11 Golan, R., Gepner, Y. and Shai, I., 2018. Wine and Health–New Evidence. *European Journal of Clinical Nutrition*, 72(S1), pp.55–59.

12 Lieberman, H., 2007. Hydration and Cognition: A Critical Review and Recommendations for Future Research. *Journal of the American College of Nutrition*, 26(sup5), pp.555S–561S.

13 Health.clevelandclinic.org. 2022. 22 Facts About Sleep That Will Surprise You – Cleveland Clinic. [online] Available at: <https://health.clevelandclinic.org/22-facts-about-sleep-that-will-surprise-you/amp/> [Accessed 21 June 2022].

14 – Sleepfoundation.org. 2022. Sleep Statistics Facts and Data About Sleep 2022 | Sleep Foundation. [online] Available at: <https://www.sleepfoundation.org/how-sleep-works/sleep-facts-statistics> [Accessed 21 June 2022].

15 Sleepfoundation.org. 2022. Common Myths and Facts About Sleep | Sleep Foundation. [online] Available at: <https://www.sleepfoundation.org/how-sleep-works/myths-and-facts-about-sleep> [Accessed 21 June 2022].

16 -Schuch, F. and Stubbs, B., 2019. The Role of Exercise in Preventing and Treating Depression. *Current Sports Medicine Reports*, 18(8), pp.299–304.

17 Eckstrom, E., Neukam, S., Kalin, L. and Wright, J., 2020. Physical Activity and Healthy Aging. *Clinics in Geriatric Medicine*, 36(4), pp.671–683.

18 Banno, M., Harada, Y., Taniguchi, M., Tobita, R., Tsujimoto, H., Tsujimoto, Y., Kataoka, Y. and Noda, A., 2018. Exercise can improve sleep quality: a systematic review and meta-analysis. *PeerJ*, 6, p.e5172.

19 Lahart, I., Darcy, P., Gidlow, C. and Calogiuri, G., 2019. The Effects of Green Exercise on Physical and Mental Wellbeing: A Systematic Review. *International Journal of Environmental Research and Public Health*, 16(8), p.1352.

20 Colberg, S., Sigal, R., Fernhall, B., Regensteiner, J., Blissmer, B., Rubin, R., Chasan-Taber, L., Albright, A. and Braun, B., 2010. Exercise and Type 2 Diabetes. *Diabetes Care*, 33(12), pp.e147–e167.

21 Beavers, K., Brinkley, T. and Nicklas, B., 2010. Effect of exercise training on chronic inflammation. *Clinica Chimica Acta*, 411(11-12), pp.785–793.

22 Nomikos, N., Nikolaidis, P., Sousa, C., Papalois, A., Rosemann, T. and Knechtle, B., 2018. Exercise, Telomeres, and Cancer: "The Exercise-Telomere Hypothesis". *Frontiers in Physiology*, 9.

23 Reimers, C., Knapp, G. and Reimers, A., 2012. Does Physical Activity Increase Life Expectancy? A Review of the Literature. *Journal of Aging Research*, 2012, pp.1–9.

24 Reimers, C., Knapp, G. and Reimers, A., 2012. Does Physical Activity Increase Life Expectancy? A Review of the Literature. *Journal of Aging Research*, 2012, pp.1-9.

25 Esposito, K., Maiorino, M., Bellastella, G., Chiodini, P., Panagiotakos, D. and Giugliano, D., 2015. A journey into a Mediterranean diet and type 2 diabetes: a systematic review with meta-analyses. *BMJ Open*, 5(8), p.e008222.

26 Widmer, R., Flammer, A., Lerman, L. and Lerman, A., 2015. The Mediterranean Diet, its Components, and Cardiovascular Disease. *The American Journal of Medicine*, 128(3), pp.229–238.

27 Hernando-Requejo, O. and García de Quinto, H., 2021. Mediterranean Diet and Cancer. *Nutrición Hospitalaria*.

28 Rodriguez, N., 2015. Introduction to Protein Summit 2.0: continued exploration of the impact of high-quality protein on optimal health. *The American Journal of Clinical Nutrition*, 101(6), pp.1317S–1319S.

29 Morton, R., Murphy, K., McKellar, S., Schoenfeld, B., Henselmans, M., Helms, E., Aragon, A., Devries, M., Banfield, L., Krieger, J. and Phillips, S., 2017. A systematic review, meta-analysis and meta-regression of the effect of protein supplementation on resistance training-induced gains in muscle mass and strength in healthy adults. *British Journal of Sports Medicine*, 52(6), pp.376–384.

30 Kahneman, D. and Deaton, A., 2010. High income improves evaluation of life but not emotional well-being. *Proceedings of the National Academy of Sciences*, 107(38), pp.16489–16493.a

Acknowledgements

I'm grateful to so many on this journey. There are so many people to thank. But here are the people that have been the closest to me on the journey and have helped more than they know.

Mum – you gave me everything you could have and more. But importantly the thing that always sticks out as the best advice you gave me is: 'Do whatever it is you want to in life, son, I'll always be here to support you, whatever happens.' Unconditional love and support. Thanks, Mum.

Dad – you taught me how to focus and work hard to reach the top of a trade, always placing great importance on education. Without you being in the military, I never would have spent most of my childhood having such good schooling. Thank you.

My wife and kids – you've taught me the true meaning of a good life – love, laughter, connection, adventures. Whatever I do in life it will be OK, because I have you. You're the best things in my life. Period.

My grandad Gordon – for always being a fan and giving your support, and for giving me £3000 to help start my first business. Sorry it took so long to pay you back!

Paul Chek – Your book was the catalyst for my journey in 'how to eat, move and be healthy'. Thank you.

Ben Gray – for originally recommending the book above to me, and for being a supporter and good friend through all that I've done.

Michael Heppell – for inspiring me to write this book many years ago. Michael wrote a similar book called *How to be Brilliant: Change Your Ways in 90 Days*. I read it, did all the work, did my homework, and it made me more brilliant. Thank you. The format and style of book inspired this one.

Ryan Holiday – thanks for writing so many books I've learned from. My goal is to follow your path as an author and impact people in the way you do. Keep doing what you do.

Miss Pearson – when I was at school Miss Pearson was the only English teacher that would help me. Everyone else wrote me off as a hopeless case. You pushed me to keep writing and to be better. I'm now a published author, so thank you.

My team – success usually has a team, so thanks to my team for always being there, supporting my work and holding everything together behind the scenes, especially Charlotte.

Phillip Benson and Guy Wallace – when I was building my first business in the Enterprise Centre at the University of Hull I hit a business crisis and pulled down my first business. It was a failure, but I needed help building what was next. You helped me by sitting me down and taking me through all the right steps to get the next business right. And we still talk today. Thanks, boys.

My brother Jack – you've always been there and often helped clean up my mess in business. Thanks for the ongoing support, bro. Sorry we fought so much as kids, but we ended up all right and I'm glad we spend more time together now.

Phil Marshall – you did more for me as a lecturer at Hull than any other. I must have been one annoying student, but I was keen and I think that's why you gave me so much support and opportunities. Thank you.

Andy MacKay – you were my mentor at my first ever job, but we spent more time arguing about health and nutrition. It inspired me to explore than avenue more deeply, so thank you. j

Matt Lovell – as the England Rugby Nutritionist, you kindly gave me an internship. You didn't have to and it gave me a great insight into the planning that goes into researching, writing and building nutrition protocols. Thank you.

My colleagues – I've made a lot of good friends in the industry – on the events circuit, from podcasting, and from just getting around and networking. It's been a pleasure getting to know you all, genuine good eggs in our field: Anna Sward, Rachel Godfrey, Simon Herbert, Mark Edwards, Rachel France, Phil Learney, Phil Graham, Sheli McCoy, Mark Laws, John Chapman, Leon Bustin, Troy Martin, to name but a few.

Tom Bainbridge – for being an amazing head of education to our students and being a podcast co-host for so long. Being in your presence has made me cleverer!

My podcast guests – to everyone who has been on the *Ben Coomber Radio* over the years and shared their experience and knowledge. Thank you. You've elevated the show and helped it get seen and heard and become a number-one-rated show. I've learned a ton from you all. I love podcasting.

My followers – thanks to all the followers of my work who have supported me over the years. For all the likes, shares, and comments, and buying this book! Amazing. Thank you for your support.

My publisher – for giving me my book deal. Thank you.

There are many more, but the list has to end somewhere. Thank you, one and all.